D1345405

INTERNAL MARKETS

Bringing the Power of
Free Enterprise
INSIDE
Your Organization

**William E. Halal,
Ali Geranmayeh, John Pourdehnad**

Foreword by Russell L. Ackoff

John Wiley & Sons, Inc.
New York • Chichester • Brisbane • Toronto • Singapore

Coventry University

This text is printed on acid-free paper.

Copyright © 1993 by John Wiley & Sons, Inc.

All rights reserved. Published simultaneously in Canada.

This publication is designed to provide accurate and
authoritative information in regard to the subject
matter covered. It is sold with the understanding that
the publisher is not engaged in rendering legal, accounting,
or other professional services. If legal advice or other
expert assistance is required, the services of a competent
professional person should be sought. *From a Declaration
of Principles jointly adopted by a Committee of the
American Bar Association and a Committee of Publishers.*

Library of Congress Cataloging in Publication Data

Halal, William E.
    Internal markets : bringing the power of free enterprise inside your
organization / William E. Halal, Ali Geranmayeh, John Pourdehnad.
        p.   cm.
    Includes index.
    ISBN 0-471-59364-8 (cloth : acid-free paper)
    1. Organizational change.   2. Corporate reorganizations.
3. Organizational effectiveness.   4. Decentralization in management.
I. Geranmayeh, Ali.   II. Pourdehnad, John.   III. Title.
HD58.8.H353   1993
658.4'06—dc20   93-19581

Printed in the United States of America

10 9 8 7 6 5 4 3 2 1

To all those brave but lonely entrepreneurs
who have struggled within large organizations
to make their dreams a reality.
Whether they have been called employees, professionals,
managers, intrapreneurs, or just plain mad,
we hope this book will at last provide the freedom
they have needed to use their creative talents.

Acknowledgments

Our greatest gratitude goes to Russell Ackoff, an unparalleled scholar, teacher, consultant, and colleague, whose inspiring leadership guided the development of the internal market perspective. Erik Winslow, Chairman of the Department of Management Science at George Washington University, deserves heartfelt thanks for supporting the 1991 Conference on Internal Markets, as well as the publication of this book. John Mahaney and his staff at John Wiley & Sons performed their usual heroic job in patiently attending to the birth of the manuscript and then nursing it through publication into this superb final form. We are especially grateful to the many contributors who collaborated with us for years, from agreeing to present their work at the 1991 conference to revising chapters endlessly; they provided the substance of the book. John Charlton of Esso Petroleum deserves particular attention for his constant encouragement and enthusiastic support from the start to the conclusion of this project. Many people gave their time and thought to reviewing parts of the manuscript, including Chris Friedemann, at McKinsey & Company; Rick Forschler, of the Boeing Corporation; Professors Pradeep Rau and Jeff Lenn, at George Washington University; and Sharon Frederick, Jean Osgood, and Anita Micossi, at Digital Equipment Corporation. Our students, associates, consulting clients, and other innocent bystanders gracefully tolerated hearing about these ideas during their formative stages. We feel a special affection for our families, especially our wives, for putting up with the demands posed by this long undertaking.

W. E. H.
A. G.
J. P.

Contents

Foreword

If the United States is to regain its preeminent position in the global economy, it will have to do a great deal more than imitate the Japanese. Adopting total quality management, just-in-time acquisition of purchased goods, forming strategic alliances, reducing layers of management, or increasing spans of control, and so on, just won't do it. The Japanese did not attain their enviable position by imitating us, but by leapfrogging—innovating not imitating.

Although the Japanese have achieved many innovations in management and organization, many of their ideas originated in the United States. They added to and embellished these concepts, but they did relatively little that we did not know about before-hand. We still know a great deal that neither they nor we have used, and utilizing this knowledge could catapult us into a position of world economic leadership once again. Such applications, however, require fundamental changes in the way we manage and organize work, and we are disinclined to make these changes. We are sufficiently satisfied with our present position to hesitate risking it. We rationalize this lack of courage either by predicting the imminent deterioration, if not the demise, of the Japanese economy or by arguing that it is not doing as well as it appears to be. The issue, however, is not how well or poorly the Japanese are doing, but how poorly we are doing—the deterioration of the American economy. Our economy has been growing, but not developing, because growth has been obtained by continuous borrowing; it has not been a self-sustaining growth. The result is a formidable national debt that keeps getting larger and increasingly appears to be uncontrollable.

The United States has four major capabilities that, if used, could revitalize our economy and enable it to develop once again.

1. We should democratize our institutions, public and private, for-profit and not-for-profit. The more educated our work force has become, the better its members know how to do their jobs. There are few workers in the United States today who cannot do their jobs better than their bosses. This implies that supervision is a decreasingly appropriate function of management. Management's appropriate functions today are:

a. To create a work environment and conditions that enable subordinates to use as much of their relevant knowledge as possible—to do as well as they know how.

b. To enable their subordinates to do better tomorrow than the best they can do today by facilitating and encouraging their development.

c. To manage the interactions (rather than the actions) of their subordinates, of their organizational unit with other units in the containing organization, and with relevant external organizations.

Democratization of the workplace can do more to increase the quality of work life—hence, the quality of outputs—than any of the currently popular quality improvement programs. Without a high quality of work life, no quality program directed at products or services can succeed. With a high quality of work life, quality of output often improves without the use of formal programs.

2. Increase the ability of organizations to learn and adapt more rapidly and effectively. In a dynamic environment, a person's knowledge is not nearly as important as the ability to learn to cope quickly and accurately with new conditions or short-lived crises. Decision makers must be able to (a) identify their mistakes (because people learn from making mistakes, not from doing things right), (b) determine what explains these mistakes, and (c) take corrective action. That is, they can identify, diagnose, and prescribe cures for mistaken decisions. To do so requires not only information systems, but knowledge and understanding systems as well. The management support system to make all this possible is not yet completely computerized, but it can be and has been designed and implemented.

3. Employ planning that involves the design and implementation of a desirable future. Too often, management predicts a future that is seemingly beyond the organization's control and then makes plans to exploit its opportunities and minimize its threats. Most of an organization's future is determined by what it does, not by what is done to it. Therefore, the planning should focus on what the organization can do to shape its future, not on what will be done to it. The principal obstructions between where an organization is and where it most wants to be lie inside the organization, not outside.

4. Convert to an internal market economy. The current spate of downsizing efforts by corporations, euphemistically called "rightsizing," is strong evidence that their internal economies have been less than responsive to changes in their businesses and environments. The internal nonmarket economies of most organizations encourage the development of internal bureaucratic monopolies that create make-work—for example, red tape—which is not only inefficient, but also obstructs those who have productive work to do.

An organization with an internal market economy has no need for benchmarking because its internal units are forced to compare themselves continuously with external suppliers of similar products or services. An organization's need to benchmark is an indication that something is seriously amiss. Why should it take a crisis for an organization to discover how inefficient it is? What keeps it from making this discovery before a crisis arises? An answer to this question can be much more valuable than the benefits of benchmarking.

Moreover, if we were to combine the best practices relevant to each part of a system—and every organization is a system—we would not get the best system. We might not even get a good one. This is apparent from the following example:

> Suppose we were to buy one of each type of automobile available in the United States and place them in a large garage. Then we hire a group of the best automotive engineers in the world. We give them the following problem. Which of these cars has the best engine? Suppose they find that the Rolls Royce does. We note this and then ask them to do the same for the transmission. Suppose they find that the Mercedes has the best transmission. We note this and continue until we know which car has the best example of each part required for an automobile. When this list is complete, we give it to the engineers, ask them to remove the parts listed from the respective automobiles, and assemble them into the best currently possible automobile. Theoretically, such an automobile would be made up of the best available parts. But in fact, we would not even get an automobile, let alone the best one, because the parts don't fit.

Management should focus on interactions rather than actions. Practices selected by benchmarking seldom take interactions into account. The only type of benchmarking that avoids such an error, is benchmarking of systems taken as a whole, systemically, not as aggregations of independent parts.

The failure to take intraorganizational interactions into account does not occur in an organization with an internal market economy. In such an economy, a major function of management is to evaluate the effects of the buying and selling decisions of subordinate units on each other and on the organization as a whole.

A number of organizations have made the transition to an internal market economy. The most conspicuous recent conversion occurred at IBM. According to the *Wall Street Journal* (January 11, 1993, p. B1), ". . . its own managers speak of the 'perestroika' under way at IBM." This book includes descriptions of several advanced conversions, presented by executives in the example organizations, not by external consultants or journalists. In reading these presentations, it becomes apparent that the transformations proposed in this volume cannot be reduced to a handbook. The design of an internal market economy and its implementation must reflect each organization's unique characteristics. External consultants may facilitate the process, but the conversion must be designed and implemented by those who will be most affected by it.

Of the four types of change, the most crucial one is the fourth, to an internal market economy. This transformation is more likely to lead to the others than any of the others is likely to lead to it. Although all four changes, or any combination of them, can be implemented simultaneously, any one of them can be put into effect without the others. However, the effects of combined implementation are greater than the sum of the effects of each taken separately. They have a multiplicative effect.

This book is more than a description of some pioneering efforts in organizational design: It is a challenge, a dare. American management has the competence required to make the transition to internal market economies. But does it have the courage to do so?

RUSSELL L. ACKOFF

BALA CYNWYD, PA

Introduction

The Single Most Important Change in Management Today

William E. Halal, Ali Geranmayeh, and John
Pourdehnad

As the world rushes into an information age of complex technologies, global markets, intense competition, and turbulent, constant change, the institutions that worked in the past are failing everywhere. Witness the collapse of communism; a crisis in government bureaucracies around the world; and the decline of corporations such as General Motors, IBM, and Sears, which were once models of successful management.

The enormity of this problem becomes evident by comparing it with the similar upheaval created by the industrial revolution two centuries ago. Just as the medieval castle, the monarchy, and other institutions of an agrarian era were transformed by the relentless advance of industrial technology into our present world, now the relentless advance of information technology is transforming society once again.

1

And today's breathtaking changes are merely a prelude to what is coming soon. The information revolution continues to roar ahead, steadily multiplying computing power by a factor of 10 every few years with no end in sight. John Scully, the visionary chairman of Apple Computer, put it this way: "So far we have been racing to the starting line. The really interesting stuff begins in the 1990s."[1]

The impact of this revolution amounts to a social earthquake, toppling our old pyramids of power to clear the landscape for new economic structures able to master a knowledge-based global order.[2] This book describes the economic foundation of management that is emerging to meet this challenge, a dramatically different system that harnesses the power of free markets *WITHIN* organizations—*INTERNAL MARKETS*.

NEW QUESTIONS ABOUT OLD BELIEFS

This unprecedented upheaval has forced executives to drastically restructure their companies. Massive layoffs, downsizing, and the elimination of layers of management have pruned most organizations back to their essential parts. These hierarchical skeletons are being fleshed out with a maze of cooperative ventures among competitors, alliances between suppliers and customers, research consortia uniting entire industries, and other innovative corporate structures.

Yet, the decline of big business continues unabated because these changes miss the heart of the problem. With a few notable exceptions, CEOs in industry after industry are feeling mounting frustration as their traditional wisdom proves ineffective in coping with an avalanche of confusing change. Where corporate Goliaths such as IBM and AT&T once gained crushing competitive power from their vaunted economies of scale, now size is proving a liability against nimble Davids such as Apple, Microsoft, and MCI—who may in turn suffer the same fate as they grow bigger.

A conceptual barrier is blocking our best efforts, causing a serious reexamination of basic assumptions about the nature of enterprise itself; new questions are being raised about the very notion of what a corporation or government agency consists of and how it should be organized and managed. Is size now fatal? Must the growth that accompanies success necessarily bring decline? How can small firms manage in a global economy? If large organizations are decentralized into federations of smaller companies, how can they be coordinated without impairing flexibility? Can *any* structure remain useful for long in a world of constant change?

Consider a few other examples of this conceptual dilemma. Large corporations comprise economic systems that are more extensive than all but the largest national economies. Yet most executives and scholars think of these corporate economies as "firms" to be managed with centralized controls. Listen to any typical discussion of corporate strategy and you will hear learned people talk of moving the resources of corporations about like a portfolio of investments, dictating which factories around the world should produce which products at which prices, setting annual and even quarterly targets for individual units, hiring and firing managers. How does this approach differ from the central planning that failed so utterly in the Communist bloc? Why would centralized controls be bad for a national economy but good for a *corporate* economy?

The great size of most corporations requires breaking them down into manageable divisions that constitute complete companies in their own right. Many of these divisions would rank in the Fortune 100 if considered separate firms, and some global corporations, such as Asea Brown Bovari (ABB), have thousands of profit centers. These units usually have their own distinct markets, clients, and competitors. At various times, they may sell their products to other divisions within the parent corporation, compete against one another for the same customers, and even award contracts to outside competitors. Again, troubling questions are raised about the nature of enterprise. What is best for the parent corporation as a whole? For the divisions? How do these "collections of small enterprises" differ from an ordinary market economy? Why should they remain together at all? In short, what truly *is* a corporation?

Our final example is from the public sector. The concept of educational choice is gaining acceptance, in which competition holds individual schools accountable for performance. Will this be sufficient to improve the old educational bureaucracy? Should schools be closed if they cannot compete? Should *all* public agencies allow their clients to select among competing units?

Although these unorthodox new issues violate tenets of traditional management principles, they are becoming commonplace. The effect of such heresy has been to challenge the prevailing paradigm of centrally planned, hierarchical organizations, which we believe is now obsolete. When Max Weber based today's "theory of bureaucracy" on principles of authoritarian hierarchy as the industrial age began, the concept was revolutionary because it brought huge gains in rationality, efficiency, and order. Now it means almost exactly the opposite: irrational adherence to petty rules, inefficient and unwieldy systems, and disregard for mounting chaos. The most damning thing a critic can say about an organization today is to call it a "bureaucracy."

The very system that once caused great success is now the cause of great failures. As our familiar old institutions began declining recently, the age of hierarchical organizations ended. What will take their place?

ORIGINS OF THE NEW MANAGEMENT PARADIGM

This book, *Internal Markets*, presents a new way of thinking about modern organizations. It is a collection of the pioneering work of notable executives, academics, and consultants who are creating a strikingly different, more powerful perspective of large institutions for a new economic era governed by the imperatives of information technology. Internal markets are *meta* structures, or *super* structures, that transcend ordinary organizational structures. Rather than being fixed structures, they are *systems* designed to produce continual, rapid, structural change to manage the unusual demands of today's complex, turbulent world.

A variety of well-known related concepts are emerging—flat organizations, intrapreneurship, organizational networks, reengineering, groupware, the virtual corporation, and many other creative innovations. How does this book differ from the wave of other publications offering a flood of such hot new business ideas?

The concepts described here are compatible with this literature, but they go beyond it to put today's innovations in perspective as part of a larger management revolution. *Internal Markets* carries today's evolution of management thought to its logical conclusion by providing a broader conceptual foundation based on the principles of free enterprise: complete internal market economies that bring all the advantages of free markets *INSIDE* large organizations, just like external economies.

Some of the ideas that led to this perspective have their origins in the classic works of famous scholars and practitioners. Alfred Sloan invented the concept that a large corporation should be decentralized into semiautonomous divisions, but his vision was lost as the General Motors bureaucracy grew to its present overblown condition.

The first widely published formulation of internal markets seems to have been made by Jay Forrester of the Massachusetts Institute of Technology in a 1965 article[3] that is reprinted in this book. At about that time, other pioneering scholars, such as Warren Bennis,[4] were warning of the impending demise of "mechanistic" bureaucracies and the need for "organic" structures, a term that nicely captured the spirit and feel of the coming revolution in management. Some creative executives, such as Robert Townsend, CEO of Avis, struggled to free their firms from the growing encrustation of bureaucracy.[5]

But the organic concept remained too vague for effective implementation because it lacked the central idea of market mechanisms. It also seems that the need for such great changes was not yet urgent enough to challenge deeply entrenched management beliefs. In 1984, Townsend issued a poignant summary of the problem:[6]

> The folks in the mailroom, the president, the vice presidents, and the steno pool . . . [are all] trapped in the pigeonholes of organization charts, they've been made slaves to the rules of private and public hierarchies that run mindlessly on because nobody can change them.

In retrospect, these early attempts at change generally failed because the transition to a new structural form constitutes a historic shift, and history is not driven by logic but by necessity. Major institutional change usually occurs only when environmental forces threaten survival.

Not until the turbulent 1980s did the United States finally experience an onslaught of corporate restructuring. The economic crisis of 1982, an invasion of Japanese firms onto American soil, a rush of technological change, and other such traumas forced executives to seriously rethink corporate designs. During this decade of creative change, Russell Ackoff, William Halal, Ali Geranmayeh, and John Pourdehnad were independently constructing their individual versions of the new management paradigm that converged into the work leading to this volume.

Ackoff had been building the concept of internal markets at the Wharton School, and in 1981 he outlined its key principles from the view of management science with the publication of *Creating the Corporate Future* (Wiley). Meanwhile at George Washington University, Halal started from a different perspective of strategic adaptation to a changing environment but reached a similar conclusion in 1986 with his book, *The New Capitalism* (Wiley). Ali Geranmayeh and John Pourdehnad, Ackoff's colleagues at INTERACT: The Institute for Interactive Management, were implementing these concepts through their consulting practice to develop a tested methodology of organizational transformation.

These different paths joined in 1990 when a consulting project undertaken by INTERACT occasioned a visit to Halal's office. Because the idea of internal markets was quite unknown at that time, it soon became apparent that a major meeting was needed to attract national attention. This realization led to the 1991 Conference on Internal Markets at Washington, DC, jointly sponsored by George Washington University and INTERACT.

To the best of our knowledge, this was the first meeting ever devoted to the topic. The conference attracted 100 leaders from business, government, academe, and consulting, most of whom had been experimenting with their own applications of the same idea. Once underway, the participants soon verified that the internal market perspective was intellectually sound, practically workable, and badly needed.

Later, all agreed that the relevant papers should be collected for publication, along with the work of others who could not attend. This book is the result of that effort. It is not a report of the conference proceedings, but rather a collection of what we consider to be the best available thought on the subject.

The following summary briefly describes the essence of the new management paradigm in terms of three central principles:

- *An Organization Is Composed of Internal Enterprise Units.* An organization is composed of numerous "internal enterprises" that form the building blocks of the corporate system. All internal enterprises, including line and staff units, are accountable for performance but gain autonomous control over their operations, as in any ordinary "external enterprise." This concept can also be carried down to the grass roots by decentralizing enterprises into autonomous work teams. Alliances between internal enterprises and work teams in different corporate systems link individual organizations together to form a global economy.

- *Corporate Executives Manage the Organizational Infrastructure.* Rather than managing operations through the chain of command, corporate executives design and regulate the infrastructure of their "organizational economy" just as federal governments manage national economies: establishing common systems for accounting, communications, financial incentives, education, governing policies, and the like. Top management may also encourage the formation of various business sectors that would exist in an economic system: venture capital firms, consultants, distributors, and so on.

- *Leadership Fosters Collaborative Synergy.* This system is more than a laissez-faire market, but a "community of fellow entrepreneurs" that fosters collaborative synergy by encouraging joint ventures and alliances, the sharing of technology, solutions for common problems, and mutual support among both internal and external partners. Corporate executives are the senior members of this community, so they provide the leadership to create a collaborative corporate culture, resolve obstacles, and guide this internal market in its shifting development of various strategies.

This brief summary cannot convey the full implications involved, nor can it answer the difficult questions we raised at the onset, especially because the internal market concept entails a paradigm shift that completely reorganizes prevailing management thought. That task is left to the following chapters. However, if one grasps the central concept that an internal market economy replicates the features of an external market economy, the remaining elements and behavior of market superstructures become fairly straightforward. The many examples of progressive corporations and governments that have adopted such systems demonstrate some striking results.

As a community of entrepreneurs uses its freedom to launch new products and services, hire and fire, buy and sell, both internally and externally, the same self-organizing, creative interplay occurs that makes all market economies so advantageous. Powerful solutions to difficult problems emerge quickly and almost spontaneously, spawning a rush of economic growth that could not conceivably have been foreseen, much less planned, by the most brilliant hierarchical system. Markets have their drawbacks, of course, but they are spreading around the globe because they excel over the only other alternative—central planning—whether in communist governments or capitalist corporations.

In both nations and organizations, planned economic systems are too cumbersome to cope with the avalanche of confusing, chaotic change now rushing down on society. The internal market paradigm is advantageous under these turbulent conditions because it is a *conceptual system for creating strategic organizational change.* Free enterprise, whether internal or external, remains the only economic philosophy able to produce an unending stream of adaptive change rapidly and efficiently.

TAKE AN INTELLECTUAL JOURNEY THROUGH *INTERNAL MARKETS*

Because the world is experiencing a historic upheaval, the most formidable challenge facing all of us is to reframe our prevailing beliefs. It is hard for most people to conceive how organizations can work without central control because we live in a culture based on hierarchy. The ideas in this book are valuable because they provide this vision, but they also require us to seriously consider a new mode of thought that seems illogical from our current point of view. When the concept of market metastructures is presented to groups, the first reaction often is that the idea is unworkable and bizarre.

The following chapters present this new paradigm in the most coherent, easily understood manner possible, but this will mean little unless you can make a mental shift in your present beliefs about the way organizations work. The authors of these chapters challenge the reader to temporarily accept the possibility of understanding organizations from a dramatically different perspective that violates many commonly accepted rules: Control can be best achieved through freedom; security is increased by accepting risk; structure is enhanced by change; and so on. By permitting yourself to explore this intellectual journey into a different world of market-based superstructures, you may return with a far more powerful, dynamic, and liberating perspective of institutions.

Part One provides a conceptual overview of this new management perspective. Russell Ackoff begins by asking us to consider the similarities between corporate and national economies, with the striking conclusion that capitalist corporations should be making the same structural changes now underway in former Communist governments. William Halal then shows how various trends all suggest that market systems represent the paradigm of the information age, with their own advantages and disadvantages, management imperatives, forms of behavior, and leadership. Jay Forrester updates his seminal 1965 article with current thoughts about the most crucial changes needed in American corporations. Raymond Miles and Charles Snow examine the strengths and limits of various organizational networks, presenting a different view of the internal market perspective. Peter Senge points out the limits of internal market structures, showing how learning processes are also badly needed. Finally, Ali Geranmayeh and John Pourdehnad tackle the difficult questions raised by internal markets to help readers evaluate practical applications of the concept.

Part Two offers the firsthand experiences of pioneering executives who have led their corporations through the transition to internal market systems and related metastructures. Bert Roberts and John Zimmerman outline the principles of their corporate culture that have made MCI such a dynamic organization. John Starr describes how internal markets revitalized Alcoa by reintroducing the company to economic reality. James Rinehart offers highlights from his career at General Motors and Clark Equipment to suggest that even the CEO's office should become a profit center. David Noer recalls the lessons he learned in converting Control Data's support units into internal consulting firms. Julio Bartol and Ali Geranmayeh draw on their experiences with Armco's Latin American division to present a practical approach for linking internal markets and corporate strategy. John MacLean shows how a decentralization strategy transformed Canadian Imperial Bank of Commerce. Joseph Gamble, Michael Sheehan, and Seton Shields examine the problems and benefits they encountered forming subsidiaries to jump-start Blue Cross/Blue Shield. And John Charlton offers plans under way to make the R&D function at Esso Petroleum of Canada a self-supporting enterprise. All of these personal accounts include frank analyses of the challenges these companies faced, the issues they wrestled with, and their successes and failures.

Part Three then provides similar firsthand accounts that extend this discussion to the public sector. James Pinkerton passes on to the Clinton Administration the "New Paradigm" of government that he proposed during the Bush Administration. David Osborne applies the principles of this entrepreneurial form of government to sketch out a plan for Washington, DC. William Halal, Charles Blake, and Kathryn Sheldon Hammler conclude with a study showing that the federal government is adopting internal markets.

A CORPORATE PERESTROIKA FOR THE INFORMATION AGE

These chapters have their limits individually, but taken together, they show that the transition from hierarchy to enterprise is well underway, with profound implications. In a decade or so, our prevailing notion of management may seem as archaic as the medieval belief in the divine right of kings. Instead of today's fervent conviction that organizations must inevitably be top-down, hierarchical pyramids of power and constraining rules, the idea of market metastructures should create a different form of entrepreneurial management based on the same principles that guide external market systems.

There are caveats. No organizational design can be perfect, so internal markets incur risks, inequalities, and other messy problems of market systems. Like all broad management frameworks, the market perspective offers a conceptual approach, rather than detailed solutions, which each manager must adapt to his or her own needs. In fact, this approach may not be appropriate for some organizations. And, as Peter Senge points out, structural change does not address behavioral issues directly, which is why an internal market must be designed as a total system that includes new processes for organizational learning, decision making, and other behavioral factors.

Russell Ackoff reminds us in the Foreword, however, that a market orientation is the first imperative for revitalizing institutions because it defines the structural foundation supporting all other aspects of management. By organizational *structure*, we mean the way managers design operating units, join them together in working relationships, set up reward systems, form communication channels, and so on; organizational *behavior* describes how people act within this structure. A sound structure does not *assure* effective behavior, but it is an essential starting point. It is necessary but not sufficient. As we continually point out in this book, talented employees, collaborative leadership, inspired strategies, and other factors are also needed to create excellence. However, these are secondary causes because it is difficult for people to work effectively in a faulty structural foundation. *Structure is the first requirement for good management.*

That is the basic problem facing managers today. Capable, well-intentioned people working in General Motors, IBM, the federal government, schools, hospitals, and other organizations are struggling against outmoded bureaucratic structures. American society must redesign its institutions into modern superstructures built on market concepts appropriate for a new economic era.[7]

This impending shift to a dynamic model of organization forms the single most important change taking place in economics today. Modern nations such as the United States are in the throes of a management revolution that presents roughly the same challenges and opportunities posed by today's restructuring of socialist economies—a "corporate Perestroika for the Information Age." To quote John Scully[8] again:

> The command-and-control model of running a large organization no longer works . . . the single biggest theme in the world of business during the 1990s . . . [will be] the reorganization of work using information systems to compete in the marketplace.

If the United States can rise to this challenge, we could harness the creative power of American individualism to regain competitive leadership in a global economy. A hopeful factor is that this would be a logical extension of the American principles of democratic free enterprise that are now creating revolutions around the world. Internal market metastructures offer the same powerful advantages of free markets that have overthrown communism: myriad opportunities for achievement, liberation from authority, accountability for performance, entrepreneurial freedom, creative innovation, high quality and service, self-organization, ease of handling complexity, fast reaction time, flexibility for adaptive change, and great personal and financial rewards.

To realize these possibilities, however, we must recognize the crucial but difficult new idea that organizations can be more effectively understood, designed, and managed as market economies in their own right to create a far more dynamic, liberating, and productive new class of organizational metastructures. The evidence in the following chapters shows that powerful forces are moving in this direction, but confusion reigns because a useful concept has been lacking to capture this new economic reality now emerging quite rapidly. This book presents that concept.

PART ONE

THE PERSPECTIVE OF INTERNAL MARKETS

1 Corporate Perestroika

The Internal Market Economy

Russell L. Ackoff

Perestroika, the Russian word for "restructuring," is applied to the recent efforts of the former Soviet Union to convert from a centrally planned and controlled economy to a market economy. A centrally planned and controlled national economy has never attained as high a level of economic development as that reached by national market economies. Although not every national market economy has flourished, all truly vital economies have been market economies.

Curiously, in our country, which has a market economy, most organizations, institutions, and government agencies operate with centrally

Russell L. Ackoff is chairman of INTERACT: The Institute for Interactive Management; August A. Busch Jr. Visiting Professor of Marketing at John M. Olin School of Business, Washington University; and professor emeritus of Management Science of The Wharton School, University of Pennsylvania. Among his many publications are his widely known books, *Creating the Corporate Future* and *Management in Small Doses* (New York: Wiley).

planned and controlled economies. Their internal economies are more like the national economy that the former Soviet Union is trying to get rid of than the national economy that we have. Unfortunately, many, if not most, of our corporate and institutional economies are currently in decline largely because, like the old Soviet Union, they contain and are constrained by many units that are bureaucratic monopolies.

In search of economies of scale, centrally planned and controlled economies in nations and corporations tend to create monopolistic providers of goods and services. For example, in corporations, accounting, personnel, and R&D departments are usually deliberately organized as subsidized monopolies. They are subsidized in the sense that the users of their products or services do not pay for them directly; the supplying units are supported financially by funds allocated from above. The pool for these funds is filled by a "tax" assigned to the units served. Subsidized monopolistic units are generally insensitive and unresponsive to the users of their services, but they are sensitive and responsive to the desires of the higher level units that subsidize them. These higher level units, which are even more removed from the units being served, are often unaware of, or unresponsive to, the needs and desires of such users of monopolistically provided goods and services.

However, this is only the beginning of the problems that centrally planned and controlled economies create within nations, institutions, and public and private organizations. Other problems include oversizing, excessive layers of management, and spans of control that are too small. Bureaucracies try to ensure their survival by becoming as large as possible; they operate on the (not unreasonable) assumption that the larger they are, the more difficult they are to eliminate. As a result, oversizing has become a congenital problem in many American organizations. Centralized economic planning and control allow subordinate organizational units to become bloated largely because those in control are rarely aware of the overpopulation in each of the units they control and because their status is often judged to be proportional to the number of people subordinate to them. Companies operate using the so-called information supplied by the managers of these bureaucratic units, but managers usually generate this information to justify whatever their units are doing, however inefficient it may be. The current rash of down- and rightsizing activities in American corporations reflects the growing awareness of centralized management's complete lack of population control. The large cuts at IBM and Kodak are only two of many recent examples.

Bloating is especially prevalent in corporate headquarters. For example, when Clark Equipment Company got into serious financial difficulty and converted from a centrally planned economy to an internal market, its headquarters was reduced from about 450 people to about 70, and its performance improved.

In addition, because salaries are usually attached to ranks in American organizations, people are often promoted to managerial ranks, not because a manager is needed, but because this is the only way to award them additional compensation. To justify the promotion, one or two people are assigned to them. This makes for very small spans of control, leading in turn to excessive layering. On average, the United States has approximately two and a half times as many managers and layers of management as the Japanese have.

Centrally planned and controlled economies also stimulate the growing costs of internally provided products and services because the supplying units do not need to compare their costs and prices with those of external suppliers of the same products and services. As a result, they seldom know what their internal costs actually are. Therefore, they have no systematic way of benchmarking those costs. In contrast, units operating in a competitive economy cannot survive without knowing and meeting the prices at which their competitors are providing comparable goods and services.

Transfer pricing, which is the surrogate for market pricing in a centrally planned and controlled economy, produces intense internal conflict and competition. Peter Drucker once observed that competition within corporations is much more intense than competition between them and, moreover, is a lot less ethical. Corporate units usually have much more cooperative relationships with their external suppliers than with their internal sources of goods and services.

It is almost impossible to determine the economic value of a subsidized internal monopolistic provider of a service or product—for example, a corporate computing or telecommunication center, a centralized R&D unit, or a human resources or organizational development department. In a market economy, users, not subsidizers, evaluate suppliers and express their evaluation in a way that counts, by their purchases.

The managers of most so-called business units within corporations do not know what their total costs are. In particular, they seldom know how much capital they employ and what the cost of that capital is. Their cost of capital is usually hidden in costs allocated to them from above. Allocated costs are sometimes as high as 40 percent of total unit costs.

How can managers reasonably be held responsible for the financial performance of their units when they neither know nor can control a large portion of their costs, in particular, their costs of capital?

MACRO- VERSUS MICROECONOMIES

The macroeconomy of the United States involves relatively autonomous competitive suppliers of goods and services. Some regulation of these units is required because, among other things, they do not have perfect information about the market. Further, they do not always behave ethically or in the best interests of their stakeholders, their environments, or the systems that contain them, including society at large. To the extent there is centralized control, it is supposed to provide only enough regulation to enable the market to operate effectively.

Why do we have one type of economy at the national level and another at the organizational level? Some argue that the economic problems of a nation are of a different magnitude and complexity than those of companies. This is not so, however; IBM and AT&T are among the largest economies in the world. Very few nations have larger economies. Even fewer are as complex.

Such considerations lead to the question: What would be the effects of organizing corporations and public institutions around internal market economies? Would their performance be better or worse?

INTERNAL MARKET ECONOMIES

In an internal market economy virtually all organizational units, including executive offices, operate as profit centers. The only exceptions to this requirement are units whose output cannot or should not be provided to any external user and that have only one internal user. The corporate secretary, for example, serves the chief executive officer and no one else. Therefore, this secretary should operate as a cost center attached to the executive office, which in turn should operate as a profit center. A unit that produces a product whose composition is secret for competitive reasons would also not be expected to operate as a profit center and therefore would be a cost center that is a part of a profit center.

Not all profit centers are expected to be profitable, but their profitability is taken into account in evaluating their performance. For example, a company may retain an unprofitable unit because of the prestige it brings the parent (e.g., Steuben Glass at Corning) or because its product is used as a loss leader. An unprofitable unit may also manufacture a product or provide a service that is required to complete or round out a product or service line.

Subject to the minimal constraints discussed in this chapter, profit centers should have the freedom (1) to buy any service or product they want from whatever source they choose, and (2) to sell their outputs to whomever they want at whatever price they want or are willing to accept. Because some corporate units may lack relevant information about other corporate units and, more importantly, about the complex interactions among units, they might not act in the best interests of the corporation as a whole. Therefore, higher level units must be able to intervene when lower level units fail to act in the best interests of the whole of which they are part. The only justification for a corporation that consists of units operating as business units, is the value that the corporation adds to them. One way it can do so is to require internal purchasers of goods or services that are provided by another internal unit to give the internal supplying unit the opportunity to meet externally quoted prices. However, even if the internal supplier meets or goes under an externally quoted price, the internal buyer can elect to use the external supplier for other than cost reasons, for example, because of the quality of products or services provided.

A corporation with an internal market economy can only add value to its units if it can intervene effectively in their buying and selling decisions, but it should use this authority only when doing so benefits the corporation as a whole. This can be accomplished through executive interventions of the type discussed next.

Executive Overrides

At times a corporate executive may believe that a purchase made by a subordinate unit from an external source even at a lower price than that of an internal supplier, would be harmful to the corporation. In such a case, the executive can require that the purchase be made from the internal supplier, but that executive must pay for the difference between the internal and external price. This means that the buying unit will not have to pay more than it would have paid had it been free to buy from the external source. In addition, since an executive who overrides a subordinate unit will also be a profit center, he or she will have to consider explicitly the benefits as well as the costs of such interventions.

In one case, an executive vice president consistently required one internal unit to buy a major component of its product line from another internal unit. In many cases, the component could have been obtained externally for less money. As a result, at the end of the year the vice president had been charged several million dollars for his overrides. He then reevaluated his policy and decided to free the units to do as they wanted the following year. Not only did each improve its financial performance, but these previously antagonistic units became friendly and cooperative, and the executive stopped feeling like the referee of a prize fight.

When a corporate executive believes that a sale an internal unit wants to make to an external customer is not in the corporation's best interests, he or she can override that sale, but only by providing the internal unit with the amount of profit it would have made from that sale. This means that a selling unit will never have to sell its output at a price lower than it has negotiated.

When a manager believes an external purchase or sale should never be made, he or she can act like a government relative to his or her subordinate units by establishing appropriate restrictive rules or regulations. The federal government of the United States prevents the sale of certain (e.g., military) products to certain foreign countries because it considers such sales to be against our national interests. Corporate managers may act similarly. Coca Cola is not about to allow an external supplier to make Coke syrup.

The Executive Unit

As noted earlier, the executive unit operates as a profit center. It incurs costs when it overrides purchasing or selling decisions of subordinate internal units. It also incurs other costs for obtaining consulting or staff services, for interest on money it has borrowed, and for taxes and dividends it has to pay.

The executive unit also has two major sources of income. First, it charges for the operating and investment capital it supplies to subordinate units. These units then know what capital they are using and pay for that capital at a cost related to their riskiness and what that capital costs the corporation. (Where a subordinate unit is set up as a wholly owned but separate corporation, it may be given the option of obtaining capital wherever it wants.) The second source of income to the executive unit is a tax it imposes on the profitability of each unit. This tax should cover the operating cost of the executive unit. The tax rate should be established in advance of the period in which it is to be applied, and with the participation of the taxed units. That is, there should be no taxation without representation. (The "circular organization" facilitates such representation.[1])

Operating an executive unit as a profit center helps assure that it is efficient and that the tax it levies is kept low.

Profit Accumulation

Each profit center should be permitted to accumulate profit up to a level set for that unit (this level may vary by unit). Profit up to the limit should be available to the unit for any use it desires as long as that use does not have an adverse effect on any other part of the corporation or the corporation as a whole. Accumulations of capital in excess of the specified amount should be passed up to the next higher level of the organization for its use or for transmission to a still higher level. Excess accumulation of capital by a unit indicates its inability to invest it profitably. Therefore, it should be handed over to a part of the organization that can so invest it. This policy tends to elevate the status of "cash cows" in an organization because it underscores that they are the engine of growth and development.

A unit that provides its excess profit to a higher level unit should be paid interest on it by that higher level unit at a rate no less than that obtainable outside the corporation.

PUBLIC SECTOR APPLICATIONS

The use of internal market economies is by no means restricted to private for-profit organizations. It can and has been used effectively in the public sector. For example, a voucher system for supporting public schools was developed by Christopher Jenks of Harvard University and publicized by Milton Friedman. In this system, schools obtain their only income from cashing vouchers paid to them by parents of children who have applied to and been accepted by the school. Children and their parents can apply to any school they want. Local governments supply parents with the vouchers. The vouchers can also be used to cover all or part of the tuition required by private schools.

The voucher system not only puts public schools into competition with each other, but it also makes them compete with private schools.

To survive, schools must provide a service sufficiently valued by students and their parents to induce them to turn over their vouchers.

If, in such a system, schools had to select among applicants at random, segregation in schools would become a nonissue. This could be modified by a requirement to accept any student living within a specified area of responsibility; schools would then select at random only from applicants living outside that area.

In another example, a centralized licensing bureau in Mexico City had a terrible record of inefficiency and poor service. It was broken up into small offices in each section of the city. The income of each office was derived exclusively from a fee paid to it by the city government for each license it issued. (The amount varied by type of license.) Those wanting a license could obtain it from any office. Unlike the former centralized bureaucratic monopoly, the new offices could only survive by attracting and satisfying customers. Service time decreased, service quality increased, and overall costs and corruption within the offices decreased.

An internal market economy can be employed by many government service agencies, and to the extent that it is, the public's pressure to privatize these services might significantly decrease.

POSSIBLE OBJECTIONS

Proposals for the introduction of a market economy in an organization usually give rise to four types of concerns.

First, skeptics argue that the additional amount of accounting required by such a system would be horrendous. Not true. The amount of accounting required is actually reduced. Most of the accounting and reporting currently done by organizational units is to facilitate their control by higher level units. In an internal market economy, only profit-and-loss statements and balance sheets need to be provided to higher level units. Any additional information requested by higher level units should be paid for by those units. This requirement has a strong tendency to reduce the amount of unnecessary accounting information flowing within organizations, particularly up.

Second, some argue that an internal market economy will increase conflict and competition between internal units. Again, not true. Most organizational units have much better relations with their external suppliers than they do with internal units (1) whose services or products they are forced to use, or (2) with which they also compete for scarce resources. Internal suppliers who must compete with external suppliers for internal customers' business are much more responsive to these customers than monopolistic internal suppliers.

The corporate computing center of one very large corporation provided services to all units of the corporation without charge. Its costs were covered by corporate headquarters. These funds were extracted from overhead payments made by every corporate unit. The units using the center complained continuously about the poor service it provided and wanted to engage more responsive external services. Units making little or no use of the center resented the overhead assessment that did not take their lack of usage into account. On the other hand, the computing center head complained about the unreasonable requests and expectations of users of his center. These dissatisfactions led to the CEO's request for an evaluation of the center's output to determine whether it was worth its high cost.

Despite heroic efforts to determine that unit's worth, it could not be done. The schedules of production operations, which constituted the major output of the center, were significantly modified by plant managers before they were applied, and no record was kept of these modifications.

Following the suggestion made to him, the CEO converted the computing center into a profit center whose services had to be paid for by using units at a price set by the serving unit. However, users were allowed to use external services, and the center was permitted to sell its services to external customers.

Within a few months, the number of computers in the center was reduced by half. Nevertheless, the center was doing almost all the work required by internal units. Now that they had to pay for it, however, these units significantly reduced the amount of computing they requested. Moreover, they were much more satisfied with the services they received. In addition, the center acquired a number of external customers whom it served very profitably. It obtained a return on the investment higher than that obtained by any other unit in the corporation.

In another case, a diversified food manufacturer had a large market research unit with a monopoly on corporate work. Most of the units that had to use it regarded it poorly because they felt the research unit was unresponsive to their needs and offered inferior service. It too was converted into a profit center with the requirement that it become profitable within two years or else be eliminated. However, it was given freedom to sell its services to whomever it wanted. On the other hand, its internal users were given freedom to obtain their market research wherever they wanted. Every one of them initially moved to external suppliers. As a result, the internal unit was forced to look for external work. It eventually succeeded, but only after significantly improving the quality of its services. In time, it became a thriving business. Internal units became curious about its success and began to try it again. This time they found it responsive to their needs. Internal demand became so great that the unit had to reduce, but not eliminate, its external work. It did not have to sacrifice profitability to do so.

A third argument for rejecting the adoption of an internal market economy is that it cannot be installed in a part of an organization, only in the whole. This, it is asserted, may be very difficult, if not impossible, to arrange. Difficult, yes, but impossible, no. In 1988, the Kodak Apparatus Division—Kodak's manufacturing arm that produces copiers, X-ray equipment, medical devices, cameras (i.e., everything but film)— converted to an internal market economy. Its first problem was that the corporation of which it was a part did not want to convert to an internal market economy. As a result, KAD had to operate as a market-oriented economy within a centrally planned and controlled economy.

Kodak continued to charge KAD for services, and KAD could not break the charges down into those for services it used and those it didn't. Therefore, KAD had to develop surrogate costs. It treated the estimated cost of corporately provided services that it did not use as a tax. Furthermore, it had to continue reporting to the corporation as it had before converting to an internal market economy. Therefore, it had to maintain one set of books for the corporation and another for itself.

One year after its conversion, KAD's effectiveness had increased so much that the corporation began to pay attention to it. The corporation as a whole did not convert to an internal market economy, but KAD's experience led to changes in the corporate bookkeeping system that allowed it to operate more easily with an internal market economy. Other Kodak units have since followed suit.

Like KAD in Kodak, the research and development unit of Esso Petroleum Canada also converted to an internal market economy within a centrally controlled corporate economy, but in this case the containing unit tried to facilitate the conversion. It did so because it considered the conversion to be a trial which, if successful, would lead it to support similar conversions of other of its units, and eventually of the whole.

A fourth reason often given for not taking the idea of an internal market economy seriously is that certain internal service functions cannot "reasonably" be expected to obtain external customers. Accounting and legal departments are often cited as examples. Nevertheless, one corporation headquartered in a small city in the Midwest converted both its accounting and legal departments into profitable business units. Many local small and medium-sized companies lacked access to high quality professional accountants and attorneys and wanted their services badly. This enabled the accounting and legal departments to sell services externally at a very good price. As a consequence, the quality of their services improved significantly to retain external customers. The external contacts also led to the formation of several significant strategic alliances.

Another company that occupied a number of buildings in a suburb of a major metropolitan area converted its facilities-and-services department (buildings, grounds, and utilities) into a profit center that operated within a corporate internal market economy. All of its internal users shifted to outside agencies from which they obtained better services at a lower cost than had been provided by the internal unit. As a result, the service department gradually shrank and was eventually eliminated at a considerable saving to the company.

ADVANTAGES OF AN INTERNAL MARKET ECONOMY

A number of the benefits of an internal market economy have already been identified: in particular, increased responsiveness of internal suppliers, better quality and lower cost of internally supplied services and products, continuous rightsizing, elimination of fluff, debureaucratization, demonopolization, and so on. A few other advantages are worth mentioning.

First, because virtually every corporate unit operating within an internal market economy becomes a profit center, similar measures of performance can be applied to all of them. This makes it possible to compare performances of units that were previously not comparable, for example, manufacturing and accounting.

Second, the manager of a profit center within an internal market economy is necessarily a general manager of a semiautonomous business unit, which provides all unit managers with opportunities to improve and display their general management skills. Therefore, executives are better able to evaluate the general management ability of their subordinates.

Third, when units are converted to profit centers and acquire autonomy, their managers are in a much better position to obtain all the information they require to manage well. They become more concerned with finding the information they need than with providing requested information to their superiors.

CONCLUSIONS

Because conversion to an internal market economy raises a number of problems of adaptation, it is not a task that attracts the fainthearted; it requires considerable courage. Moreover, conversion to an internal market economy is risky for those managers whose units either are unable to compete effectively in the open market or are no longer needed within the corporation. Such units are very likely to be eliminated in an internal market economy. That they should be eliminated offers little solace to those who are affected. The possibility of creating activities that will use excess personnel productively is seldom considered in such circumstances. Nevertheless, the managers who are responsible for the excess are generally retained and moved to another unproductive activity.

A major obstruction to the conversion to an internal market economy is the reluctance of many higher level managers to share with their subordinates information to which they alone have had access. To be sure, information is power, and many managers are not willing to share their power. Unfortunately, they fail to recognize that there are two kinds of power: power-over and power-to. Power-over is authority to command, whereas power-to is the ability to implement. The relationship between these two types of power becomes increasingly negative as the educational level of those managed and the technical content of their jobs increase. Internal market economies may decrease managers' power-over, but they more than make up for this loss by increasing their power-to. This truth is no consolation to those who value power-over for its own sake. Those who want authority for its own sake and ignore its consequences do not fit into a democratic organization.

Installing internal market economies in American corporations can allow them to increase their effectiveness by an order of magnitude. Such restructuring is as important to our country on the microeconomics level as it was to the Soviet Union on the macroeconomics level. Without it, we are destined to experience continued economic stagnation.

2 The Transition from Hierarchy to . . . What?

Market Systems Are the Paradigm of the Information Age

William E. Halal

How can we explain the remarkable fact that American institutions began failing at about the same time the Soviet Union collapsed? In 1991, blue-chip companies began ousting their CEOs, the federal government was in gridlock, health care was heading toward a financial crisis, and the educational system was heavily criticized. In 1993, IBM, once regarded as the best managed corporation in the world, recorded the biggest business loss in history, which was shortly exceeded by General Motors.

William E. Halal is professor of management at George Washington University. Portions of this chapter are adapted from the author's publications: "Corporate Perestroika," *Christian Science Monitor* (August 6, 1991); "Internal Markets: Bringing Free Enterprise *Inside* the Organization," Proceedings of 1990 Annual Meeting of the Academy of Management; and *The New Capitalism* (New York: Wiley, 1986).

The basic problem in all these cases is not the people but the *system*. These institutions are suffering from the same crippling illness that has become one of the biggest problems of our time—a bureaucratic inability to cope with today's turbulent new world. In an ironic twist of history, capitalist corporations as well as Communist governments are both trapped in centrally planned, hierarchical structures of the past, and so Americans and Russians face the common challenge of moving to a new management system.

Many creative changes are underway to solve this problem, but we badly need a better way to think about the transition from the hierarchy to the . . . to the what? Therein lies the central issue. What *IS* the new model of organizational structure evolving for the information age? Surely, there must be a more precise, useful concept than the terms we hear so often: "flat structures," "lean management," "flexible organizations," and other vague notions that only modify the existing system. The biggest reason economies are stalled today is that we lack a well-defined model, theory, or paradigm for the way modern organizations work, so we are all confused about what we should be doing.

My colleague, Russell Ackoff, and I agree the answer lies in extending our analogy between corporations and centrally planned economies. Just as the old Communist bloc knows it must adopt markets, so too have leading-edge corporations been moving to market systems—internal markets. The blur of management fads flooding the media can be confusing, but one of the most striking trends of the past decade is the growing use of "intrapreneuring," "internal customers," and other internal equivalents of free markets. Some firms have even been using internal leveraged buyouts (LBOs) to let managers gain control of their units.[1]

There are many less obvious trends toward internal markets as well. Former monolithic hierarchies such as AT&T and IBM have been decentralizing into small "internal enterprises"—like the privatization of state enterprises in the old Communist bloc. Pay-for-performance systems are linking employee rewards to contributions—roughly the way the Russians are introducing incentive pay. Corporate staffs are being converted into profit centers that sell their services to line units—as are Communist apparatchiks having to compete now. Tom Peters urged: "Force the market into every nook and cranny of the firm."[2]

Now, I realize this idea seems fraught with conflict, duplication of effort, and other controversial issues, and it is certainly true that internal markets incur the same risks, turmoil, and other drawbacks of any market system. But that is precisely the point. The concept represents a badly needed shift to a different mode of organizational logic that we must learn to understand if we hope to master the complexity of a knowledge-based global economy.

Organizations have been dominated by top-down control because bureaucratic structures were needed to manage an industrial past. What could be more reasonable in an age of machines than to construct institutions themselves as "social machines?" But in an information age, a new type of "metaorganization" is emerging to match the structural form of the future—the social networks, groupware, virtual organizations, and other superstructures made possible by information technology (IT). Just as factories gave rise to the chain of command, IT is connecting people from diverse locations to work together on common problems. And the heart of all these metasystems is the use of market mechanisms. Internal markets provide a sound economic foundation for modern management based on the dynamic principles of free enterprise.

The result is that a revolution is imminent in the way organizations work. Modern corporations are no longer pyramids of employees working from 9 to 5 at fixed locations, but self-organizing clusters of roaming entrepreneurs connected together by social and information networks. Across these superstructures, the universal foundation of free market economics is linking organizations together into a worldwide web of business alliances to form a global economy. Without any planning, a central nervous system for the planet is emerging in which power, initiative, and control originate among ordinary people from the bottom up.

This chapter describes the transition to internal market systems, focusing on how the concept can create internal equivalents of all external market functions. Next, it examines how today's revolution in information technology is driving this transformation, the pros and cons of the idea, and the role of workers and leaders in such an organization. Finally, we see how the concept offers a model for the global corporation.

THE INTERNAL MARKET MODEL

The beauty of the internal market model is that it is a simple idea with profound ramifications—the goal is to replace hierarchical controls with market forces. This key principle leads to the possibility of replicating within organizations the same features we have long used successfully in external markets, thereby creating entire internal market economies. This is not simply an academic theory but represents a growing body of successful business practice, as attested by the experiences of creative CEOs.

The Decentralization Contract: A Paradox in Power

Like most crucial problems in management, the basic issue is power. The old hierarchical system centralized authority up the chain of command, so we assumed that maintaining control over subordinates was synonymous with good management. Peter Drucker quipped, "So much of what we call management consists of making it difficult for people to work." Robert Levison, an operating executive at a major company,[3] described the usual result:

> I am tired of the waste that our centralized forms of management create. Big companies have become almost socialistic. The division manager is summoned to corporate headquarters every so often for a "review," typically by 25 corporate executives [questioning] your operation. The payoff? Humiliated division managers, who learn once more that their job is to execute orders, not to make decisions, and a hodgepodge of numbers to juggle in order to make them come out the way the experts thought they ought to. Management people throughout the U.S. [should] rise up in rebellion.

Everyone suffers from this authoritarian business culture. CEOs are forced to carry the impossible burden of monitoring virtually everything to gain a godlike omniscience in knowing "each sparrow that falls," and they bear the main responsibility for getting things done. The result is that managers throughout the chain of command often become bottlenecks choking the flow of action, and the chief executive is usually the chief bottleneck. One manager described the resulting bureaucratic labyrinth that had to be negotiated at IBM: "All day long, it's a constant round of meetings where nothing gets done."[4]

At the bottom of the hierarchy, subordinates lack sufficient challenge and rewards, so they allow the organization to drift into inaction. The most notorious instance is the paternalistic system of Communist economies that discouraged initiative, but the situation is not too different in many corporations. Here's the way employees described it at IBM: "As long as you shined your shoes and said good morning to your boss, you had a job for life."[5] The time is ripe for changing this out-moded system, and Jack Welch, GE's brash but charismatic CEO, who is widely considered one of the most dynamic executives in the United States, agrees:[6]

> In an environment where we must have every good idea from every man and woman in the organization, we can no longer afford management styles that suppress and intimidate.

The solution is a "decentralization contract" combining control of performance with freedom of operations, or what Peters and Waterman called "simultaneous loose–tight properties." Hewlett-Packard is famous for its entrepreneurial management that holds employees accountable for results but gives them wide operating latitude. As one HP executive described it, "The financial controls are very tight, what is loose is how (people) choose to meet those goals." This sharply focused understanding enhances both control and freedom to provide two major advantages:

1. It ensures accountability for performance of all units.
2. It encourages creative entrepreneurial action.

Major forces are now relentlessly restructuring corporations in this direction. Competition is producing great pressure to reduce administrative overhead and permit innovation, while powerful information systems are automating middle-management functions. As a result, roughly two million middle-management jobs were eliminated during the 1980s, about every third manager,[7] wiping out the heart of the old corporate hierarchy. Jack Welch described the change at GE: "We used to go from the CEO to sectors, to groups, to businesses," he said. "We now go from the CEO to businesses. Nothing else is in between."[8]

However, providing a sharp, sound focus on controlling the performance of operating units while minimizing intrusions on their autonomy poses a difficult challenge. There is wide agreement that a combination of performance measures is needed to ensure a realistic balance that avoids overemphasizing short-term profit: customer satisfaction, product quality, and the like.[9] Managers are then held accountable through incentive pay, bonuses, stock plans, budget allocations, or outright dismissal.

If this difficult combination of accountability and freedom can be developed, a crucial paradox occurs in the use of power: a superior form of control can be achieved—not by curtailing freedom, but *through* freedom—by encouraging large numbers of autonomous enterprises to nibble away at complex problems. The result is an organization that is almost self-managing because people may use their own judgment as long as they produce results.

Converting Support Units into Profit Centers

Decentralizing line units into autonomous profit centers is fairly common now, but the concept is also being applied to corporate staff units, manufacturing operations, research and development, marketing and sales offices, and even the CEO. Raymond Smith, CEO of Bell Atlantic,[10] expressed the logic best:

> We are determined to revolutionize staff support, to convert a bureaucratic roadblock into an entrepreneurial force. Staffs tend to grow and produce services that may be neither wanted or required. I decided to place the control of discretionary staff in the hands of those who were paying for them . . . line units. . . . The most important thing is that spending for support activities is now controlled by clients.

The chapters in this book show that many corporations have been extending internal markets into this new domain. For instance, David Noer's experience in converting support units at Control Data into profit centers was fraught with trouble, but it also introduced a healthy discipline and sense of achievement.[11]

Corporate Information Resource Management (IRM) units are moving strongly in this direction. The old approach is to have the CIO's office impose its choice of IT equipment on passive users. The internal market perspective redefines the situation so that line units buy their own equipment and services from the CIO's office or outside competitors. Many corporations find that converting the IRM function into a profit center dramatically improves IT performance,[12] which is confirmed in a later chapter on the federal government.

The concept can also solve difficult problems in manufacturing. State-of-the-art manufacturing facilities are productive but expensive, so it is essential to use them effectively. The chapter by John Starr shows that the solution is to treat these facilities as "internal job shops" that produce goods for internal and external clients. Bruce Merrifield at the U.S. Department of Commerce notes that manufacturing is "becoming a service function. Plants are making different products for different companies in different industries."[13]

Likewise, R&D can be defined as a service that assists line units in developing products. In a following chapter, John Charlton describes how Esso Canada is converting its research department into a profit center. The concept of "core competence"[14] also fits nicely into this larger schema. Firms must focus on a few core competencies, but how should these units be managed? All such technical groups should be treated as service units, working under contract to provide technical knowledge or producing inventions to be sold through licensing agreements.

On the downstream end of any business, marketing, sales, logistics, and customer service units can be reorganized into the internal equivalent of distributorships. Like ordinary distributors, these profit centers represent the full line of a company's products for some particular region to provide the integrated service that individual business units cannot. Johnson & Johnson established "customer-support centers" that handle sales, distribution, and other services for the company's retailers.[15]

In a later chapter, Jim Rinehart contends that even the office of the CEO should be a profit center to set an example for the rest of the firm. Revenue comes from the return on assets invested in profit centers (similar to a venture capital firm), and from a portion of all sales (like a "tax" of the "corporate government"). Some CEOs may not want to go this far, but it underscores the key principle for creating internal markets: All functions of external markets can be replicated within organizations.

These concepts can be applied in a variety of ways, but an essential discipline results from allowing all units the freedom to conduct normal business transactions both inside and outside the firm. Without that freedom, internal units are subject to the monopoly power, bureaucracy, and administrative overhead of their business partners, roughly the way apparatchiks overcontrolled the Soviet economy. Tom Peters put it this way:[16]

> Insist that every element of the firm—even staff—demonstrate "fitness to compete" by selling a substantial share of their products or services on the outside market . . . and by purchasing goods and services on the outside.

Self-Organizing, Internal Market Economies

Thus, the most critical element for transforming a hierarchy into a market system is linking freedom to accountability, thereby allowing units to move through the system freely, taking on responsibilities they choose and drawing on capital, facilities, personnel, and information to accomplish their task. The role of executives is to create a superstructural framework of performance controls, incentives, and communications, and then to provide encouragement, support, and other forms of leadership to assist the internal market in allocating resources spontaneously instead of by administrative fiat.

Figure 2–1 illustrates the internal market system that would result from decentralizing a 3-dimensional matrix with product, functional, and geographic structures. The heart of the system consists of new ventures spun off by product divisions to become independent business units that develop and market their own products. Functional support units are profit centers that sell their assistance to other units or external businesses. Geographic areas are also profit centers,

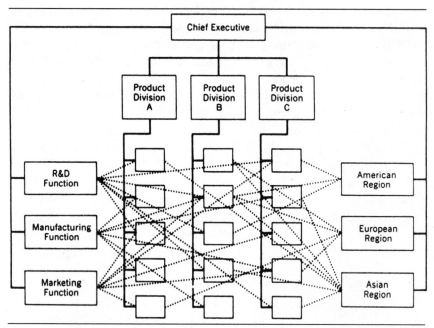

FIGURE 2–1.   Example of an internal market organization.

distributing products and services from various divisions to clients in their region.

This system could be thought of as an organizational network, but the internal market concept offers a more encompassing model. Markets do create networks of business relationships, but the reverse is not true; networks say little about the transactions involved in these relationships. The key ingredient in creating the organization of the future is to base such metastructural systems on an internal market economy in which all units behave as internal enterprises coordinated by market mechanisms.

By drawing on these dynamic, creative qualities of internal markets, we may then be able to manage a new age of complexity in an organic, self-organizing manner.[17] From this view, the organization is no longer a hierarchy of power but a web of changing business connections held together by clusters of internal enterprise—as in any market. This portrait may appear radically different, but it simply represents an extension of the trend that began decades ago when large corporations decentralized into product divisions. The examples in Box 2–1 show that this central organizing concept provides the powerful competitive edge marking excellent companies.[18]

These are simply a few prominent examples, but a recent survey of corporate practices in the United States, Europe, and Japan shows widespread acceptance of the key features in this model, as shown in Table 2–1.[19] Of 47 executives we interviewed, 90 percent agreed that these changes are necessary, 76 percent felt they would dominate management in the late 1990s, and 85 percent thought that firms which do not adopt the concept will fail or suffer a marginal existence.

TABLE 2–1. Corporations in Transition

Internal Market Feature	Not Practiced	Partially Practiced	Fully Practiced
Pay for performance	0%	27%	73%
Employees free to develop new ideas	4	9	87
Autonomous profit centers	30	30	40
Support units accountable for results	21	0	79
Units can buy and sell outside	65	12	29
Networking among all units	45	27	27
Great organizational flexibility	13	30	57
Unit managers decide strategy	0	19	81

INTERNAL MARKET ECONOMIES

- *Cypress Semiconductor* is one of the best exemplars of an internal market. Each business unit is a separate corporation with its own board of directors, and support units from manufacturing subsidiaries to testing centers all sell their services to line units. CEO T.J. Rodgers says "We've gotten rid of socialism in the organization," while Tom Peters claims the company demonstrates "perpetual innovation."

- *Johnson & Johnson* (J&J) is organized into 166 separately chartered companies that sell a particular product line. These autonomous internal enterprises are not only permitted, but expected, to pursue their own strategies, working relationships with suppliers and clients, and all other normal aspects of an independent business. CEO Ralph Larsen says the system "provides a sense of ownership and responsibility that you simply cannot get any other way."

- *Au Bon Pain* After management had struggled for years to run this chain of bakery-cafés in the traditional bureaucratic manner, performance took off with the conversion to an entrepreneurial model in which each store manager became a part-owner of his or her unit and gained wide control over its operations. Sales and earnings spurted up, turnover disappeared, and store managers earned as much as $100,000 per year.

- *Nucor Corporation* has become so famous for its management system that it is widely regarded as "the closest thing to a perfect company in the steel industry." Minimills are run by small teams of workers, technicians, and managers who have almost complete control over all operations and receive bonuses that can double their income. CEO Ken Iverson claims, "We're eliminating the hierarchy."

- *Merck & Company* has been rated the top Fortune 500 company four years in a row largely because of its unusually flexible system for organizing scientists into effective project teams. Researchers from 12 scientific disciplines are completely free to pool their efforts in any project they choose, spontaneously merging the intellectual talents and financial resources of various units into a committed team. CEO Dr. Roy Vagelos described the system, "Everybody here naturally gravitates around a hot project. It's like a live organism."

- *Sun Microsystems* hollowed out its nonessential functions by subcontracting chip manufacturing, distribution, and service functions to focus its energies on designing advanced computers. Its remaining divisions are independent subsidiaries with contractual authority over these allied business partners, giving them more control while providing the flexibility and focus on core competence that has made the company a leader in the competitive work station market.

INFORMATION TECHNOLOGY SHORT-CIRCUITS
THE HIERARCHY

Such examples pale in comparison with what should occur soon as the IT revolution short-circuits today's hierarchy. Box 2–2 illustrates how more powerful and inexpensive IT is encouraging the formation of an electronic web of lateral relationships, operating from almost anywhere, that cuts across the old hierarchical chain of command.

Box 2–2
GROWTH OF TELEWORKING

- *Decreasing IT Costs* IT costs are dropping by a factor of 10 every few years. For instance, a teleconferencing system that costs $1 million in 1982 could be bought for $100,000 in 1992, and transmission time has gone from $2,000 per hour to $200.

- *Telecommuting* Five million Americans are full-time telecommuters, but the number leaps to 35 million if part-time telecommuters and self-employed people are included. Roughly 60 percent of all office products are sold to individual lawyers, stockbrokers, sales executives, and other entrepreneurial workers who conduct their work at home, while traveling, at vacation resorts, and at many other locations.

- *Teleconferencing* Teleconferencing is growing 40 to 60 percent per year, which is why AT&T and MCI are both introducing video phones.

- *Information Networks* As of 1992, there were 10 million "electronic mailboxes" and 21 million personal computers (PCs) in the United States, wired together by 6,000 bulletin boards. Shell saves $100 per year on each of its 23,000 mailboxes while providing the entire firm instantaneous contact. Cellular telecommunications and fiber optic cables are growing at 50 percent per year to connect everything from phones to TVs to portable PCs into one great digital soup.

- *All Business Functions* The use of IT now covers the entire span of business activity: electronic banking and shopping, corporate TV networks, electronic publishing, and computerized supplier-distributor linkages; other functions are being added to this list daily. Roughly 70 percent of all managers used a PC as of 1992.

Source: William Halal, "Teleworking" (*Information Strategies Group Report,* 1992).

These trends suggest that the new practice of "teleworking" may become widely accepted as an alternative way to conduct business within a few years, dramatically altering the way organizations work. Can anyone imagine being without a fax machine today? Yet fax was rare just a few years ago. The same wave of popular use may make other forms of IT de rigueur as soon as a critical mass of users is reached. Computer journals claim teleworking is ready to take off: "Videoconferencing is at the threshold of a dramatic expansion"; " Business conditions are ripe for [change] . . . telecommuting could hit its peak in the mid–1990s"; "The videoconferencing market is set to soar."[20]

Resistance abounds because the idea breaks with tradition; and it's true that IT also can isolate people. Teleworking is unlikely to *eliminate* direct interaction because people are social beings who will always want personal contacts. Rather, it should become a viable *alternative* as IT becomes more user-friendly and inexpensive, offering a convenient way to augment normal working relations. White collar workers would then be able to do their jobs almost anywhere, in addition to working in the office, introducing what could be thought of as the "virtual organization." *BusinessWeek* described it as "electronic corporations made up of individuals and groups scattered all over the country."[21] In the United Kingdom, a computer services firm employs more than 1,000 consultants but has no offices because everyone works out of the home through computer networks.[22]

These trends, however, pose the unavoidable challenge of constructing a new type of organization around the IT that now forms the central nervous system of the modern firm. Paul Strassman, who has been called the "high priest of MIS," is concerned that the vast capital investments in IT are not paying off because "they simply take a rigid bureaucratic structure and ossify it further by enshrining it within a layer of computer code."[23] IBM itself used IT to exert tight hierarchical control, with the results we now witness in the firm's decline.

Modern business will not be able to use IT effectively without a sound working model of the modern organization, and that model is free markets. From this view, only a few essential standards are needed to ensure compatibility of hardware, financial records, communication systems, and the like. All else should be left to the discretion of internal enterprises, just as enterprises in the open market are free to choose the office technology they prefer. Even these requirements may disappear as the move toward open systems makes all IT interchangeable. Studies by Thomas Malone show that IT "should lead to a shift from [management] decisions within firms to the use of markets."[24]

This imperative of IT is so powerful that it cuts across nations. For instance, although IT systems are still crude in the socialist bloc, they were largely responsible for the collapse of centrally planned economies. Lech Walesa grasped intuitively the underlying force that powered the revolution he merely guided in Poland: "How did these reforms appear?" he asked. "The result of computers, communication satellites, television." The lesson seems clear: IT is replacing hierarchies with markets everywhere.

ASSESSING THE PROS AND CONS

Figure 2–2 illustrates the evolution of organizational structure to put today's transition to markets in historic perspective.

The hierarchical model emerged during the relatively simple conditions of the industrial age because it was good at controlling the routine tasks of manufacturing and for managing a work force of "economic men." Organic structures began to emerge in the 1950s with the matrix, and were further advanced by recent innovations such as flat organizations,

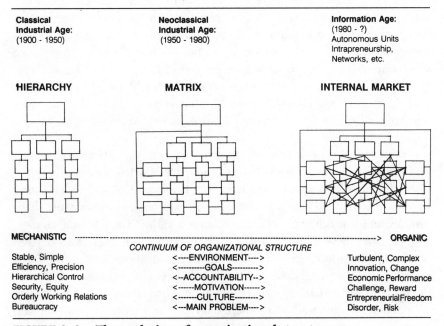

Classical Industrial Age: (1900 - 1950)	Neoclassical Industrial Age: (1950 - 1980)	Information Age: (1980 - ?) Autonomous Units Intrapreneurship, Networks, etc.
HIERARCHY	**MATRIX**	**INTERNAL MARKET**

MECHANISTIC --> ORGANIC

CONTINUUM OF ORGANIZATIONAL STRUCTURE

Stable, Simple	<----ENVIRONMENT---->	Turbulent, Complex
Efficiency, Precision	<----------GOALS---------->	Innovation, Change
Hierarchical Control	<--ACCOUNTABILITY-->	Economic Performance
Security, Equity	<------MOTIVATION------>	Challenge, Reward
Orderly Working Relations	<-------CULTURE--------->	Entrepreneurial Freedom
Bureaucracy	<---MAIN PROBLEM---->	Disorder, Risk

FIGURE 2–2. The evolution of organizational structure.

intrapreneurship, and networks to adapt to today's complex technological and economic changes.

This historic movement from mechanistic hierarchies to organic superstructures is one of the most striking trends in management. The development of complete internal market economies is likely to form the next major phase in this evolution, and we estimate it should enter the corporate mainstream somewhere about the year 2000 when the information age fully arrives.

This brave new world of computerized internal markets incurs the same drawbacks of external markets—messy working relationships fraught with risks, social inequities, and outright failures, as some of the experiences reported in this book attest. However, the advantages are more compelling.

Economists have long argued that hierarchies are superior because markets incur "transaction costs" in searching for alternatives and managing financial transactions.[25] But today's IT revolution is reducing transaction costs, and cost increases can be offset by decreased overhead and gains in innovation. Western Airlines eliminated 500 managers, which saved many millions of dollars per year and improved performance because of the decrease in bureaucracy.[26]

Even the troublesome aspects of internal markets often actually represent signs of useful organizational adjustments. Is a supervisor unable to staff his or her unit with volunteers? In the outside world, this means that working conditions should be improved. Are some units suffering losses? A market would let them fail because they do not produce value. Do differences in income exist? Wage inequalities can motivate good performance, and they urge poor workers to shape up. Thus, as John Starr reminds us in Chapter 8, what appears to be disorder in a market is often vital information about economic reality that should be heeded.

Finally, the evolution of internal market superstructures seems unavoidable because it offers the only feasible way to successfully introduce the rapid change needed to compete globally. A disenchantment has set in with strategic planning because any top-down form of "planning" usually produces more bureaucracy rather than actual change. The organic, lifelike behavior of superstructures, however, goes beyond planning altogether because these metaorganizations transcend fixed structures and central controls; they are systems or processes that produce a constant stream of structural change throughout the organization as autonomous units adapt to their environment. Instead of having top executives struggle to forecast long-range business conditions and force the organization to move in some wholesale direction, the individuals in an internal market feel their way into the future like the cells of some superorganism that possesses a life of its own.

These advantages are useful for most institutions, but there are no perfect organizational designs. Centralized hierarchies may avoid disorder, but they also inhibit creative freedom. Conversely, organic systems can foster entrepreneurial change only at the cost of enduring some chaos. Internal markets are no panacea, therefore. They are inappropriate for some situations such as military operations and space launches, that demand the close coordination of thousands of people and complex plans in precise, split-second timing. I hold no illusions that the internal market model is some universal ideal that should be applied in an all-encompassing way.

To illustrate the relative nature of these pros and cons, think of the organizational continuum in Figure 2–2 as a scale ranging from 0 to 10. Most bureaucratic firms would lie at about 2 or 3 on this scale, whereas the more flexible ones would be at about 7 or 8. These are differences of degree, and even the most entrepreneurial institutions will retain some hierarchy as a rudimentary skeleton supporting the markets that form their living tissues.

Many structural forms are emerging along this organizational spectrum to suit the unique needs of differing institutions, as the following chapters illustrate. Ray Miles and Chuck Snow describe the different network forms that are appropriate in different cases, and MCI has developed an especially interesting approach that relies on shaping a vital corporate culture. Charles Handy's typology of new organizational forms describes other variations.[27]

So it's a complex world, and we will always have to trade off the costs and gains of various organizational designs. Although the balance seems to be shifting toward internal markets, the advantages of enterprise can only be gained by tolerating greater levels of organizational disorder.

ENTREPRENEURIAL MANAGEMENT: WORKING AND LEADING IN AN INTERNAL MARKET

The drawbacks of internal markets seem especially severe now as market forces are upsetting the lives of workers and of managers themselves.

Mergers, bankruptcies, downsizing, and other changes of the past decade have caused massive unemployment and have ended the loyalty that once made organizations work. Even IBM is laying off workers for the first time in its history. If internal markets introduce more of the same, there is a keen need to develop a different management culture that can allow people to work and lead comfortably at the grass-roots level of such organizations.

From Employees to Internal Entrepreneurs

CEOs are not firing loyal workers simply to be harsh, but because the world is in the throes of a massive economic restructuring which exerts two major new demands: strict accountability for performance in order to survive, and organizational flexibility in order to adapt to these chaotic changes—the very advantages of internal markets.

This helps explain the new role that is evolving for individuals. Whereas it made sense to treat people as *employees* in a hierarchical system, internal markets require people to assume the central role that powers a market system—*entrepreneurs* (or intrapreneurs). Not all employees can fill this role, but, under the prodding of the brutal changes summarized here, a new form of "market-based" management is emerging. Intrapreneuring, pay-for-performance, and autonomous work teams are replacing the old employment relationship in which people were paid for holding a *position.*[28] This newly evolving management system focuses on providing people, not with a job, but with an *opportunity* to earn a return on their creative efforts, with all the freedom, self-control, risks, and rewards associated with being an entrepreneur.

This trend is highlighted by the many people who are redefining their working roles. The "contingent work force" of part-time employees, temporaries, subcontractors, and self-employed workers constituted one-third of American workers in 1990, and it is far larger in Europe. These "personal entrepreneurs" are taking charge of their own careers by packaging themselves as self-employed contractors able to move from company to company, consultants working for various firms, and individuals starting their own businesses.[29] About 20 percent of all professionals now work as "temps," including lawyers, doctors, and even executives. "The temporary executive [has become] a permanent fixture in American corporate life," claimed an executive recruiter.[30]

Internal Labor Markets

To assist in this conversion, big companies will have to become hospitable to creative entrepreneurs by emulating the hundreds of business incubators that have sprung up during the past few years to nurture young ventures. A good example is the system used at Teknekron, which has produced 10 successful ventures out of 12 attempts, for an average corporate growth rate of 40 percent per year.[31] Lumbering giants such as AT&T, IBM, and GM are forming similar small ventures that operate within superstructures. One of IBM's most successful actions was the Independent Business Unit concept that created the PC in 1½ years. GM's entry into the electric car market is spearheaded by a team of 200 people working outside the normal chain of command.

The development of concepts such as pay-for-performance may in time create internal labor markets that encourage workers to be more mobile, creative, and productive. Roughly 70 percent of American businesses now use some form of incentive system that links pay to performance. Just as any market requires entrepreneurial freedom, internal labor markets should allow employees to select their jobs in self-managed units that contract for work.

An interesting case occurred when Crown-Zellerbach started a system whereby loggers formed their own work teams, which were simply paid for the amount of timber they produced. The result was the elimination of job classifications, work rules, supervisors, and other complex arrangements that hindered all parties. Loggers were strongly motivated because they could "run their own business" as they saw fit and ⁺hey earned more, while management was pleased with the increase in productivity and the decrease in administrative overhead.

Harnessing the Talents of the Younger Generation

The challenges facing intrapreneurs of balancing a variety of complex tasks, braving the uncertainty of the market, and finding the will to be self-reliant are not for everyone. But these problems have always confronted those who want to carve out their own niche in life, and the proportion of such persons is growing now. The younger generation tends to prefer autonomy, opportunities to advance, and personal fulfillment in lieu of routine jobs and security.

Requiring such people to work for assigned bosses at assigned jobs is an outmoded carryover from a past when people believed power imparted control. Today, there is a wider understanding that power is an illusion. It usually drives behavior underground to energize the "informal organization" that smolders beneath the surface of most workplaces, actually causing managers to lose control.

Channeling the raw energy released by organic structures into constructive action is not going to be easy, but permitting employees autonomy *along with accountability* may turn hidden problems lurking beneath the surface into useful forces, rather than fueling an illicit underground system. Young people could then direct their stifled ambitions into intrapreneurial outlets instead of fighting their way up a disappearing hierarchy. William O'Brien, CEO of Hanover Insurance Company, put it this way:[32]

> The fundamental movement in business in the [future] will be in the dispersing of power, to give meaning and fulfillment to employees.

The New Business Ethic of Competition and Cooperation

Internal enterprise will always be difficult, but it can be ameliorated by good leadership that shares critical policy decisions with its organizational members and provides support. This is the "democratic" half of our democratic free enterprise heritage that is now extending cooperation into economic life,[33] creating a dynamic tension between competition and cooperation.

Both modes of behavior are destined to become far more intense. An entrepreneurial ethic is deeply ingrained in American culture, and now competition is surfacing in companies that have been managed as bureaucracies. But teamwork is another traditional American trait, and it is also becoming more prevalent now because collaborative problem solving is needed to solve complex problems in an information age. The result is a different environment is evolving in which we must often both compete and cooperate with one another. GM, Ford, and Chrysler compete ferociously with Toyota, Fiat, and Renault—while they also work together as partners with these same adversaries.

There is no avoiding this new reality, and so a new business ethic must be developed that can handle competition in a constructive, friendly way that allows people to also work together cooperatively. Excessive internal competition can be contained where necessary by agreeing to form consortia, joint ventures, and other "internal strategic alliances," just as we do now in external markets.

Ultimately, the relentless force of economic realities will require all of us to assume the primary responsibility for our own welfare, with the support of democratically managed metaorganizations. Managers that can develop this new blend of competition and cooperation will be positioned to realize the vast opportunities opening up in a world that is spawning multitudes of new business possibilities.

Freeing Executives to Become Leaders

Entrepreneurial management also raises tough new questions about the role of executives and the very nature of corporations. If an organization is no longer a well-structured social machine but a fluid tangle of autonomous units going their own way, what distinguishes it from the outside marketplace? What gives it an identity that makes it more than the sum of its parts? In short, what are leaders really managing?

In addition to creating an internal market economy, executives must nourish two essential strengths in managing any metaorganization: acquiring vital new knowledge, and developing a cohesive corporate community.

The first strength requires improving the organization's technology, marketing, and other crucial knowledge that has now become a strategic factor in modern business. In an industrial age, capital-intensive companies manufactured goods, but in an information age, data-intensive firms "manufacture" knowledge. As Peter Senge points out in Chapter 5, today's corporation must become a learning organization, led more like a research lab or a university, in which the leader enhances this store of knowledge, helps solve critical issues, and offers ideas.

The other leadership focus is to inculcate those beliefs, values, and other cultural traits that unify a corporation into a cohesive whole and drive it to success. Modern leaders avoid getting immersed in day-to-day operations in order to concentrate on higher needs that only they can provide. They instill a vision of the future, ensure accountability, resolve conflicts, encourage cooperation, and motivate people to reach for ambitious goals.

Instead of relying on their old authority as decision makers, then, executives find that superstructures free them to become leaders, assisting their fellow entrepreneurs in creating successful ventures. Some worry that this freedom will result in a loss of control. The key to understanding superstructures is that they require a different kind of control that is more subtle but more effective. Rather than taking an unrealistic responsibility for "each sparrow that falls," modern CEOs focus on the strategic factors that really count because they transform a mere collection of individuals into a powerful, problem-solving system.

Thus, a internal market system is more effective than either an authoritarian hierarchy or a laissez-faire economy. It is a community of entrepreneurs who shape their private market into a controlled vehicle for reaching goals—a "guided market."

THE GLOBAL CORPORATION IN A GLOBAL ECONOMY

Similar changes are taking place in other institutions and other regions. Chapters in Part II describe applications in Canada and South America, and Part III shows how an entrepreneurial form of government is emerging in which agencies compete to serve clients better. The change is most visible in education where students are being offered a choice of schools in order to replace the old educational monopoly with a market system.

Public utilities that were considered "natural monopolies" are also moving to enterprise. The electric power industry is rapidly introducing competition among suppliers. One of the healthiest things that ever happened to AT&T was the competition from MCI, Sprint, and other young phone companies that has rejuvenated the industry. How would the United States have entered the information age if AT&T had retained sole control over the nation's phone system?

There are signs that Japanese corporations, which have traditionally been organized as collaborative hierarchies, are submitting to this same imperative. The old system of lifetime employment is loosening up as employees switch jobs, and auto companies recently eliminated layers of middle management and initiated merit pay. One Japanese executive said, "The era of waving the company flag to motivate people is over."

The global implications of these ideas are crucial for competing in a global economy. For instance, Japan's dominance of the microelectronics industry strikes at the heart of the United States' economic strength, so it has provoked a heated debate over the relative advantages of large versus small firms. Silicon Valley is populated by many small, creative enterprises, but they are no match for the Japanese *keiretsu* and they are eating each other alive with unconstrained competition. On the other hand, the bureaucracy of large American firms such as IBM has hindered their ability to compete as well.[34]

In fact, economic structures are evolving to resolve this conflict, and the only real barrier is our failure to understand what is happening. The growth of R&D consortia, supplier-manufacturer-distributor partnerships, joint ventures, and a host of other strategic alliances are rapidly connecting American corporations together, as shown in Figure 2–3.[35] The one thing lacking is a central concept to give this new economic strategy a sharp focus—the internal market paradigm. Internal markets transform the corporation from a hierarchy of decision makers to what Norman Macrae called a "confederation of entrepreneurs." Here's how GE described their new corporate structure that combines the creativity of small enterprises with the power of global organizations:[36]

> We're trying to reshape GE as a band of small businesses . . . to take the strength of a large company and act with the agility of a small company.

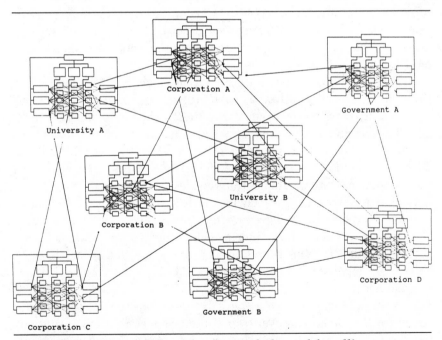

FIGURE 2–3. The global market network formed by alliances among internal market organizations.

In addition to resolving the old conflict between global size versus entrepreneurial flexibility, the internal market model also provides a logical foundation for forming the alliances that are crucial for world competitiveness, as also shown in Figure 2–3. Redefining a large corporation as a cluster of small enterprises allows each unit to engage in external transactions on a sound business basis. Further, everyone in a market organization is accustomed to forming alliances because that is how internal relationships are managed. And executives are freed from operating matters to focus on strategies that harness internal and external enterprises into powerful new combinations.

The Japanese may not think of their system as internal markets, but the essence of the *keiretsu* embodies many of the same principles: a family of independent companies free to conduct their business as they think best, yet bonded together by their collective ability to assist one another. All nations and corporations are developing their own unique structures for competing in a global economy, and they can be understood as variations on this central idea.

For instance, the similarities between internal market superstructures and Asea Brown Boveri (ABB) Corporation are shown in Box 2–3. The CEO, Percy Barnevik, has been described as "moving more aggressively than any CEO in Europe, perhaps the world, to build the new model of competitive enterprise."

Imagine failing American corporations such as GM rebuilt along these lines. Instead of a few divisions reporting to a top management team that makes most major decisions, these behemoths should encourage their entrepreneurial engineers and managers to start hundreds of fledgling ventures like GM's Saturn. Yes, many of them might fail, but many more would succeed, and the winners would have met the test of the market rather than administrative rules.

IBM is moving aggressively in this direction now as the company's product divisions are being converted into independent businesses.[37] IBM intrapreneurs are now entering each other's once sacrosanct markets, staff units are being turned into profit centers, and cheap clones of IBM PCs are being purchased by some IBM office units. Now, that's an internal market!

Americans cannot rely on emulating the Japanese talent for making collective decisions. However, the United States can draw on its entrepreneurial heritage to mine that rich lode of creative talent now languishing beneath the bureaucratic layers of its big institutions. Internal

---
Box 2-3
ABB'S MARKET MODEL OF THE GLOBAL CORPORATION

- *A Confederation of Entrepreneurs* "We are a federation of national companies . . . a collection of local businesses with intense global coordination."

- *Multidimensional Structure* "Along one dimension ABB is structured into 50 or so business areas operating worldwide. Alongside this structure sits a country structure of 1,100 local companies that do the work of business areas in different countries."

- *The Decentralization Contract* "Our managers need well-defined responsibilities, clear accountability, and maximum degrees of freedom. I don't expect them to do things that hurt their business but are good for ABB. That's not natural. We always create separate legal entities. Separate companies allow *real* balance sheets with *real* cash flow and dividends. Managers inherit results year to year through changes in equity."

- *Support Units as Profit Centers* "You can go into any centralized corporation and cut its headquarters staff by 90 percent. You spin off 30 percent into freestanding service centers that perform real work and charge for it. You decentralize 30 percent by pushing them down into line organizations. Then 30 percent disappears through reductions."

- *Small Internal Enterprises* "Our operations are divided into 1,200 companies, which are divided into 4,500 profit centers with an average of 50 employees. We are fervent believers in decentralization. People can aspire to meaningful career ladders in units small enough to understand and be committed to."

- *A Strategic Information System That Unites the Firm* "We have a glue of transparent, centralized reporting through a management information system called Abacus."

- *Employee Entrepreneurs* "I don't sit like a godfather, allocating jobs. What I guarantee is that every member of the federation has a fair shot at the opportunities."

- *Providing Leadership* "I have no illusions about how hard it is to communicate clearly and quickly with thousands of people around the world. Real communication takes time, and top managers must be willing to make the investment . . . meeting with the company CEOs in an open, honest dialogue."

Source: William Taylor, "The Logic of Global Business," *Harvard Business Review* (March–April 1991).

markets can create an American form of global corporation based on the power of enterprise—an "American Keiretsu."

This transition is formidable because it requires a social transformation, rather like the transition the former Communist bloc is attempting. To fully appreciate the problem, put yourself in the shoes of Boris Yeltsin or Lech Walesa. How would you convert their nations into market systems? By suddenly applying shock therapy? Or by gradually feeling your way along through the economic minefield? Would you focus first on creating individual enterprises or the infrastructure they need to succeed? And how would you calm fears and inspire change?

The experiences in this book offer some guidelines for making the transition to internal markets. In general, the best approach is to gain a solid grasp of the possibilities and the problems involved by first learning about the idea. Then recruit willing, enterprising volunteers who can see the project through. Provide them thorough training in the new business skills needed to succeed in a market environment. Take care to plan the change collectively and to sketch out a realistic vision of how it would work. Prepare the organization by shaping a culture that is receptive to enterprise. Start small with pilot programs limited to part of the organization, and then expand on the basis of success. Most importantly, gain commitment to the idea and give it top priority. Percy Barnavik described ABB's approach: "We took ten of our best people, the superstars, and gave them six weeks to design the restructuring. We called it the Manhattan Project."

The change is difficult despite the best planning, but more organizations are moving in this direction because economic realities demand it. Corporations are getting larger, yet they must also master an intensely competitive global economy that requires massive technical and social innovation, and their employees are educated people who dislike bureaucracy. If we hope to survive, much less thrive, under these extraordinary new conditions, it is imperative to restructure institutions for a fundamentally different era.

As this imperative of the Information Age unfolds during the next decade or so, today's stagnating bureaucracies should become alive with myriad internal ventures that pass resources, employees, and information throughout organizational superstructures and across their permeable boundaries, connecting institutions in an economic web that forms a unified global economy. The resulting conditions—numerous small competing enterprises, the freedom to pursue individual interests, and limitless market information—constitute the requirements that economists have long defined for "perfect markets."

The economic implications are path breaking. Today's advent of electronically-mediated relationships promises a great new world of more fluid and effective market economies that can weave the lives and work of an emerging global order together into a seamless whole. And the construction of this global business network begins by building a metastructural foundation for large institutions based on the same market principles that are now flowering around the world—internal markets.

3 Reconsidering "A New Corporate Design"

Jay W. Forrester

Editors' Note: In 1965, Jay W. Forrester wrote a paper titled "A New Corporate Design," which anticipated the outlines of the internal market paradigm. The editors are pleased to reprint that article in the Appendix to this volume, and to present this commentary by Professor Forrester, "Reconsidering 'A New Corporate Design,'" which updates his thoughts on corporate structure in the light of what has transpired during the 28 years since he published his seminal 1965 work.

What is most remarkable about the 1965 article is its incisive vision of major trends that were beginning to revolutionize organizational structures almost three decades ago, but that have only recently been recognized by the business community. The key features of Jay Forrester's "New Corporate Design" provide an uncanny anticipation of the very concepts gaining popular currency today.

Jay W. Forrester is Germeshausen professor emeritus and senior lecturer, Sloan School of Management, Massachusetts Institute of Technology. He is well known as the founder of systems dynamics, the scientific discipline of modeling systems, which led to many creative applications including the famous *Limits to Growth* study of the Club of Rome.

Forrester recommended replacing the paternalistic superior–subordinate relationship with a more effective form of control in which employees became free agents contracting to deliver agreed-upon performance goals—what we now call "pay-for-performance." He urged redefining an organization as a collection of autonomous profit centers to improve accountability and entrepreneurial innovation—today's "confederation of entrepreneurs." In 1965, when computers still filled an entire room, Forrester saw that information technology was producing a different mode of organizational behavior in which temporary working liaisons cut across the hierarchical chain of command—today's popular preoccupation with "groupware" and "organizational networks."

Not only did "A New Corporate Design" accurately anticipate the major features of today's internal market paradigm, Jay Forrester also understood the enormous obstacles to the acceptance of this idea because it amounted to a social and economic revolution. Listen to the prescient opening to his 1965 article, which cuts to the heart of the problem we still face in developing a new model of organizations:

> During the last fifteen years there have emerged several important new areas of thinking about the corporation, its purpose, and its management. When brought together, these ideas suggest a new kind of organization that promises major improvements in the way the corporation can serve the needs of man. As yet, no such synthesis has been implemented.
>
> In technology we expect bold experiments that test ideas, obtain new knowledge, and lead to major advances. But in matters of social organization we usually propose only timid modifications of conventional practice and balk at daring experiments and innovation. Why? Surely it is not that present organizations have proven so faultless. . . . Perhaps we are reluctant to permit changes in the framework of our existence. But it is time to apply to organizations the same willingness to innovate that has set the pace of scientific advance.

This statement remains as valid today as it was 28 years ago. It is unfortunate that American business did not consider the implications of "A New Corporate Design" more seriously when it was first published because much of today's agonizing over economic decline might have been avoided. If the nation could have somehow enlisted the abundant talent of its managers and workers in creating innovative organizational systems during the past two decades when the fertile ideas of scholars like Jay Forrester were emerging, the United States could today be leading the world toward a new economic order. The following update to "A New Corporate Design" and the original article in the Appendix offer us another opportunity to remedy this loss.

COMMENTARY ON UPDATING "A NEW CORPORATE DESIGN"

Rereading "A New Corporate Design" left me with several reactions. First, the paper fails current standards for "political correctness" with its use of masculine pronouns throughout and its references to managers and employees as "men." Even as a reader who feels present changes in writing style have gone to extremes, I still found the paper jarring.

I was especially struck once again by how difficult it is to change existing paradigms. The management paradigm based on an authoritarian structure is so deeply embedded in people's thinking that alternatives cannot even be imagined. Radical alternatives are rejected as not discussible.

THE AUTHORITARIAN PARADIGM

I use "paradigm" here in the sense of Thomas Kuhn,[1] meaning a frame of reference or a microscope through which to view the surrounding world. A paradigm restricts a person's vision to seeing only what is expected and to accepting only what prior conditioning makes believable. Seldom do the holders of a paradigm change, even in the face of powerful evidence that the paradigm is faulty. More frequently, change arises through a new generation of people who find the old view unsatisfactory and who seek an alternative paradigm that better fits the social and natural world. The slow revision of paradigms is illustrated by the extreme case of Galileo, who in the year 1633 was convicted of heresy by the Roman Catholic Church for his forceful and persuasive arguments that the earth is not the center of the universe but rather revolves around the sun. It was not until 1992, more than 350 years later, that the Church officially acknowledged that Galileo had been right.

The unshakable belief that "organization" inherently requires and implies an authoritarian hierarchy fits the concept of a paradigm. People believing in the authoritarian paradigm do not see or accept any other possibility.

Visualizing a radically different alternative to the authoritarian form of organization inside a corporation appears almost impossible for people who have been conditioned since birth by living in an authoritarian universe. Families, schools, and corporations operate on the basis of superior–subordinate relationships. The resulting authoritarian paradigm is overpowering.

Repeatedly, we see the contradiction of prominent executives making speeches about the advantages of a free-enterprise economic system while they are running some of the largest authoritarian socialist bureaucracies in the world. In fact, modern large corporations are the breeding ground for socialism. Several characteristics describe the typical corporation today:

1. Centralized ownership of productive resources by the organization.
2. Assignment of individuals to tasks by those higher in authority.
3. Rewards to individuals determined by subjective judgment and personal interest of superiors.
4. Barriers to emigration in search of a better life (through vesting in pension plans).
5. Maintenance of personal power by restricting availability of information.
6. Appointment of leaders to office without democratic election by the workers in the society.

Are not these the descriptors of an authoritarian socialist, or communist, or dictatorial government?

Corporate executives are usually unable to imagine an organization that operates without the superior–subordinate relationship. When I ask an executive for an example of an organization that operates without the superior–subordinate structure, a law partnership may be suggested. When I ask for a very large system operating without the superior–subordinate structure, nothing is forthcoming. Instead, such is considered impossible.

A FREE ENTERPRISE PARADIGM

Is it not remarkable that executives, who are captives of the authoritarian paradigm, almost never identify the largest nonauthoritarian economic system, as a possible organizational alternative to the typical corporate structure? That well-known alternative is the constitutional government of the United States. Our largest economic structure, the national economy, rests on free enterprise negotiations in which there is no superior–subordinate relationship among legal entities—automobile companies, dentists, drugstores, consultants, individuals in their private lives, and construction companies all have equal status under the law; none can dictate to another merely through power arising from a superior administrative position.

Free enterprise as a basis for economic organization has existed for several hundred years in nations of the English-speaking world and Western Europe, but it has yet to be accepted by most other countries or as a basis for the internal organization of corporations. If our largest economic systems operate successfully as free-enterprise societies, why cannot such structures exist within corporations?

"A New Corporate Design" represents an alternative to the authoritarian form of organization. The "design" starts by totally eliminating superior–subordinate relationships as basic organizational building blocks. Rebuilding from what might otherwise be chaos leads to a structure that parallels the constitutional organization of the U.S. national economy.

A free-enterprise corporation would:

- Eliminate all superior–subordinate relationships.
- Forbid internal monopolies, even at the point of allocating financial resources. As in the outside economy, there must be several internal competing "investment bankers" who are continually searching for people within the organization who will act as entrepreneurs to organize products, services, and markets. Conversely, people who have innovative proposals would have several alternative sources of support so that they would not be subject to the prejudices and caprice of a single allocator of funds.
- Reward people on objective measures of return-on-investment applied to the entire time that an individual is associated with a project or program. Individuals should receive financial compensation automatically on the basis of known formulas for completed return-on-investment results above some specified threshold.
- Assure mobility and freedom of association within the corporation by requiring that every separate accounting center receive no more than 40 percent of its annual income from any

one source. This means that each center would have at least three clients and could shift work toward the most constructive relationships.

- Develop a constitutional and contractual relationship with all participants such that no individual or small group would have the power to change the structure of the organization. As in a national democracy, change could come only through votes of corporate citizens. Fundamental concepts, as with a national constitution, would require more than a majority vote.

I now would like to alter the impression created in the section of my original paper entitled "Individual Profit Centers." One sentence there points in the right direction: "Since emphasis should focus on the total life cycle of an undertaking—a successful beginning, successful mid-life management, and successful termination or transfer—profit center accounting for determining personal compensation should usually occur at the closing of an account and be measured against a compounded return-on-investment basis that extends over the total life of the activity." But most of that section on profit centers can easily but unintentionally be read as endorsing measures of success based on current short-term profits.

Management must avoid rewards based on current operations. We should move away from present corporate practice in which salary and bonuses are based on the current year's performance. Such rewards favor short-term decisions for immediate personal advantage instead of long-term success of the organization. Instead, all rewards should be based on a final accounting. That final accounting could be at the completion of a specific task, such as the design of a circuit. But for a product manager responsible for carrying an idea from design through marketing, reward should be at the completion of the product life and closing of the activity, or at the "sale" of the activity as a going business to a willing buyer in the company who would assume the existing financial status with the "purchase" price added to the seller's assets and to the buyer's obligations. Only with program termination built into the accounting will individuals have incentive to stop activities at the optimum time.

I also do not believe that money is the primary source of motivation. Instead, freedom, recognition for a task well done, and absence of frustrations imposed by others are among the conditions that induce dedication to the task at hand. However, clearly defined financial rewards for all individuals throughout the organization will force clear organizational design that creates freedom, recognition, and absence of frustrating bureaucratic intervention.

CLINGING TO THE AUTHORITARIAN PARADIGM

The reluctance to give up authority over others stands as the major barrier to creating true internal markets within a corporate structure. People hold a most unsymmetrical view of how authority should be exercised. Each individual believes that power should be decentralized down to that person's level and centralized up to that level.

Several of my experiences at about the time "A New Corporate Design" was being written illustrate both the need for changing corporate structure and the difficulty in doing so.

Digital Equipment Corporation

For the first 10 years of its growth, I was on the board of directors of the Digital Equipment Corporation; its founders had worked for me while building the first digital computer at the Massachusetts Institute of Technology (MIT) and later while designing and coordinating the installation of the SAGE (Semi-Automatic Ground Environment) System for North American air defense. As a board member, I pressed for two radical changes from traditional management practice. The first, using system dynamics modeling to design growth policies, had a lasting impact. The second, to introduce the "New Corporate Design" organization, produced one very successful experiment, but was never tried again. It may be of interest to review briefly these two departures from conventional management.

When joining the board of directors, I did not adequately understand the reasons for the successes and failures of the proliferating high-technology companies. Success did not correlate with quality of products, or management education of the founders, or available funding. Our prior work at MIT on the instability of production, distribution, and marketing interactions suggested that growth was a systems problem that depended on how corporate policies influence one another. Such feedback channels of influence represent a very complicated dynamic system. I constructed a system dynamics simulation model having some 250 variables that represented policies and connections in a high-technology company and its interactions with customers and competitors. Only about 10 percent of the variables dealt with physical quantities such as products, capital plant, employees, and inventory. Most of the model represented information streams about attitudes toward customers, leadership characteristics of management, effect of the company's own history and traditions on current decisions, policies for maintaining quality, and the market response to product quality, availability, selling effectiveness, price, and design. When run with policies that could be identified in various successful and unsuccessful companies, the model exhibited the kinds of behavior seen in actual companies. The modeling study yielded insights about growth policies governing pricing, quality, and plant expansion that continued to be followed in Digital for many years.

Even though it did not survive in the company, another management experiment in the early days of Digital is more directly relevant to "internal markets" and to "free enterprise within the corporation." The ideas presented in "New Corporate Design" were first formulated in the context of my work on the board of Digital. The paper had been redrafted several times over an interval of two or three years for discussion with board members before it was published. I had been recommending an internal free-market structure, complete with the return-on-investment emphasis, as discussed earlier, with evaluation of an individual only at the completion of an undertaking. Finally, with considerable uneasiness, the management agreed to an experiment.

A new product, with development expected to cost a few hundred thousand dollars, lay ahead. An engineer, who also had a business school degree, was a candidate for taking charge. He was offered a challenging combination of responsibility and authority. He would have complete control of the project, nothing would be charged to his account except what he authorized, he would have an approved total budget in advance, he would set the market price, and he would be evaluated by the final compounded return on investment offset by sales. In lieu of overhead, he would be responsible for 6 percent per month return on investment compounded monthly. That compounded return means that a $1,000 obligation doubles in a year. At that time, perhaps even now, such a return was reasonable for an innovative high-value product, if expenditures were tightly managed. Such a return on investment puts a high premium on precise timing of expenditures. If materials or services are purchased too soon, return on their investment climbs while waiting for them to be incorporated into the program. On the other hand, procuring too late will incur a return-on-investment charge on the entire project investment while waiting for a crucial input.

The negotiation in advance of the project's approval and acceptance was most interesting. Extended discussions in several sessions between the candidate and board members established the managerial framework for the project. Through three meetings and seven cumulative hours, the prospective manager failed to recognize the essence of the proposition. He continued presenting his plans in a typical engineer's "snow job," as if he were trying to justify support from a reluctant management. On several occasions he was told that his presentations were not consistent with the purpose of the meetings. He was explicitly told that we were not there to decide whether or not to give him the money; we were meeting only to determine whether or not he wanted it. Finally, in the seventh hour of meetings, he stopped in the middle of a sentence; suddenly, the fundamental nature of the proposal had penetrated, and he said, "Oh! You mean you want me to run this as if it were my own company!" He had been told that in every possible way, but the idea was so unconventional that he could scarcely understand it.

He accepted the challenge. He succeeded well beyond the 6 percent per month compounded cumulative return.

In spite of both the technical and financial success of the project, management would not allow a repeat of even the experiment, and certainly not its diffusion into the entire company.

The project had been much more of a challenge to management than to the project leader. Objection to the experiment was explained on the basis that it had made the leader uncooperative. At some point in the program, there had been a crisis elsewhere in the company, and management had asked this project leader to drop what he was doing and help salvage someone else's mistakes. He had refused, quite properly, because he had a contract with his return-on-investment clock running. It was as if a banker, with a loan to a small successful company, had insisted that the management of that company put everything on hold and help the banker recover from difficulties in some other investment. Management discovered that it had bargained away its right to interfere and to micromanage the project. The deal had erased the superior–subordinate relationship. Unusually high financial and product success were not sufficient reasons to induce management to give up prerogatives for day-by-day decision-making control.

In retrospect, Digital grew and succeeded during the expansion of the computer industry and during the rising phase of the economic long wave. The long wave (also known as the Kondratieff cycle) is the name given to the major capital-goods expansions that occur some 60 years apart. Those economic expansions have reversed into the great depressions of the 1830s, 1890s, 1930s, and now the 1990s. The long wave is internally driven within the economy by the mutually interacting influences of capital expansion, debt, real interest rates, speculation, and extrapolation of past economic trends. In the downturn phase, the long wave exerts extreme pressures on businesses that have become inefficient and lost resiliency and flexibility to respond to change.

When the large central-machine nature of the computer industry matured and simultaneously the long-wave downturn arrived, Digital was unprepared. The company had not encouraged, or even permitted, the nurturing of strong, entrepreneurial, high-visibility leaders inside. There was top management belief in delegating responsibility, but responsibility was not accompanied by corresponding authority nor by a commitment of resources for the delegated responsibility. With delegated responsibility goes the burden of being blamed for failure; but without corresponding authority and funding, there is little opportunity to prevent failure. Under such circumstances, a company evolves toward political maneuvering, infighting, and empire building. The shortage of people operating "as if this were my own company" prevents redirection into newly emerging markets that top management fails to perceive. The high overhead and bureaucratic inefficiencies, which were tolerable during and obscured by growth when there was excess market demand, became unsustainable when the direction of the economy reversed and the computer industry shifted from large machines to personal, networked, desktop machines.

But Digital was not alone in its overdependence on authoritarian control. The Soviet Union, General Motors, Sears, and IBM also were unwilling to give up their authoritarian hierarchies until internal rigidities, inability to innovate, and inefficiency drove them belatedly to restructuring. But will restructuring at such a late stage succeed in any of these faltering economic systems? It takes a very long time to build a new culture, even if the design for the new culture is clear. From the Magna Charta to the U.S. Constitution took more than 500 years. The challenge: Can corporations change more quickly? Weaknesses in corporate organization have already been debated for 100 years. When do we move from debate to action?

International Business Machines (IBM) Corporation

The debilitating influence of authoritarian bureaucracy creates a cumulative spiral toward less efficiency and less innovation. Such a system not only discourages free-enterprise attitudes, it also filters people by repelling strong and innovative leaders and attracting and holding those who are less venturesome. This personnel-sorting process became evident in IBM about 30 years ago when I was advisor to staff responsible for organization and training.

At that time, IBM had twice developed unsuccessful products for the digital control of chemical plants. I came on the scene at the beginning of the third attempt. They were about to repeat the compartmentalized sequence of testing an idea in research, passing the concept to a development group, turning demonstration units over to production designers, delivering the designs to manufacturing, and finally expecting the sales department to bring in orders. In such a subdivided organization, the participants rarely think favorably of what they have received from those earlier in the chain, nor do people have great interest in the suitability of their output for those to whom their work will be delivered. I suggested setting up the third attempt in a different manner.

The proposal was to pick someone who passionately believed in computers for chemical processing and make that person responsible for the entire program from research through sales. The reaction was surprising, "We don't have anyone in the company to whom we dare give that much responsibility." They felt compelled to follow the standard managerial formula even after two prior failures.

In response, I suggested that they make a list of the people in IBM who could take on the entire program from beginning to end. No one was to be excluded; it did not matter whether a person could be spared or would want the job. We were trying only to identify the kind of person who was needed. They managed to arrive at a half-dozen names, but each candidate had a serious limitation—little experience in some major area, such as research, marketing, or manufacturing. There was no well-rounded and fully qualified candidate.

Then I asked for a list of any qualified individuals who had worked for IBM but were no longer with the company. "Oh!, there is so-and-so, and also _____, and _____, and _____." A dozen names appeared on the list without reservations. Examining the individuals was revealing. All had carried through important successful projects without management approval, sometimes against orders to stop the work. They had gotten money from outside, or diverted it from other inside activities without anyone noticing. They had broken new ground in technology and also in effectiveness in getting much done with few resources. But they had stepped on toes and evaded regulations. They had operated on the basis of not asking permission ahead of time but only asking forgiveness afterward. But a bureaucracy seldom forgives actions that threaten the legitimacy of authority. The individuals had either been sent to the corporate equivalent of Siberia, or they had known that they could never again enjoy the freedom to succeed that they had experienced. For either reason, they all eventually left the company.

In a different series of discussions, I tried pushing the "New Corporate Design" ideas as a way to make IBM more entrepreneurial and innovative. Those I worked with saw the unfavorable corporate trends toward lack of innovation and rising costs. They agreed that something fundamentally different should be done. Yet, they felt, probably correctly, that they dared not introduce a radical change in management concept that might upset the big money-making mainframe divisions. Instead, they suggested that they should expect and accept that those profitable divisions would die. To replace the currently profitable divisions, they would start innovative free-enterprise divisions that would grow and take over in the more distant future. What actually happened was that the big old divisions did begin to die, but the company never implemented a replacement culture that could keep pace with changes in the industry and the economy.

Those in IBM who saw the handwriting on the wall were unable to initiate investment in future salvation. As happens in almost every technical and organizational disaster—for example, the Challenger spacecraft explosion—many people see the calamity coming and know how to prevent it but are suppressed by authorities who focus on immediate issues. A fundamental principle in the behavior of systems asserts that policies favoring the short run almost always degrade the long run and vice versa. But few people will accept the short-run price in exchange for the long-run good.

CROSSCURRENTS IN TRANSFORMING PARADIGMS

Many managers are trying to compensate for corporate weaknesses arising from an authoritarian organization. But are such reorganizations getting at the fundamental source of the problems, or only trying to alleviate symptoms? Addressing symptoms without reaching under-lying causes of inefficiency and lack of innovation will fail to achieve the improvements that are possible. I suggest that the authoritarian superior–subordinate building block is the deeply embedded root from which the current economic weaknesses are growing. Are any corpo-rate reorganizations replacing the authoritarian structure with a real internal market?

Most of the publicized reorganizations begin from the top. Decen-tralization reaches down only one or two levels to operating divisions. But the smaller units continue in the authoritarian organizational pat-terns. Usually, the reorganization keeps management in a superior posi-tion to set incentive pay, bonuses, stock plans, budget allocations, and transfer prices. Real entrepreneurship does not extend to the level of individuals. Would we say that political concepts had changed if the for-mer Soviet Union merely becomes separate countries each governed as a Communist dictatorship?

If individuals are not included in the internal market concept, there is no training ground where a person can learn how to combine authority and responsibility in conducting business. Sometimes the ap-pearance of divisional independence includes separate boards of direc-tors of operating units. But often such boards consist of senior officers of the holding company; this is the equivalent in the outside economy to the government appointing the boards of all corporations. Is that free enterprise? At the level of most individuals, such decentralization re-tains the authoritarian structure.

It is true that an authoritarian organization can exist in many fla-vors. It can be more or less restrictive depending of how the chief exec-utive allocates authority, responsibility, and resources. It is possible to build a high esprit de corps within the traditional corporation. But such an organization exists at the sufferance of the executive. It can take 10 years to instill the intended values in a company, while a successor who is not a believer can destroy the fragile structure in 10 weeks. We must ask of such a vision: What guarantees that it will be enduring?

Although most reorganizations within corporations fall far short of the "New Corporate Design" concept, a growing movement does point to the power of networking truly independent entities. The terms "virtual" corporation and "modular" corporation are now applied to a fluid mix of independent companies and individuals assembled for a specific purpose by a central unit that makes plans, lets contracts, and provides leadership. The central unit operates between the independent participants and the market and is disciplined by market forces. The independent participants compete with potential participants to maintain their places in the network. But why can't a corporation do the same thing within its own boundaries?

The present legal structure under which corporations operate is incompatible with an internal free enterprise form of democracy. A new kind of corporate "constitution" must be devised. The rights of various constituencies should be rebalanced. Those working within a corporation create far more of its wealth and success than do stockholders, but the relative contributions are not reflected in the legal rights.

THE CHALLENGE

The time has come to shift responsibility for successful enterprises from chief executive officers who are operators to creators of corporations who are "enterprise designers." A fundamental difference exists between an enterprise operator and an enterprise designer. To illustrate, consider the two most important people in successful operation of an airplane. One is the airplane designer and the other is the airplane pilot. The designer creates an airplane that ordinary pilots can fly successfully. Is not the usual executive more a pilot than a designer? A manager is appointed to run an organization. Often there is no one who consciously fills the role of organizational designer.

Organizations built by committee, intuition, and historical happenstance often work no better than would an airplane built by the same methods.

Correct design can make the difference between a corporation that is vulnerable to changes in the outside business environment and one that exhibits a high degree of independence from outside forces. Correct design can improve the stability of employment and production. Correct design, in the balance of policies for pricing, capital plant acquisition, and sales force, can often make the difference between growth burdened by debt and growth out of earnings. Correct design can help avoid the adoption of policies offering short-term advantage at the expense of long-term degradation. Correct design can help prevent expenditure of managerial time in debating policies that are inherently of low leverage and therefore unimportant. Correct design can help identify the very small number of high-leverage policies capable of yielding desirable change. Correct design can develop and release human initiative.

The dynamic behavior of a corporation is far more complicated than any of the technical products that corporations produce. In creating new products, the designers use computer simulation to study behavior and build prototypes to test concepts because people realize they cannot reliably anticipate how a proposed design will perform. Why not do the same with designs of social systems? The groundwork has been laid in the field of system dynamics.[2]

System dynamics simulation of corporate dynamics goes far beyond the "systems thinking" that has now become a popular subject of conferences. The difference between "systems thinking" and "system dynamics modeling and design of policies" is as great as the difference between talking about the vision of a new chemical plant and actually doing the design, computer simulation, and pilot plant experimentation. To become a corporate designer will require a professional training as demanding as becoming an engineer or a medical doctor. Are not successful corporations as important as bridges and clinics? Should their design not be taken at least as seriously?

As the ideas in "A New Corporate Design" are developed further, the national legal structure governing corporations will need revision. Present beliefs and laws about labor unions will not be appropriate. If the corporate citizens are to have control in the same sense that citizens do in a democracy, then ownership should lie with those who are creating the corporate wealth. Such corporations must be immune from the short-term disruptions and financial manipulations experienced in the mergers and leveraged buyouts of the 1980s. Those externally imposed maneuvers left many companies in a weakened condition.

There should be sustained debate and experimentation with organizational ideas that are much more radical than the decentralization now being practiced. A company can decentralize, or even spin off divisions into independent companies, but that does not change the organizational nature of the smaller units. Indeed, the smaller units may become more manageable hierarchies, but they retain the original fundamental weaknesses.

Learning to be an entrepreneur in a free market requires years of experience. Unless each individual begins gaining that experience as soon as he or she enters the work force, there will be no training ground for *free market* leadership. Until the internal market concept reaches all individuals at every level of skill and experience, organizations will drift back to the traditional authoritarian hierarchy.

4 Internal Markets and Network Organizations

Raymond E. Miles and Charles C. Snow

The creation of internal markets to improve organizational responsiveness is a major part of a broader revolution that is dramatically reshaping Western organizations—the advent of network organizations. This chapter explores three main topics concerning internal markets and other types of network organizations generally:

1. It places the internal market structure alongside two related forms that rely on networks of *external* partners supplying customized services at market prices.
2. It illustrates how and why these new forms have evolved from earlier organizational models.
3. Most importantly, it uses our knowledge of earlier organizational forms to understand how managerial actions can influence the success or failure of today's network organizations.

Raymond E. Miles is professor of organizational behavior and former dean, the Haas School of Business, University of California, Berkeley. **Charles C. Snow** is professor of business administration, the Smeal College of Business Administration, The Pennsylvania State University. This chapter is adapted from their article, "Causes of Failure in Network Organizations, *California Management Review* (Summer 1992).

INTRODUCTION

It is widely recognized that we are in the midst of an organizational revolution. Throughout the 1980s, organizations around the world responded to an increasingly competitive global business environment by moving away from centrally coordinated, multilevel hierarchies and toward a variety of more flexible structures that closely resembled networks rather than traditional pyramids. These networks—clusters of firms or specialist units coordinated by market mechanisms instead of chains of command—are viewed by both their members and management scholars as better suited than other forms to many of today's demanding environments.[1]

Despite the current success of network organizations, the most likely forecast is that their effectiveness will decline rather than improve over time. In fact, there is already evidence of deterioration in some network organizations—failures caused not by the inappropriateness of the network form but because of managerial mistakes in designing or operating it.

Indeed, the evolution of the network form of organization appears to be following a familiar pattern. Historically, new organizational forms arise to correct the principal deficiencies of the form(s) currently in use. As environmental changes accumulate, existing organizational forms become less and less capable of meeting the demands placed on them. Managers begin to experiment with new approaches and eventually arrive at a more effective way of arranging and coordinating resources. The managers who pioneer the new organizational form understand its logic and are well aware of its particular strengths and weaknesses. However, as the use of the new form increases, so too does the potential for its misuse. When design and operating flaws multiply, the form loses its vitality and begins to fail.

EVOLUTION OF THE NETWORK FORM

Over the course of American business history, four broad forms of organization have emerged. First, the *functional organization* appeared in the late nineteenth century and flourished early in the twentieth century. This new organizational form allowed many firms to achieve the necessary size and efficiency to provide products and services to a growing domestic market. An early example of the vertically integrated functional organization was designed by Andrew Carnegie. By controlling both raw material supplies and distribution, he was able to keep his steel mills running efficiently on a tightly planned schedule. A current example is Wal-Mart, Inc., one of the nation's largest retailers. Across the country, Wal-Mart focuses on a well-defined, homogeneous target market as it locates its stores in small towns and suburbs of medium-sized cities. For these highly similar markets, Wal-Mart makes maximum use of on-line computerized sales data from over 1,200 stores to feed what is recognized as one of the most efficient inventory and distribution systems in the country. Like its functional predecessors, Wal-Mart performs a limited set of functions extremely well, using the specialized talents of planners, logistics specialists, and store personnel. Wal-Mart is tightly integrated from its warehouses through its store shelves, and because of its buying power, it can coordinate an army of suppliers eager to respond to its forecasts and schedules.

The *divisionalized organization* appeared shortly after the end of World War I and spread rapidly in the late 1940s and into the 1950s. Among the earliest divisionalized structures was that designed by Alfred Sloan at General Motors, where specific automobile brands and models were aimed at distinct markets differentiated primarily by price. Product divisions (Chevrolet, Pontiac, Cadillac, etc.) operated as nearly autonomous companies, producing and marketing products to their respective customers, while corporate management served as an investment banker for growth and redirection. A modern divisionalized firm is Rubbermaid, whose 10 operating divisions account for over 200 new products a year. Each division has its own target market and its own research and development (R&D) team focused exclusively on that market, allowing maximum responsiveness in a diversified product arena.[2]

The third organizational form—the *matrix*—evolved in the 1960s and the 1970s, combining elements of the functional and divisional forms. An early matrix structure was created at TRW, which sought to make efficient use of specialized engineers and scientists while adapting to a wide range of new product and project demands. Technical and professional personnel moved back and forth from functional departments to product or project teams, and from one team to another, as their skills were needed. Many modern matrix organizations are even more complex, such as the one used by Matsushita, which combines global product divisions with geographically based marketing groups.

Movement toward the *network* form became apparent in the 1980s, when international competition and rapid technological change forced massive restructuring across U.S. industries. Established firms downsized to their core competence, delayering management hierarchies and outsourcing a wide range of activities. New firms eschewed growth through vertical integration and instead sought alliances with independent suppliers and/or distributors.

Within this general trend toward disaggregation and looser coupling, managers experimented with various organizational arrangements. Instead of using plans, schedules, and transfer prices to coordinate internal units, they turned to contracts and other exchange agreements to link together external components into various types of network structures.[3] As illustrated in Figure 4–1, some networks brought suppliers, producers, and distributors together in long-term stable relationships. Other networks were much more dynamic, with components along the value chain coupled contractually for perhaps a single project or product and then decoupled to be part of a new value chain for the next business venture. Finally, inside some large firms, internal networks appeared as managers sought to achieve market

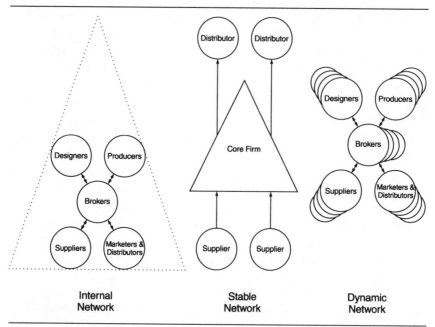

FIGURE 4–1.   Common network types. From C. C. Snow, R. E. Miles, and H. J. Coleman, Jr., "Managing 21st Century Network Organizations," *Organizational Dynamics,* **Winter, 1992, pp. 4–20.**

benefits by having divisions, smaller business units, and even corporate staff units buy and sell outside the firm as well as within the firm.[4]

Network organizations are different from previous organizations in several respects. First, over the past several decades, firms using older structures have preferred to hold in-house (or under exclusive contract) all the assets required to produce a given product or service. In contrast, many networks use the collective assets of several firms located at various points along the value chain.[5] Second, networks rely more on market mechanisms than administrative processes to manage resource flows. However, these mechanisms are not the simple "arm's length" relationships usually associated with independently owned economic entities. Rather, the various components of the network recognize their interdependence and are willing to share information, cooperate with each other, and customize their product or service—all to maintain their position within the network. Third, while networks of subcontractors have been commonplace, many recently designed networks expect a more proactive role among participants—voluntary behavior that improves the final product or service rather than simply fulfills a contractual obligation. Fourth, in an increasing number of industries, including computers, semiconductors, autos, farm implements, and motorcycles, networks are evolving with characteristics that in some way resemble those of the Japanese *keiretsu*—an organizational collective based on cooperation and mutual shareholding among a group of manufacturers, suppliers, and trading and finance companies.[6]

Although the network organization exhibits characteristics that are different from previous forms, the stable, dynamic, and internal networks shown in Figure 4–1 nevertheless incorporate elements of the prior organizational forms as their main building blocks. For example, a functionally organized firm may realize that it needs to outsource the manufacture of certain components or ally with specific distributors in order to focus its attention only on those operating activities for which it is best equipped. The result of such changes is a stable network organization: a core firm linked forward and backward to a limited number of carefully selected partners. Upstream stable networks linking suppliers to a core firm are common in the automobile industry. Downstream networks often link computer hardware manufacturers and value-added retailers.

Alternatively, a large multinational matrix organization made up of various design, manufacturing, and distribution units may decide to replace centrally determined transfer prices with genuine buying and selling relationships among these units. The result is an internal market type of network.[7]

Lastly, in some industries, rapid technological and market changes may encourage a divisionalized firm to disassemble into a multiplayer dynamic network of designers, suppliers, producers, and distributors instead of holding all of these assets internally. This is what has occurred over the past 20 years in most publishing firms.

In sum, the network organization in its several variations has sought to incorporate the specialized efficiency of the functional organization, the autonomous operating effectiveness of the divisional form, and the asset-transferring capabilities of the matrix organization—all with considerable success. However, the network form itself has inherent limitations and is vulnerable to misapplication and misuse. To understand the real and potential weaknesses of the network, we need to examine the problems that have plagued (and continue to befall) its predecessor forms.

CAUSES OF FAILURE IN EARLIER ORGANIZATIONAL FORMS

As noted earlier, a similar evolutionary pattern can be seen in each of the earlier organizational forms. Widespread initial success occurred as the new form provided an innovative arrangement of a firm's resources and a new operating logic responsive to the emerging environment. However, a growing list of failures eventually followed. Some of the causes of failure were obvious—for example, the new form was increasingly, perhaps faddishly, applied in settings for which it was never intended or suited.

The more intriguing failures arise from two types of subtle managerial "mistakes": individually logical *extensions* of the form that, in the aggregate, push the form beyond the limits of its capability; and *modifications* of the form that, while reasonable on the surface, nevertheless violate the form's operating logic. To fully understand these causes of failure, it is necessary to first restate the logic of the functional, divisional, and matrix forms and then examine major types of preventable failure against that logic (see Table 4–1).

The Functional Form

The functional form of organization can be thought of as a special-purpose machine designed to produce a limited line of goods or services

Table 4–1. Causes of Failure in Traditional Organizational Forms

Organizational Form	Operating Logic	Primary Application	Extension Failure	Modification Failure
Functional	Specialized assets centrally controlled by plans and budgets	Efficient production of standardized goods and services	Vertical integration beyond capacity to keep specialized assets fully loaded and/or to evaluate contributions	Product or service diversification that overloads central planning mechanisms
Divisional	Decentralized operation of divisions with centralized evaluation and investment	Related diversification by product and/or region	Diversification (or acquisitions) outside area of technical and evaluative expertise	Corporate interventions to force coordination or obtain efficiencies across divisions
Matrix	Dual focus on standardized and customized products	Shared assets between standardized products and prototype contracts (e.g., many aerospace firms)	Expanding number of temporary contracts beyond ability of allocation mechanisms	Modifications that distort the dual focus (i.e., favor one type of market or product over another)
		Shared assets between worldwide product divisions and country-based marketing divisions (e.g., some global firms)	Search for global synergy limits local adaptability	

73

in large volume and at low cost. The logic of the functional form is *centrally coordinated specialization*. Departments staffed with specialized experts are integrated into the firm's overall effort in accordance with a common schedule that is fully and predictably operated. Firms in the late nineteenth and early twentieth centuries frequently integrated forward, creating new wholesaling and retailing channels to assure that their output could be efficiently distributed and sold, and they often integrated backward to assure themselves the steady flow of materials and components essential to efficient operation. Today's functional paragons, such as Wal-Mart, are masters at obtaining these kinds of efficiencies, but typically they are not as vertically integrated.

Although vertical integration assures input and output predictability, it does not come without costs. The further backward and forward a firm integrates, the greater the costs of coordination among a larger number of specialized assets demanding full utilization. Ultimately, it becomes difficult to determine whether any particular asset along the value chain is making a positive contribution to overall profitability. In fact, the recent trend toward disaggregation (e.g., buying rather than making components, outsourcing sales or distribution) reflects the recognition by many firms that coordination costs and asset underutilization are offsetting the benefits gained.

An example that illustrates these trade-offs involves the turnaround efforts made at Harley-Davidson in the early 1980s. The motorcycle manufacturer discovered that much of its production inflexibility, along with excessive costs, was caused by attempting to produce virtually all its own parts and components. A move to a just-in-time inventory system allowed Harley-Davidson to outsource many parts and supplies, reducing its total cycle time and bringing new products to the market quicker while lowering overall costs. What is interesting about organizational "failures" such as that at Harley-Davidson is that managers need not do anything wrong—at Harley, the company's functional structure encouraged internal production to assure control. Rather, such systems often fail because managers do too many things right.[8]

Alternatively, the functional organization form will also fail if it is modified inappropriately. The functional organization's logic of central control does not easily adapt to product or service diversity. While some limited diversity is possible, if the number of products offered becomes too large, or if demand variations interfere with efficient scheduling, the functional form begins to prove inflexible and costly to operate.

For example, after World War II, the Chrysler Corporation rapidly expanded its product line in an attempt to match General Motors' strategy of a "product for every pocketbook." However, while its models proliferated (actually exceeding the number of GM models at one point), Chrysler did not adopt the divisional structure then used by its competitors, ultimately suffering from losses in efficiency and coordination costs. Here, managers modified key aspects of Chrysler's functional structure for apparently logical reasons, but the addition of more than 70 different models demanded a total restructure—the adoption of a new (the divisional) form.

The Divisional Form

The divisional organization can be thought of as a collection of similar special-purpose machines, each independently operated to serve a particular market and all coordinated centrally. The operating logic of the divisional form is thus *the coupling of divisional autonomy with centrally controlled performance evaluation and resource allocation.* The divisional form achieves both flexibility and economies of scope by rapidly focusing clusters of assets on new or expanding markets. The divisional form also may develop mechanisms for transferring new technology and managerial know-how across divisions as well as to newly created or acquired operations.

Markets for differentiated goods and services grew rapidly in the 1920s and again after World War II. As described earlier, General Motors used a divisional structure to focus different automobile models on distinct markets. Similarly, Du Pont identified different types of markets in which its several divisions could use their technical know-how in applied chemistry, and Sears Roebuck used managers across the country to independently operate "hometown stores with nationwide buying power."

Although divisionalized firms are adept at moving incrementally into related areas, they are also vulnerable to overextension. Most divisionalized firms have moved into some markets that initially appeared to be appropriate but ultimately proved to be outside their area of expertise, weakening the firm's ability to appraise performance and make investment decisions. For example, General Mills, a highly successful divisionalized firm, at least twice extended itself into areas that proved to be beyond its zone of expertise, first into electrical appliances and later into toys and fashion goods. In both cases, the firm recognized its own shortcomings and either divested the divisions or moved back from direct operation.[9]

Divisionalized firms are also vulnerable to modifications that begin with good reason but subsequently undermine the firm's operating logic. For example, the creation of cross-division units to share technology and process improvements, may genuinely prove valuable. However, excessive coordination requirements eventually constrain the divisions' flexibility to meet the demands of their respective markets and to accurately assess the effectiveness of each division. Just such extensive coordination requirements constrained, in fact destroyed, the operating autonomy of the separate automobile divisions of General Motors. Under the threat of growing competition, GM's complex, interdivisional structure grew to the point of delaying new product development, and its intrusive coordination mechanisms contributed to unit costs above those of its competition. Most recently, to produce a "truly new" car (Saturn), GM had to circumvent its own convoluted structure by creating an entirely new division.

This type of problem is common today because, unfortunately, fewer and fewer firms appear to be willing to leave the logic of the divisional form intact. Indeed, many firms that refer to themselves as divisionalized, in fact, have extensive corporate staff coordination and minimal divisional autonomy. Such operations actually produce all the costs and rigidity of the functional form while adding the cost of divisional duplication of resources. Again, individually sound decisions may add up to overall operating inefficiencies and ineffectiveness.

The Matrix Form

The matrix organizational form can be thought of as a complex machine simultaneously generating two or more outputs. The operating logic of the matrix is similar to that of the functional form, centrally coordinated specialization. To these dual aspects of its operating logic, the matrix form adds the requirement for *balance among the components to produce mutually beneficial allocations of resources*.

For example, in one type of matrix, an aerospace firm may produce a line of standard products in the functionally structured portion of the organization, while simultaneously organizing a series of project teams for customized products. In this case, the matrix structure allows members of the various project teams to be drawn from functional units and, when a project is completed, returns them to their home departments for reassignment. The result is a capacity to expand and contract in response to new market opportunities while maintaining crucial human assets.

In another matrix application, a multiproduct, multinational firm may combine worldwide product divisions with national or regionally based marketing groups. Again, the key in a global matrix is to gain the benefits of local operating flexibility while employing resources "owned" by the product divisions.

As with the functional and divisional forms, the matrix form can be overloaded by simply extending a firm's operations beyond the capability of its structure. For example, in the aerospace matrix, each additional project places new demands on the resource-allocation capacity of the firm. Ultimately, resources are held but are not kept fully employed, and the firm achieves something akin to negative synergy— each new logical addition brings with it coordination costs that exceed its benefits.

Equally troublesome are failures of the matrix resulting from modifications that violate its operating logic. The purpose of the matrix form is to let two different types of market forces shape operations; many firms, however, are unwilling or unable to maintain balance between conflicting market demands. For example, if worldwide product divisions cannot influence the marketing priorities of national marketing groups, operating efficiency may be totally subordinated to local responsiveness.

In sum, considerable evidence suggests that an organizational form performs optimally only within certain limits. When a particular form's logic is violated, even by apparently reasonable extensions or modifications, failure may result.

POTENTIAL CAUSES OF FAILURE IN NETWORK ORGANIZATIONS

Like its predecessor forms, the network organization can fail because of alterations made by well-intentioned managers. The network form has an operating logic associated with each of its variations, and violations of this logic are likely to limit the form's effectiveness and, in the extreme, cause it to fail.

The Stable Network

The stable network has its roots in the structure and operating logic of the functional organization. It is designed to serve a predictable market by linking together independently owned specialized assets along a given product or service value chain. However, instead of a single vertically integrated firm, the stable network substitutes a set of component firms, each tied closely to a core firm by contractual arrangements, but each maintaining its competitive fitness by serving firms outside the network.

The most common threat to the effectiveness of the stable network is an extension that demands the complete utilization of the supplier's or distributor's assets for the benefit of the core firm. If the several suppliers and distributors in the stable network focus their assets solely on the needs of a single core firm, price, quality, and technical innovation are not improved by market competition. This process of asset overspecialization and overdedication by network partners is frequently incremental and can therefore go unnoticed. Continued, step-by-step customization of a supplier's processes, either voluntarily or at the core firm's insistence, can ultimately result in the inability of the supplier to compete in other markets and an obligation on the part of the core firm to use all of the supplier's output (see Table 4–2). For maximum effectiveness, both the core firm and its stable partners must explicitly consider the limits of dedication and force themselves to set restrictions on the proportion of assets that can be so utilized.

A highly effective stable network has been put together by Nike, the athletic shoe and apparel giant. Founded in 1964, as a U.S. dealer for a Japanese shoe firm, Nike began developing its own product line in 1972 and has built a $3 billion business on a strategy of working closely with, but not dominating, a wide range of suppliers in Korea, Taiwan, Thailand, and the People's Republic of China. Nike wants its suppliers to service other designers so that they can enhance their technical competence and so that they will be available when needed but not dependent on Nike's ability to forecast and schedule their services. A major factor in Nike's continuing market leadership is its ability to introduce new models quickly to meet (or create) market trends. Perhaps most importantly, Nike has maintained its technical competence and leads the industry in R&D investment.[10] Nike personnel work directly with suppliers to build and maintain their capability, verifying product quality in process as well as after the fact. To assure their own expertise in

Table 4–2. Causes of Failure in Network Organizations

Type of Network	Operating Logic	Primary Application	Extension Failure	Modification Failure
Stable	A large core firm creates market-based linkages to a limited set of upstream and/or downstream partners	Mature industries requiring large capital investments. Varied ownership limits risk and encourages full loading of all assets	Overutilization of a given supplier or distributor may lead to unhealthy dependence on core firm	High expectations for cooperation can limit the creativity of partners
Internal	Commonly owned business elements allocate resources along the value chain using market mechanisms	Mature industries requiring large capital investments. Market-priced exchanges allow performance appraisal of internal units	Firm may extend asset ownership beyond the capacity of the internal market and performance appraisal mechanisms	Corporate executives use "commands" instead of influence or incentives to intervene in local operations
Dynamic	Independent business elements along the value chain form temporary alliances from among a large pool of potential partners	Low tech industries with short product design cycles and evolving high tech industries (e.g. electronics, biotech, etc.)	Expertise may become too narrow and role in value chain is assumed by another firm	Excessive mechanisms may develop to prevent partners' opportunism or exclusive relationships with a limited number of upstream or downstream partners

79

manufacturing (and to prevent costly design mistakes), Nike has continued a small domestic manufacturing operation focused on leading-edge designs.

The stable network can also be damaged by thoughtless or even inadvertent modifications. In the search for assurance that suppliers can meet quality standards and delivery dates, some core firms attempt to specify the processes that the network member must use. Deep involvement in a supplier's or distributor's processes can occur through innocent zeal on the part of the core firm's staff and may be enthusiastically endorsed by the component's staff. Within limits, close cooperation to assure effective linkage is valuable. However, the core firm can ultimately find itself "managing" the assets of its partners and accepting responsibility for their output. Moreover, when the operating independence of the network member is severely constrained, any creativity that might flow from its managers or staff is curtailed—and the core firm is not getting the full benefit of the component's assets. In effect, the core firm is converting the network into a vertically integrated functional organization.

The Internal Network

The logic of the internal network, or internal market in the terms used by Ackoff and Halal, requires the creation of a market economy inside a firm. Here organizational units buy and sell goods and services among themselves at prices established in the open market. Obviously, if internal transactions are to reflect market prices, the various components must have regular opportunity to verify the price and quality of their wares by buying and selling outside the firm. The purpose of the internal network, like its predecessor the matrix form, is to gain competitive advantage by permitting wide entrepreneurial freedom along with accountability for performance. But, also like the matrix, the internal network can be damaged by extensions that overload its internal market mechanisms and by modifications that unbalance the relationships between buyers and sellers.

For example, the giant multinational firm ABB (Asea Brown Bovari) has grown quickly to over $25 billion in revenues and nearly a quarter of a million employees through a concerted program of mergers and acquisitions that has given it unmatched local and global synergy in the electrical systems and equipment market. To this point, the firm has increased shareholder value by thoughtfully specifying the market domain of each of its components and creating the internal mechanisms by which they can exchange goods and services in mutually beneficial ways under overall market discipline. However, it would be easy for such a firm to be seduced by its current success into an attempt to move further and further afield. At the moment, the CEO and key managers of ABB have a well-articulated concept of how the firm's global internal market operates.[11] However, each new business line, and each new geographic area addressed, must be carefully interconnected throughout the global grid, a task whose difficulty increases not arithmetically but geometrically.

Internal networks thus can fail from overextension, but they can fail perhaps even faster because of misguided modification. The most common managerial misstep in internal networks is corporate intervention in resource flows or in the determination of transaction prices. Not every interaction in the internal network can and should flow from locally determined supply and demand decisions. Corporate managers may well see a benefit in having internal units buy from a newly built or acquired component, even though its actual prices are above those of competitors in the marketplace. Such prices may be needed to sort out the operation and develop full efficiency. However, the manner in which corporate management handles such "forced" transactions is a crucial factor in the continuing health of the network. Ideally, rather than dictate the transfer price and process, corporate executives should provide a "subsidy" to assist the start-up component in showing a profit or should provide buyers with incentives to match the costs from lower priced competitors. Obviously, such subsidies or incentives should be time bound and carefully monitored to prevent abuses. Although this process is demanding, it protects the logic of market-based internal transactions so that they do not revert to centrally determined transfers. Unfortunately, instead of preserving the ability to evaluate components on actual performance, many corporate managers "command" component behaviors and risk destroying agreement on the concept of an internal market itself.

Despite potential problems, the shift from complex, centrally planned hierarchies to internal market structures is a growing movement, and IBM's recent announcements provide one more large, highly visible example. IBM's plan is to turn each of its major units into self-managed businesses, with outside buyers and sellers as well. The 1991 Conference on Internal Markets at George Washington University reported experiments in building internal networks in organizations ranging from services (Blue Cross-Blue Shield), to materials (Alcoa), to low- (Clark Equipment) and high-tech (Control Data) manufacturers. Not surprisingly, these applications tend to demonstrate both the benefits and the types of resistance anticipated here. However, it is too early to tell whether these and other internal network structures will avoid major managerial mistakes.[12]

The Dynamic Network

The operating logic of the dynamic network is linked to that of the divisional form of organization which emphasizes adaptability by focusing independent divisions on distinct but related markets. Central evaluation and local operating autonomy are combined in the dynamic network, where independent firms are linked together for the one-time (or short-term) production of a particular good or service. For the dynamic network to achieve its full potential, there must be numerous firms (or units of firms) operating at each of the points along the value chain, ready to be pulled together for a given run and then disassembled to become part of another temporary alignment.

The availability of numerous potential partners eager to apply their skills and assets to the upstream or downstream needs of a given firm is not only the key to success of the dynamic network, it is also a possible source of trouble. For example, if a particular firm in the value chain overspecializes—refines but also, over time, restricts its expertise—it runs the risk of becoming a "hollow" corporation, a firm without a clearly defined, essential contribution to make to its product or service value chain.[13] Firms need to occupy a wide enough segment of the value chain to be able to test and protect the value of their contribution. A designer needs to retain its ability to build prototypes, a producer may need to experiment with new process technologies, and so on. Firms with a contribution base that is either too narrow or weakly defined are easily overrun by their upstream and/or downstream neighbors. Indeed, examples of firms (and industries) pushed into decline and ultimate failure by excessive outsourcing abound. From radios to television sets to video recorders, outsourcing decisions by U.S. corporations allowed foreign suppliers to acquire the technical competence to design and sell their own products, eventually capturing the bulk of U.S. domestic markets.[14]

Conversely, firms with a clear competence-based position on the value chain, maintained by continuing investment in technology and skill development, can afford to interact confidently with upstream and downstream partners. Nevertheless, there is a constant temptation for firms to go beyond the development of their own competence as the means of ensuring their viability. They may seek to add protection through an excessive concern for secrecy, heavy emphasis on legalism in contractual relations, a search for preferential relationships with particular partners, and so on. In fact, potentially dysfunctional network behaviors are currently multiplying across the personal and business computer industry as firms, including industry giants IBM and Apple, build an almost undecipherable maze of interconnected agreements and alliances to protect market share, enter new arenas, search for technical innovations, and promote the adoption of technical and/or system standards. Each of these efforts is designed to give the newly formed partners a competitive advantage over those players not included (who are instead building their own web of alliances).[15] Such protective modifications can constrain the primary strength of the dynamic network—its ability to efficiently allocate member firms, uncoupling and recoupling them with minimum cost and minimum loss of operating time.

In summary, the dynamic network places demands on its component firms to continually reappraise their technical competence and the scope of their activities, not only to maintain their own well-being but that of the broader network as well. No one component can know everything that is happening or everything that is needed in the broader network. However, each component can preserve its own competence and refrain from behaviors that threaten network performance.[16]

AVOIDING FAILURE: DEVELOPING THE COMPETENCE FOR SELF-RENEWAL

The preceding sections have outlined how organizational forms may lose their vitality over time as managers make what appear to be logical extensions or modifications. However, rather than improving performance, these actions may gradually obscure and subvert the operating logic of the form. What is needed is the competence not only to make adjustments to environmental shifts, but to do so either within the constraints of the operating logic of the existing organizational form, or by adopting a new form to fit a new environment.

The possibility that firms adopting network structures will improve their self-renewal competence flows from two unique characteristics of the network form: the essential relationships among components are *market transactions* (and thus highly *visible* to all parties), and these relationships are *voluntary* (and thus must reflect *explicit* commitments).

Dynamics of Market Relationships

Even when a network's components are commonly owned, the essential structure of the organization is of the type found in a marketplace—clearly specified, objectively structured contracts that guide interactions rather than internal schedules, procedures, and routines. Conversely, in hierarchical relationships, every interaction is colored by the hidden threat of organizational politics, the likelihood that power and influence rather than performance are guiding behavior. In older organizational forms cost data may be manipulated by simply changing accounting conventions—such as the way in which overhead expenses are accumulated and assigned. With market linkages, attempts at personal gain may be made, but the behavior will be much more transparent.

The visibility of network linkages does not guarantee that they will always be efficacious to each of the parties, but it does push the parties toward performance-based equity. A number of years ago, we predicted that network organizations would create "full-disclosure information systems" to assure that all decisions were made objectively and fairly.[17] Such practices are now quite common. As the CEO of Excel Industries, a major supplier of Ford, states: "They know every cost we incur."[18]

Visible market linkages among network components have perceptual as well as substantive benefits. A faulty market coupling must be dealt with, whereas purely hierarchical mechanisms can be eroding or even broken for some time before the damage demands the affected parties' attention.

Dynamics of Voluntary Relationships

Market relationships, as suggested, tend to be explicit. They specify the performance that is expected from each partner and how that performance will be measured and compensated. Explicitness, however, does not require complex, legalistic, or highly formal contracts. A contract can be as simple as a due date and a price based on disclosed costs. In the construction industry, "partnering" sessions are held among network members at the beginning of major projects to clarify responsibilities and relationships and to agree on methods of resolving disputes. Similarly, General Electric's Workout Program is designed to bring GE's managers, customers, and vendors together to create effective working relationships.[19]

Most importantly, the fact that network relationships are explicit does not mean that they are dictated by one party or another. In fact, underlying all the positive characteristics of network structures is the dynamic of voluntarism. If voluntarism is not present—if partners are not free to withdraw from relationships they believe are unfairly structured—then the value of openness and explicitness is compromised. Of course, such compromises can and do occur, as noted earlier, when business partners become overly dependent on one another and when corporate management intervenes in internal market transactions.

Nevertheless, U.S. firms are gaining experience at creating and maintaining fair and voluntary relationships. For example, Harley-Davidson claims it is no longer "waging war" with its suppliers. Harley's managers reportedly "threw the lawyers out" and produced a simple contract that clarified goals for suppliers and outlined how disputes could be resolved.[20]

The unique, positive characteristics of the network organization discussed here can assist managers in making adaptations in keeping with the operating logic of each form. Because changes are visible and clear to all parties in the network, there are likely to be multiple players tracing the impact of any change. Moreover, the key characteristic of the network form, voluntarism, is in itself a litmus test of logic violation—*any* change that reduces voluntarism is a potential threat to the overall efficiency of the network.

CONCLUSIONS

Research over the past decade has increasingly confirmed what managers and organizational theorists have long understood—organizations, particularly large, complex firms, have a difficult time responding to changes in their competitive environment. Instead of adapting incrementally as market and/or technological changes occur, managers tend to wait until environmental demands accumulate to crisis proportions before attempting a response, and then they often fail. When managers do behave incrementally, they frequently make patchwork alterations to the existing organization as each new market or technological shift occurs but without considering the ultimate systemic impact. Such adjustments gradually move the organization away from its core structural logic, creating an idiosyncratic system whose functions are highly dependent on a few key individuals or units. These organizations are not only unstable and costly to operate, they often are so convoluted that it is difficult even to determine where major change might begin—to get to the center of a complex organizational knot.

Our premise here has been that organizational forms, particularly the network form, need not be so prone to failure. If managers understand the logic of their organization's form, and if they keep that logic visible to themselves and others associated with the organization, the benefits of proposed changes can be weighed against the strains they impose on the total system. In fact, it is possible to anticipate how and why each organizational form is likely to fail. Moreover, if managers understand the operating logic of alternative forms, they can explore the possibility that environmental changes have pushed their organization outside the boundaries of one form and into those of another.

We have tried to illustrate how the network form should facilitate the manager's task of successful adaptation. By its very nature, the network organization is always in the process of renewal—its important elements are in a constant state of adjustment to market, technological, and other forces in the environment. This continual process of adaptation, coupled with the fact that network components are typically smaller and more focused than those of integrated firms, should help managers deepen their understanding of the form's operating logic and develop their renewal skills.

Whether the network form of organization is less prone to internally generated failures than its predecessors is determinable only over time. Nevertheless, its evolution provides managers the opportunity to explore and test their understanding of organizations from a new vantage point, and the continued study of networks should contribute to a better understanding of the causes of success and failure in all organizational forms.

5 Internal Markets and Learning Organizations

Some Thoughts on Uniting the Two Perspectives

Peter M. Senge

I first encountered the idea of internal markets as a graduate student when, some 20 years ago, I read Jay Forrester's prescient article, "A New Corporate Design" (Appendix). I remember the excitement I and fellow graduate students shared over the radical implications of Forrester's conception—eliminating superior–subordinate relationships, organizing all activity in terms of self-responsible profit centers, determining compensation objectively, eliminating internal monopolies, allowing freedom of access to information, and establishing a corporate constitution.

Peter M. Senge is director of the Organization Learning Center, Massachusetts Institute of Technology. He is also a well-known scholar of organizational systems who has recently attracted wide attention with his book, *The Fifth Discipline* (New York: Doubleday, 1990).

Like so many of Forrester's ideas, the new corporate design was well ahead of its time. But it inspired a generation of students to think boldly, in anticipation of when that time would come.

In the intervening years, my work and that of my colleagues has led in a somewhat different direction—toward understanding the processes whereby people in organizations make sense of their world, formulate strategy and policy, establish genuine vision, and lead themselves. Eventually, our work has come to focus on how organizations learn, what might be the "core competencies" of learning organizations, and which "leadership disciplines" are needed to develop those competencies.

So, now, 20 years later, it is a delight to have the opportunity to once again reflect on the possibilities of "internal market" structures. Perhaps, and this will be the premise I will explore, these two strands of work, on learning organizations and on internal markets, might now begin to be woven together to produce possibilities neither might enable alone.

SOME QUALMS

Before starting, I should say that I am not an unquestioning fan of internal markets. Such a structural change, however radical, does not address a range of very important issues. Bringing these qualms to the surface will foreshadow some of my suggestions for making internal markets more effective and will provide some insight into the thinking behind my suggestions.

In our work over the past 15 years, we have been guided by a premise, right or wrong, that fundamental changes in how organizations work require fundamental changes in how we think and interact. Changes in the "outer world" do not necessarily produce changes in the "inner world." And, it is the inner world of assumptions, worldviews, fundamental beliefs and attitudes, and habitual ways of interacting with one another that most limit what is possible in contemporary organizations. It is often said that most political revolutions don't change very much. After a few years, the liberators become the new oppressors. To the extent this is the case, it is undoubtedly because both oppressor and liberator are locked into common patterns of thinking and acting that lie below the surface of different espoused belief systems.

Herein lie my concerns about the internal market movement. I am skeptical of what can be accomplished by changes in structure alone.

What leads us to believe that lots of local managers focused on their own profits will be any more farsighted than a few corporate managers focused on corporate profits? Will they be any better at systems thinking? After all, "results-oriented" divisional presidents focused on quarterly division profits are notorious among nature's most shortsighted reductionistic creatures.

Similarly, why should local profit-center managers be better than their bureaucratic cousins at inquiring into highly conflictual issues without invoking defensiveness and self-protection? Traditional authoritarian firms may indeed be crippled by the poor movement of information up and down the chain of command, as advocates of internal markets point out. But, I believe they are crippled just as often by "undiscussable" issues that everyone acknowledges but no one can broach. Why should this be any different with internal markets? What good is it to have more free movement of information if people cannot discuss the information that is most important but that is also the most threatening?

I question the reasoning behind viewing internal markets as the solution to innovation and growth. Such reasoning, it seems to me, assumes that people, free of the constraints of bureaucratic hierarchies, can figure out what needs to be done to achieve those outcomes. It assumes that they are not doing so in traditional organizations because they are demotivated, lack the information needed to succeed, or are denied the freedom to act on the information they have. None of these condition seems to me wholly adequate to explain the ineffectiveness of contemporary organizations.

Managers today often have more information than they know what to do with. They lack, however, the ability to distinguish what information is important from what is not for a given set of issues. Many organizations in which I have worked encourage high levels of freedom of action (many also do not). I have often observed this freedom lead to bad decisions made enthusiastically, rather than to good decisions.

For example, one organization in which I and my colleagues worked extensively in the early 1980s was organized around a large number of small completely autonomous divisions, each a freestanding profit center. Corporate staff for an organization of 6,000 employees was 15, including the CEO, several vice presidents, a couple of lawyers, and secretaries. Morale was extremely high throughout the organization. People had freedom, strong philosophical convictions, and exciting economic opportunities. But, on closer inspection, there were also deep problems. Individual division presidents were often young and aggressive but inexperienced in growing their own company. Corporate managers found themselves trapped in a dilemma when they were uneasy with local business unit plans. If they said nothing, they tacitly endorsed plans about which they had qualms. If they intervened, they sent a signal that they lacked confidence in local decision making. When they did intervene, they were often ineffective at fostering a learning process that resulted in deeper understanding and genuine shifts in thinking and strategy. They ended up advocating strategies they could rarely explain and were reticent to enforce.

For several years the company grew rapidly. Then, it began to struggle and eventually stagnated. There has been virtually no growth for the past eight years, and more losses than profits. One division, for example, ended up highly dependent on a particular computer manufacturer as its prime customer for its specialized circuit boards. When that customer failed, so did the division. Other divisions floundered for different but similar reasons. On the whole, key decision makers were slow to learn, despite great freedom, abundant information, and enormous enthusiasm and motivation to learn.

Problems such as this illustrate deep dilemmas and challenges not solved by internal markets. In particular, individual decision makers are often poor at understanding the complex systems within which they operate. Experience may produce insight, but understanding possessed by experienced managers is usually highly intuitive and difficult to explain convincingly to others who do not share that intuition. When conflicting views arise, things often get worse. Rather than working together to develop more integrative views, differences in view are suppressed or debates lead to polarization. Either way, key decisions tend to be made based on politics rather than merit.

This is why increasing freedom of individual decision makers often does not lead to better decision making. People attempt to solve obvious problems without understanding their deeper causes. This leads to alleviating problem symptoms in ways that will simply create new, more difficult problems. When these new problems arise, they will not be connected with the earlier actions taken to resolve the earlier problems. Just as common, actions taken to resolve problems in one part of a larger system create new problems in another part. These connections often also go unrecognized, especially when there are delays before consequences in distant parts of the system emerge.

These assertions about the ineffectiveness of individual decision making are supported by rigorous experimental research. This research has focused on decision making in complex systems with multiple inter-actions and multiple delayed effects—that is, just like the situations in which most important managerial decisions are embedded. For exam-ple, in a simple production distribution system, embodying a fraction of the complexity of real distribution systems, decision makers consis-tently create wild cycles of undersupply and excess supply, even when external customer demands are stable.[1] They do so by focusing on im-mediate problems in their part of the system and ignoring the conse-quences of their decisions for other parts.[2] When the cycles arise, the decision makers blame forces outside their control.

The other critical premise advanced to support internal markets is that they lead to "creative search behavior"—that is, lots of individual decision makers exploring multiple options are more likely to hit on ef-fective strategies. This is a timeless argument for free markets and, in my judgment, a valid argument—up to a point. Two things disturb me about raising this argument in support of internal markets.

First, there is also abundant evidence that free markets often deal inadequately with complex situations where cause and effect are not close in time and space. As we can see all around us, free markets don't always promote the common good—especially when the common good goes beyond the simple transactions on which the market's actors are focused. Crowding, pollution, labor abuse, and unsustainable depletion of natural resources all arise as by-products of free market decision making. Economists agree that to be "efficient," markets often require levels of information not available in real life.

Second, experimental research is starting to show that, as in the case of individual decision makers, the problems in markets go beyond simply not having enough information. Decision makers en masse aren't necessarily much more intelligent than individual decision makers. Lab-oratory experiments with free markets show that feedback complexity systematically degrades performance relative to the optimal ideal of economic theory. People in a variety of experimental markets with time delays, multiple feedback processes, and nonlinear interactions generate business cycles, wild patterns of boom-and-bust, and speculative bub-bles quite similar to those observed in real markets. Experience, finan-cial incentives, and full information about the state of the system have but little moderating effect on these problems involving multiple deci-sion makers. People are still incapable of getting close to "optimal" outcomes in even moderately complex situations, and even when they have more information than people would have in real life.[3]

The key to the learning problems of individuals and markets is that most critical issues confronting managers in the private and public sector today are "dynamically complex." Cause and effect are often not obviously related, and "obvious" solutions often do more harm than good. These problems cannot be solved by more information. The problems lie in how we process the information we have. There are cognitive constraints to effective decision making, which are not altered by internal markets.

Cognitive constraints to effective decision making are exacerbated by interpersonal and cultural constraints. Interpersonal and cultural constraints arise, in part, because we all understand the larger systems of which we are a part from our own vantage point. All of us feel strongly about our views and thus justify our reasoning toward what should be done to improve matters. The result is that people often hold diverse, seemingly irreconcilable, views of critical issues such as how to foster innovation and growth. Bringing these differences to the surface can be highly threatening to the team spirit and apparent togetherness many organizations seek to foster. Consequently, most organizations solve this problem by covering up differences, opting for a facade of superficial agreement and saving people's real views for "corridor conversations." If more candor prevails, it often leads to a different pattern of defensiveness. People "speak out" about what's on their mind. But their minds are rarely changed. In effect, the best defense becomes a strong offense.

Interpersonal and cultural constraints on effective decision making are also not eliminated by internal markets. In traditional organizations, these constraints might have been most evident in senior management teams because that is where decision-making power was concentrated. With internal markets, defensiveness and games playing will be spread among a larger number of decision-making teams. Clear focus on profits may mitigate some of this behavior. But, insofar as such patterns are deeply embedded in cultural norms of win and avoid losing, of covering up ignorance and uncertainty, and of protecting oneself and others from embarrassment or threat, the constraints are unlikely to be altered significantly by internal markets. Experience has shown that overcoming culturally embedded defensiveness takes a long-term commitment to developing new learning skills and capabilities, in the context of a broad commitment to values of openness and inquiry.[4]

On a more parochial level, I am concerned about the internal market movement in the United States because of our extraordinary, and often unjustified, belief in the power of competition. To many, internal markets will mean no more than turning loose the forces of competition within organizations. Yet, our most effective international competitors again and again show the power of cooperation allied with competition. The Japanese and the Germans, in very different ways, have both evolved sophisticated "collaborative competition" models. For example, in Japan, the very same companies that might compete in products and services collaborate in developing new tools and methods that lead to improvements in products and services. Such collaboration has been vital to the steady advance in total quality management (TQM) methodology and practice.

Thoughtful advocates of internal markets address this concern. Ackoff (Chapter 1) points out that internal markets can be expected to lead to more cooperative behavior within companies by eliminating the games playing and internal politics created by bureaucrats. Halal (Chapter 2) calls for an "ethic of competition and cooperation."

Nonetheless, we should not underestimate our cultural predisposition to see competition as the solution to all of life's problems; this might lead to a distorted view of internal markets. This predisposition will lead many to see internal competition as a panacea, and be blind to the need for complementary changes in our management practices.

By this time, you may be wondering why someone with so many qualms about an idea is bothering to write in its support. My qualms are directed at those who see internal markets as "the answer" rather than as one piece of a larger puzzle. If seen as part of a broader array of equally fundamental innovations, the shift to internal markets might be vital.

SOME SUGGESTIONS

The implementation of internal markets is best regarded as part of a three-pronged strategy for creating a fundamental alternative to traditional authoritarian, hierarchical organizations:

1. Making basic innovations in organizational structure.
2. Rethinking the nature of managerial work.
3. Developing new tools, methods, and ultimately new competencies.

Innovations in Organizational Structure

With internal markets as a central element, a variety of innovations in organization structure and design should be explored.

Elliott Jacques has advanced an intriguing set of design ideas that might complement internal markets.[5] What becomes of management hierarchy in an organization structured around internal markets? Surely, there might still be management levels within profit centers, as well as management levels within the "corporate" or central organization. Jacques suggests a rigorous way to define levels of management hierarchy—in terms of time horizon of responsibility and levels of abstraction of people's work. Based on this perspective, he argues that there are four "domains" of work: (1) direct hands-on work domain (decision horizons of one day to several months), (2) direct operations management (time horizons from several months to 2 years), (3) management of whole business units (time spans of 2 to 10 years), and (4) corporate strategy and design across multiple business units (time spans beyond 10 years). These domains are in turn, broken into seven management strata, the generic elements of appropriate management hierarchy.

It might be that integrating Jacques' perspective into internal market organizations would help in thinking through how profit centers are organized internally, and how profit centers and corporate management interact. Presumably, whole business units would be profit centers, as might many units at Jacques' "operational domain." But, without clear distinctions regarding time horizon of responsibility, little in the internal market concept guarantees an appropriate balance of short-term and long-term thinking. Similarly, thinking of the overall organizational hierarchy as representing different levels of abstraction clarifies the types of skills and capabilities needed at different levels, another potential blind spot of the internal market approach.

There are undoubtedly many other perspectives that can help illuminate changes in structure complementary to internal markets. Interestingly, many of the areas of structural innovation today are discussed in Forrester's original paper. His emphasis on "eliminating the superior–subordinate relationship" foreshadowed the "self-managing work teams," that have gained considerably in recent years.[6] His "objective determination of compensation" relates to "gain sharing" and related innovations in reward systems.[7] The section on "Restructuring through electronic data processing," identifies many of the basic forces creating, in contemporary jargon, "network organizations."[8]

However, structural innovations by themselves are unlikely to remedy some of the deeper seated limitations in traditional organizations. There also need to be basic changes in management philosophy and a commitment to developing new learning capabilities.

Rethinking Managerial Work

The work of management is changing profoundly, especially the work of senior management. I see many senior managers today deeply disoriented. They know the world is changing. They know their work is changing. But, they are not quite sure how and are most definitely not sure what it all means for them personally. I believe few organizations have grasped the depth and extent of the changes that lie ahead.

In traditional hierarchical organizations, senior managers set the direction and made the key decisions, and designed the control systems to translate decisions at the top into coordinated local actions. The work of management was planning, organizing, and controlling. In healthy organizations of the future, I believe managers will be responsible for developing commitment, building knowledge, and designing and guiding the processes whereby the organization continually renews and improves itself, that is, learns. Elsewhere, I have talked about the "new work" of senior managers as *stewards, teachers,* and *designers.*[9] I believe these ideas are especially relevant in the context of organizations structured around internal markets.

Nurturing Commitment around Core Precepts and Aspirations

All systems of management are built upon fundamental premises about people. What might be the underlying precepts and premises appropriate to organizations structured around internal markets?

One set of core premises concerns the nature of motivation and management's role in strengthening motivation. Authoritarian organizations assume that people need to be "motivated" to give their fullest effort, to be loyal, and to be innovative. In turn, much of the time and effort spent by managers at all levels is spent trying to figure out "how to motivate people." In fact, one of the primary justifications for traditional management lies in the need to motivate people. Deep in this mental model about management is the belief that the primary sources of motivation are extrinsic, that is outside the individual.

This premise may be a deep source of the disharmony most people feel between their personal lives and their work lives. It is exactly what Dr. Deming is describing when he says, "Our prevailing system of management has destroyed our people." Deming offers an alternative premise: "People," says Deming, "are born with intrinsic motivation, self-esteem, dignity, curiosity to learn, joy in learning." They possess, in the words of anthropologist Edward Hall, a "drive to learn," which is denied by traditional management's belief that people must be "motivated."

Intrinsic motivation may be a vital premise for organizations structured around internal markets. The internal market concept places great weight on freedom of action. But, it must also tap the intrinsic motivation to learn in overcoming the cognitive and interpersonal barriers to effective decision making. Simply giving people latitude to make their own decisions does not guarantee that they will be effective decision makers unless there is a relentless motivation to continually learn, especially to better understand the larger systems within which the individual operates. I see little hope of sustaining this relentless learning activity through extrinsic rewards.

Tapping the drive to learn requires creating an environment where people are genuinely committed. "Effective knowledge creation," requires a "high degree of personal commitment," according to Ikujiro Nonaka, in his article "The Knowledge-Creating Company."[10] When people are genuinely committed in their work, they are fully engaged. They are imaginative. They feel a sense of responsibility for overall results achieved not just for "doing their job." For internal market structures to realize their potential, it is not enough for one or two "leaders" to be genuinely committed, with everyone else compliant. Large numbers of people will need to be genuinely committed in their work.

Profit-and-loss responsibility, the by-product of internal markets, is a powerful source of such commitment. Surely, many people are less engaged than they might be in traditional organizations because they feel no responsibility for the overall health of the enterprise.

But, profit responsibility is insufficient motivation because it does not, by itself, tap deep levels of intrinsic motivation. If people make money doing things that have little meaning for them, their commitment will be much weaker than if they believe in what they are doing.

This is why concepts such as *vision, values,* and *purpose* are so central to motivate real learning, and so vital for organizations structured around internal markets. I do not believe that making money brings out the highest in the human spirit. Moreover, people focused on profit will typically focus on short-term profit. Nothing contributes more to a long-term focus than people aspiring to achieve something that they regard as truly important and that can only be achieved over the long term.

This suggests two distinct leadership roles in firms structured around internal markets. Corporate management must work continually to build, in Nonaka's words, " a shared understanding of what the company stands for, where it is going, what kind of world it wants to live in, and most important, how to make that world a reality."[11] Local management must work continually to translate long-term values and missions into compelling business visions that focus people's aspirations and energies.

Building Knowledge

Much lip service is paid today to knowledge building but few managers understand the nature of the work required to lead in building organizational knowledge.

"No theory, no learning," says Deming.[12] People often claim that they learn through experience. Experimental studies suggest that pure trial-and-error learning can be very limited in complex systems.[13] If anything, this is even more true for organizations. Deming argues that building knowledge requires articulating a theory, predicting the consequences of changes based on that theory, observing the consequences of making those changes, and revising the underlying theory. By contrast, the "ready-fire-aim" orientation of most American corporations leads to much change but little knowledge.

At Ford, Fred Simon and Nick Zanuik, respectively program manager and head of product development for a major new car development program, have spent a substantial part of their time over the past year working to develop a *systemic* theory of how product development works at Ford. The theory considers the effects of resource allocation to product engineering and process engineering, the distribution of engineers' time between task completion and coordination, and the effects of schedule pressure and rework. This theory is grounded in extensive data gathering and analysis. It builds on generic theories of product development under study at the Massachusetts Institute of Technology (MIT) for several years. It is now being tested with teams within the large program that Simon and Zanuik direct. To facilitate testing, the theory is embedded within a "management flight simulator" that makes it accessible as an interactive simulation for managers to test out their own intuitions about the development process. The simulator, in turn, is part of a new product development "learning laboratory" being launched at Ford.

The important part of this story is that the theory is being developed and tested by senior line managers as part of their work. Just as we now know that assembly-line workers can both work within the line and continually work to improve the assembly process itself, so too can managers both manage within a system and work to continually improve the system itself. To do so, however, requires a significant time commitment. It also requires skills and patience. But, the payoff can be immense. Not only are the Ford managers developing insights and tools that should improve their program, they are investing in knowledge building that could potentially aid other product development efforts as well.

The same process has operated within several service companies within the MIT Organizational Learning Center. There, the work is to develop better, more systemic theories of why service companies tend to generate mediocre levels of service, higher than possible total costs, and underinvestment in service capacity. We are also trying to better understand the dynamics of implementing "value-adding service" strategies, and we are redesigning traditional operations based on standardized services (and products) to focus on solving customers' unique problems. Again, the underlying theories are being developed and tested by operations managers in diverse service businesses.

We are only just beginning to take seriously the notion that learning organizations are knowledge-building organizations. New ways must be found to distill and transmit understanding of complex issues, especially those that recur in diverse settings.[14] This task is too important to leave to chance, or to delegate to staff experts. I believe developing better theories of organizational processes and systems, and building those theories into tools and methods that many will use and test, will become a central task of management.

The new role of "manager as researcher" seems strange to many because of our traditional paradigm of manager as key decision maker and motivator. But, it points to a critical, and neglected, task for organizational learning. In organizations structured around internal markets, with large numbers of independent decision makers, this could be a primary source of value added by senior or corporate management.

Designing Learning Processes

Developing better theories is the first stage in knowledge building. Designing learning processes that bring these theories into daily use and result in continual testing and improvement is the second.

By a "learning process," I mean a systematic way whereby work at any level in an organization is improved by deepening understanding to support better decisions. Learning processes are different from training processes. A learning process is focused on the work at hand and how to do it better, whether that work be highly concrete and operational or more abstract and strategic. A training process focuses primarily on developing new skills and secondarily on applying those skills. Designers of learning processes are also interested in developing new skills and capabilities, but these develop as by-products of learning how to do our work better. All companies do training. Relatively few companies allocate significant effort to design learning processes. I believe the distinction is critical.

In many ways, the emphasis on training is an extension of the prevailing educational philosophy in the West, which separates thinking from doing, abstract skills from practical capabilities, education from personal purpose and aspiration. By contrast, the first rule in designing a learning process is that "the learner learns what the learner wants to learn." Learning is deeper and more enduring if it occurs in the context of real goals and aspirations, and real challenges that the learner is confronting. The learner is naturally motivated. The second rule is that learning occurs over time, new insights are tested out in practice, there is time to reflect on the consequences of new actions, and eventually we assimilate new capabilities into our repertoire of skillful behaviors. This is how we learned to walk, to talk, and to be thoughtful and considerate in our relationships. Unfortunately, most of our formal education process bore little resemblance to what we learned about learning as young children.

In organizations, designing learning processes means studying how work is being done and what people are truly motivated to do better, and then finding ways to support them in those goals. It starts with allowing people to articulate their aspirations, qualms, and fears. It requires reflection on current thinking and assumptions by bringing these assumptions into the open and challenging assumptions that may be limiting. Ultimately, it means nurturing new, more empowering ways of thinking and acting, translated into new policies, structures, and practices.

There are many examples of the impact of thoughtful design of organizational learning processes. For example, many total quality management (TQM) programs train people how to analyze variation. Those with the greatest impact embed that training in real-life improvement efforts, where people are actively engaged in redesigning their work processes. In the mid-1970s, Royal Dutch Shell took a set of tools that its planners had used, scenario analysis, and began to engage management teams in shaping their own future scenarios and thinking through their plans given different possible futures. The result was "planning as learning," one element of Shell's steady ascent from the bottom to the top of the world oil industry.[15] Federal Express was the first service company in the United States to win the Malcolm Baldridge award for quality, in large part because of its pioneering efforts to measure quality delivery service *and* make that information available to all employees. Every day, each of its 70,000+ U.S.-based employees learns how the company did the previous 24 hours through a short morning satellite broadcast that includes information on where problems arose and what corrections were made. Saturn Corporation has a "learning laboratory" on its manufacturing floor, where production workers test new ideas before implementing them.

In organizations structured around internal markets, managers at many levels should be involved in designing learning processes. Senior or corporate management should be setting the tone by designing processes to improve strategic thinking and policy formulation at the business unit level. They should be especially focused on building knowledge that serves people throughout the organization—generic theories of product development, product introduction, management of products through their life cycle, service quality, and similar processes and interactions that recur throughout the organization—and making that knowledge accessible for use and testing. They might also consult with business unit managers in designing learning processes within units, but implementation of these processes should be the responsibility of local managers. Likewise, business unit managers should be involved in building knowledge and designing learning processes within their organizations.

In keeping with the internal market concept, senior management's services in research and learning process design might be organized as a profit center. Rather than being able to "push" its tools and theories on the organization, it would then be in the position of having to market to a constituency it is seeking to serve. The benefits of its efforts to support learning would then be subject to continual test, as local operations had to weigh those benefits against their costs. Such an arrangement raises many questions, but they are important questions. Many of the benefits of senior management's learning support services would be in the long run. Would local management discount those benefits? How would local management assess the value of improved mental models, enhanced communication about complex issues, and clearer reasoning in support of strategies? How would tangible business results be balanced off against intangible organizational capabilities? Such questions are exactly those with which senior managers are wrestling today. So, bringing the internal market discipline to bear would push basic issues in building learning capabilities down to more local levels within the organization.

New Core Learning Competencies, New Learning Tools and Methods

None of these changes in the work of management will be easy. They are well beyond the skill set of most contemporary managers. They will only be achieved as part of an ongoing process of developing new learning competencies. New tools and methods will be required to support this developmental process.

Much of our research is focused on understanding the core competencies of learning organizations and how they can be developed. This has led, in our work, to focusing on the development of new tools and methods, the use of which can lead to new skills and capabilities.[16]

Core Learning Competencies

1. *Nurturing Personal Vision.* Most adults have lost their ability to envision what matters to them, a tragic by-product of "growing up," of spending more and more time solving problems that don't really matter, of fitting in and conforming to others' expectations. Learning organizations create a climate where people start asking basic questions

anew—questions such as "What does matter to me?" "What would I really be excited about working to create?"

2. *Building Shared Visions.* Shared visions do not come from committees. They emerge from the interactions of people's individual visions, and the capacity to listen "to the deeper music" that unifies diverse, individual views.

3. *Systems Thinking.* Learning processes will break down if people perceive themselves in a world of capricious forces out of their control. Systems thinking involves the capability to see the interrelationships and processes of change, to understand the forces shaping change and our part in those forces. Without this ability, people see themselves as victims of forces outside their control and do not see how their own actions contribute to their problems.

4. *Surfacing Assumptions, and Balancing Inquiry with Advocacy.* Most managers in Western organizations are trained to be forceful, effective advocates. This works fine until people confront problems where no one's understanding is sufficient, where groups of people have to come to new more integrated views. Inquiry skills start with cultivating reflectiveness on our own thinking, distinguishing our assumptions from direct experience, learning how to inquire constructively into others' reasoning, and encouraging others to inquire in our reasoning.

5. *Dialogue.* Ultimately, the mental models that matter most are those that are shared. For that reason, individual inquiry must eventually give way to capabilities for collective inquiry. Current research dialogue is showing that people in organizations have a great hunger to recapture the capability to truly talk with one another, to rediscover the lost "art of conversation." This research is suggesting a very different mediating process between individual thought and collective action. Rather than driving for watered-down consensus that everyone can live with, in dialogue groups of decision makers seek a deeper shared meaning. Differences are encouraged. There is no need for a superficial agreement. There is no premise of a simple "linear" process that first we reach agreement, then we make a single decision, then we implement the decision. Rather, what we are finding is that, in dialogue, people take in much more information and develop new, more subtle and adaptive capabilities for coordinated action. It is a little like a jazz ensemble that, through practice and experience, eventually develops the capability to extemporize, to truly create together.[17]

New Learning Tools and Methods

1. *System Archetypes, and Related Elementary Systems Conceptualization Tools.* What organizations most need to learn about is often the interrelatedness of what might have previously been seen as separate problems. System archetypes characterize basic patterns of interrelationships that recur again and again in all natural systems—for example, growth and stagnation, escalation, pressures for quick fixes versus fundamental improvements, delayed balancing processes, eroding goals, and competition for limited resources where everyone loses when the resource is depleted. As systems conceptualization tools are assimilated, teams begin to talk differently, formulate problems differently, and ultimately form very different perceptions of change.[18]

2. *Generic Management "Structures"* (pattern of interrelationships). The next step in complexity beyond system archetypes, these are also recurring patterns that are more specific to particular managerial situations—for example, generic theories of product life cycles involving interactions between growing demand, building capacity to meet demand, and the different determinants of profitability during rapid growth versus mature phases of the life cycle. Similar generic theories of new product development, service quality and service capacity, value-added service strategies, and cycle time in complex supply chains are currently being developed and tested. As these tools are developed and tested further, we may find that 10 to 15 generic structures will encompass a large percentage of the basic policy and strategy issues faced by managers.

3. *Management Flight Simulators.* Because they are more complex than the archetypes, generic structures are implemented in computer simulations so that managers can experiment with alternative policies and strategies and develop an intuitive grasp of important lessons. Simulators based on generic structures are the first stage in developing simulators tailored to the specifics of particular firms and market settings. Such possibilities are virtually unlimited because the underlying "system dynamics" modeling methodology is a general purpose methodology for understanding change in a wide array of social and physical systems.[19]

4. *Left-Hand Column Cases.* The most important parts of conversations, especially those that are problematic, are often what's not said. In "left-hand column cases" a problematic conversation is analyzed by

looking at both what is said (written in the right-hand column) and what is being thought and felt but not said (written in the left-hand column). The parties having the difficulty write the case themselves. Reflecting together on the case, often with a facilitator, can be a powerful way to bring underlying assumptions and feelings to the surface in a relatively nonthreatening manner. Such exercises can help individuals reflect on the dilemmas and traps that keep critical issues "undiscussable" so that they begin to create options and experiment with generating more productive conversations.[20]

5. *Action Maps.* A different conceptualizing tool from the system archetypes, action maps are better suited for interpreting large amounts of behavioral data to reveal underlying patterns of organizational defenses. Such defenses usually serve to protect individuals from pain or threat but also limit learning.[21]

6. *KJ Diagrams.* These are also known as "affinity diagrams." The KJ diagram, one of the "seven tools for management" in TQM, supports "first-level" collective interpretation of large volumes of qualitative data.[22] Because it enforces rigorous distinctions between "facts" and "opinions," it reinforces the basic discipline of working with mental models and can serve as a useful bridge to more systemic conceptualization tools such as system archetypes.

7. *Learning Laboratories.* Current research on "managerial learning laboratories" is seeking to combine diverse tools and methods into overall learning environments that can coexist with work environments. Organizations can then integrate learning into how people work together in ways that are otherwise not attainable. Learning laboratories are "managerial practice fields," where teams can reflect, experiment, and conceptualize, thereby creating a continuous cycle of "practice and performance" analogous to the cycle that drives learning in sports and in the performing arts.

A METAPHOR: "ORGANISMIC CONTROL" IN SOCIAL SYSTEMS

Internal markets are often characterized as an "organic" structure as opposed to the "mechanistic" structure of traditional authoritarian organizations. The term organic is invoked to describe the movement of many individual elements that, over time, find their way, presumably with greater success than would have been achieved if a central authority had created a plan and imposed it on individual actors.

The problem with this metaphor as it is usually employed is that it fails to distinguish organic growth from cancer. In cancer, individual actors (cells) are making their own decisions (dividing and multiplying). They "find their way"—that is they generate an overall pattern of growth. The only problem is that the pattern is counter to the well-being of the larger organism. The cancer cells are following a rudimentary decision rule: simple mitosis. Unlike normal cells, they have lost their "social identity," the ability to perceive their environment and regulate their growth to fit the larger system of which they are a part. Heart cells know that they are heart cells. Liver cells know that they are liver cells. They reproduce in ways that preserve this "social identity" and that reinforce the community to which they belong. When a tumor begins, the cells involved "retrogress" down the ladder of differentiation toward their omnipotential generic cells, with no social identity or sense of place. They simply reproduce, regardless of their environment.

If the metaphor of organismic control is to have a real meaning for internal markets it must be married to the notion of social consciousness. Autonomous actors must be continually enriching their "social consciousness" so that the decisions they make autonomously are in the best interest of the larger organism.

This cannot be taken for granted. Developing this social consciousness is a prime task of management in an internal market organization. It starts with developing overarching precepts, values, and visions that have deep meaning to people in disparate profit centers. It continues with working to build trust through openness and relationships where people can influence one another. It ultimately rests on continually enriching people's understanding of the web of interdependencies within which they operate, and helping them see the longer term, systemic consequences of their actions.

6 It's a Great Idea! But . . .

Answers to Commonly Asked Questions about Internal Markets

Ali Geranmayeh and John Pourdehnad

In consulting with a variety of companies, we find that the initial reaction of most managers to the concept of internal markets is "It's a great idea! But . . ." The "but" is usually followed by a series of objections formulated as questions, such as, How can you develop a strategic direction for such an organization? If every unit inside the company makes a profit, what happens to the costs of the corporation as a whole? How can you ensure that internal customers get the attention they deserve

Ali Geranmayeh is a director and senior partner and **John Pourdehnad** is an independent consultant and a senior associate at the Institute for Interactive Management (INTERACT). The authors are grateful to William E. Halal, Patricia Egner, and Michael Leyzorek for their help in preparing this chapter.

when their internal suppliers are busy marketing their services to outside customers?

The intensity of the debates on such questions is itself a sign that a paradigm shift may be under way. In fact, the concept of internal markets challenges so many of the prevailing views on organization and management, and does so by offering such a dramatically different perspective, that it easily qualifies as a new paradigm. The beauty of the internal markets perspective is that it is based on a very simple idea, though the consequences are profound: Market mechanisms are often the most effective way to achieve coordination among organizational units. Most of the difficult questions raised in the discussion of internal markets can be readily resolved by keeping this central principle in mind.

The market approach and the administrative-controls approach are alternative philosophies for solving organizational problems. Most managers, however, tend to seek solutions only in the realm of administrative controls. In this chapter, we invite the reader to embark on a journey of inquiry with us: to explore the consequences of designing solutions to organizational problems by adopting market principles. So, the next time you face a complex organizational problem, ask yourself how it would be resolved in a market economy. The answer is likely to be apparent, and it will usually be a far better solution than the one offered by administrative mechanisms.

The questions that follow are the ones we encounter most frequently in our consulting experience. Collectively, these questions and our answers constitute a practical guide for those interested in pursuing the market paradigm. More important, they offer a "practice field" for interested managers to explore the issues involved in a transition to a market organization and discover the potential of redesigning organizations to harness the power of free enterprise inside them.

Our answers are not intended to promote a particular blueprint to be used by every organization. Just as there are various flavors of market economies at the macro level—from Japan and Sweden to the United States and Chile—and different philosophies for managing free markets—from those advocated by Keynes to those by Friedman—so too are there many different varieties of internal markets. The accounts in this volume are a testimony to the variety of ways different companies have dealt with the issues. In fact, it is precisely this ability to create diverse solutions to complex problems that makes markets superior to hierarchies. Every organization interested in internal markets will have to design and develop its own version. Our experience shows that it is through engagement in such a process of design that the company benefits most.

Question 1: Isn't Autonomy Destructive to the Organization?

Wouldn't the establishment of autonomous profit centers that compete in an internal market have a divisive impact on the organization, possibly even tear it apart? Wouldn't it be prohibitively difficult to integrate the parts back into a cohesive whole?

Integration is indeed a major challenge in organizations, but it is not peculiar to those using internal markets. Common experience with large organizations confirms that they are far from harmonious cooperative entities. We estimate that internal conflicts consume more than half the time and energy of a typical corporation's management. Large organizations do not act as cohesive wholes but often as mere collections of isolated units, each one fiercely protecting its own "turf" and promoting its own "empire." Lack of cooperation among units is so prevalent that images of "islands," "stovepipes," and "silos" are repeatedly brought up by managers discussing interunit interactions. In such an environment, the traditional approach of hierarchical controls, attempts to create integration by management edict and administrative fiat.

By contrast, organizations using internal markets rely on the voluntary actions of autonomous units to coordinate and integrate their activities. Such organizations create an organizational framework and a management system that support *increasing* the freedom of organizational members rather than restricting it. The market approach explicitly recognizes the purposeful nature of social systems; by treating each unit as an autonomous internal enterprise, organizations with internal markets can create the same conditions internally that lead to effective voluntary integration at the macro level.

Considered in this light, voluntary association will tend to bring organizational units closer together rather than drive them apart. Integration of organizational units will be *enhanced*, not impeded, by internal markets.

Internal markets, however, need regulation and active management. This is the role that the management system of the organization must play. Top management should act as a team of designers who work with managers of internal units to establish policies governing interactions among the units. These policies would define, for example, accepted pricing practices, conditions under which a unit would be prevented from offering its services to external customers, or be forced to buy internally, when and how a higher level manager could override the decisions of a unit manager, and processes for resolution of internal conflicts.[1] These policies and the overall design of the internal market structure are aimed at creating conditions that enable managers to preserve the integrity of the whole while placing minimal restrictions on the freedom of the parts. This type of regulation of internal markets is an ongoing process, not a one-time proposition. Governing policies of internal markets require continuous redesign and enhancement to ensure their effectiveness.

Within such a framework, and with active leadership of top management, integration is achieved through contractual agreements among informed consenting parties.

Question 2: Won't the Overall Sense of Strategic Direction Be Lost?

If units in an internal market develop their own strategies, how can an overall strategy be developed for the corporation as a whole? How can the company's focus be maintained?

The problem here has more to do with the approach to strategic planning than it does with internal markets. In the traditional paradigm, strategic planning is a top-down approach. Top-level managers *formulate* the strategy and operating companies *execute* and *implement* it. Strategic planning in such organizations works with a "command and control" mind-set. While it is true that such an approach would not work in an internal market, many studies show that it fails to work even in traditional organizations[2]—and for good reason: There is little room for effective learning and adaptation in such an approach to planning.[3]

Strategic planning in internal markets takes place at all levels, not only at the top. The contents of the plans, however, differ at each level. At the level of the corporation as a whole, an overall framework is designed and a strategic direction is established that defines the role of each of the major organizational units. Within this overall framework, each unit has the freedom to develop its own strategy to meet its particular needs and satisfy the demands of its customers. This results in short feedback loops that make effective learning and adaptation possible. Strategic planning in internal markets is thus both bottom-up and top-down.

Question 3: What Happens to Core Technologies?

Accomplishing the corporate mission often requires developing and nurturing different "core competencies." Can internal markets be trusted for the development and management of such critical skills?

Three special properties of "core" technologies set them apart from other functions within an organization: (1) They are proprietary knowledge of the company and therefore a critical source of competitive advantage (a brewing process, the source code for a software package, the chemical composition for a paint); (2) their development usually requires substantial investments in research and development (R&D) with long payoff periods; (3) for technologies that are not proprietary, the external market structure is often oligopolistic.

Let us consider each in turn. As a general rule, technologies that represent proprietary knowledge of the organization should not be managed through internal markets. These technologies are relatively few in number, and the authority for exempting them from the internal market should rest only with the CEO. (Local managers tend to be overprotective of their technologies and are likely to exaggerate their importance.) Companies have come to learn, however, that the effective life span of such advantages is decreasing rapidly. Reverse engineering and the rapid pace of technological innovation have convinced many executives that the only sustainable advantage and truly "core" competence an organization may have is its ability to innovate continuously. This competence improves with exposure to competition, not with protection from it.

The second special aspect of technology is the long-term nature of the investments it requires. This aspect has been used to argue that R&D units cannot and should not operate as profit centers because markets have a short-term focus. Historical evidence is against this argument. When the first American R&D organization was founded by Edison in 1876, it operated as a for-profit "invention factory." In a fascinating historical account of the development of R&D at Du Pont, Hounshell and Smith show that Charlie Stine, Du Pont's pioneering research director, was trying to convince corporate executives in 1920 that the R&D department should offer research services to outside clients and conduct collaborative research with Du Pont's major customers.[4] Stine argued that a broad customer base was the only way for an R&D department to protect itself against budgetary effects of the short-term swings in corporate earnings.

Today, many independent for-profit R&D organizations successfully offer their services to corporate clients. Chapter 8 by John Starr and Chapter 14 by John Charlton in this volume show how R&D units can compete within internal markets. And as the evidence by Starr suggests, they are likely to increase their competence and decrease their costs when they are exposed to the realities of the marketplace. In addition, companies managing their R&D units within internal markets will more likely be able to stretch their assets because they will be more receptive to seeking alliances and partnerships with other organizations having complementary technological resources.

The third special aspect of technology is that key components or sophisticated technologies regarded as core competencies of a corporation are often available only through oligopolistic markets. Furthermore, potential suppliers of such technologies are likely to be competitors of the parent company in the end-product market. In such cases, internal markets require active guidance and possibly even intervention by corporate managers.[5] As successful Japanese companies aggressively pursue market share at the level of core components and technologies, however, companies that *protect* their technology groups from competitive pressures will soon find themselves in indefensible positions.

Although core technologies, and more generally core competencies, deserve special management attention in internal markets, this line of thinking poses the serious danger that many companies may use the "core" designation as an excuse for protecting an operation from market pressures. They jealously guard what they believe to be their "core technology," only to find that they have buried themselves in an outmoded technology.

Conversely, many technology groups are prevented from selling their products and services to external customers. Such restrictions should apply only when an external sale would jeopardize the parent company's competitive position. For example, a vertically integrated computer manufacturer should *encourage* its chip manufacturing unit to find external customers as long as those customers are not direct competitors of the parent company. With cost of product development increasing rapidly in many industries, prohibitions to spreading R&D costs by selling outside is a burden few corporations can afford.

The present approach to management of technology (central control of a cost center protected from the pressures of the market) is largely responsible for the notorious inability of American industry to convert its superb technical competence into successful commercial products. The time has come to consider a different model for managing these strategic capabilities. A market orientation on the part of technology managers is likely to help rather than hinder the development of core competencies.

Question 4: Don't Internal Markets Create a Short-Term Profit Focus?

American management has been criticized for its shortsightedness by focusing exclusively on profits. Wouldn't the creation of numerous profit centers inside the corporation reinforce this tendency, making it practically impossible to manage for long-term performance?

Managing a profit center has nothing to do with shortsightedness. Managers with a short-term orientation will run their companies that way with or without internal markets. Profitability is a measure of the system's efficiency: the difference between the value of its inputs and processing and the value of the outputs it produces. Profitability helps determine whether a unit is creating value or consuming value.

Other measures can, and should be, used to assess a unit's performance within an internal-market economy. Many companies routinely use nonfinancial measures (quality metrics, customer service, and so on) as part of their performance measurement system. One of the more exciting ideas gaining acceptance recently is use of the "market value" of a unit as a measure of its performance, generally calculated as the present value of its expected future earnings. Not only is this measure long-term oriented, but it also offers a comprehensive, systemic evaluation of each unit's performance. The objective of all managers, including that of the CEO, could be defined as increasing the value of the units they manage.

The most troubling aspect of the question is the assumed dichotomy between short- and long-term performance. In today's competitive environment, a company must perform in the short term if it has any hope of seeing the long term. Until managers realize they must manage for both short- and long-term performance simultaneously, they will continue to get their companies in trouble by fluctuating through cycles of focusing on one objective at the expense of the other.[6]

Question 5: Won't Internal Conflicts Result?

In a competitive environment, firms are expected to take advantage of market opportunities to increase their profits even at the expense of

*their customers. Wouldn't such profit-maximization orientation on the
part of internal suppliers be disastrous for the corporation as a whole?*

Interestingly enough, our experience has been that operating units
are invariably more satisfied with their external suppliers than with
their internal ones in all aspects of customer service, responsiveness,
and quality. To the great surprise of proponents of traditional organizational relationships, external suppliers provide lower costs as well.

The reason is rather simple. In a traditional organization, internal
suppliers' performance measures and rewards are only indirectly related to the satisfaction of their internal customers. The internal supplier holds a monopoly granted by the corporation. The supplier's lifeline, its budget, is allocated by higher levels of management. Since the
boss holds the lifeline, the boss—not the customers—receives the most
attention. In such an organization, internal customers having a problem
with their suppliers must go to the boss. Talking directly to suppliers is
a waste of time, because their real "customer" is the boss. Bureaucracy
triumphs and customers lose.

In an internal market, the relationship between the units is unam-
biguously established: A supplier's only source of revenues is his customers. If customers are unhappy, they do not pay the supplier. It cannot survive by appeasing the boss. The customer holds the lifeline of the
supplier. And this makes all the difference in the world. An internal
market is the best way to create a totally customer-focused organization.

Furthermore, any marketing manager can testify that win–lose approaches in sales and marketing are shortsighted and usually backfire,
particularly in the case of repeat customers. In today's environment,
both suppliers and customers are in search of long-term win–win contracts. Such contracts often specify expected cost reductions during the
life of the contract and include provisions for sharing in the expected
productivity gains. Some even include reciprocal board memberships.

Many other features can be designed into internal market systems
to reduce the likelihood of internal conflicts. The performance of each
unit can be evaluated as a function of the profitability of its internal
suppliers and customers. Indeed, each unit may share in the profits
(and losses) generated by its suppliers and customers. Better still, the
measurement system can be oriented toward the "market value" of
internal supplier units rather than their profitability. That way they
would become much more concerned with nurturing a prosperous customer base. A satisfied and loyal customer base is much more valuable
to an investor than a temporary increase in profits. Lastly, corporate

policies and "executive overrides," as described by Ackoff in Chapter 1, can be effective deterrents against the temptation for short-term profit maximization.

Question 6: What Are the Effects on Corporate Costs?

If internal suppliers make profits from internal customers, wouldn't the overall costs to the corporation increase?

No. In fact, costs are likely to decrease. By removing the shields of subsidy and protection from internal suppliers and subjecting them to the discipline of competitive markets, the corporation is far more likely to assure itself of cost- and quality-competitiveness in all aspects of its operations[7]. After all, outside suppliers make a profit too. Interestingly enough, this logic is readily accepted when applied to cost reduction in the government sector: Opening up the provision of governmental services to private-sector bidding is recognized as an effective way to reduce costs.

For a variety of historical reasons, corporations have grown accustomed to recognizing profits only at the level of end products.[8] Managers of end-product units expect components to be transferred to them "at cost" or with minimum additions. This way of thinking artificially inflates profits at one part of the organization at the expense of others, disconnects a large part of the organization (namely, internal suppliers) from the realities of the marketplace, and leads to a bias toward vertical integration. In addition, it focuses managers' attention on internal battles over transfer prices established by corporate accountants, diverting them from satisfying their customer needs.[9]

An internal market orientation, by contrast, highlights the units in which value is being created or being destroyed. It exposes every element of the value chain to the discipline of the marketplace, thereby establishing cost consciousness throughout the chain. There is nothing wrong with component manufacturers being profitable if they compete with outside suppliers. The only way they can make a profit is by being cost- and quality-competitive.

The key difference between traditional organizations and those with internal markets is simply this: Traditional organizations promote a "cost-plus" mentality, whereas internal markets promote a "price-minus" mentality. Component manufacturers in traditional organizations expect to pass on their often bloated costs to their internal customers, who are happy to be buying the components "at cost." End-product units then add up all these costs, plus a profit margin, to arrive at their offering price. In internal markets, however, end-product manufacturers start from a market price for their products and determine how much they can afford to spend on components by subtracting all other costs they have to incur—"price minus." The only relevant question for them is whether an internal supplier is able to meet their requirements, or if they need to go to external suppliers. It is up to the internal component manufacturer to manage its operations in a way that allows for a profit with the given price. The dynamics of the entire interaction are changed, and costs are reduced rather than passed on.

Corporate management should expect each part of its operations not only to be profitable, but to produce returns that exceed the cost of capital it uses. Why would a company want to vertically integrate if it is unable to generate long-term returns that exceed the cost of capital required for integration?[10]

Question 7: Isn't Entrepreneurship Risky and Inequitable?

Entrepreneurship combines the risk of failure with the promise of substantial rewards for success. Should such risk–reward situations be replicated inside the corporation?

Conventional reward systems are rather insensitive to performance: Only the very top and bottom performers of most organizations are treated differently. The top 10 percent may get bonuses, the bottom 10 percent may be put on probation, and the other 80 percent are paid for simply continuing to do a tolerable job. Furthermore, most organizational reward systems promote risk aversion because they are tuned to detection of errors of commission rather than errors of omission. Not taking advantage of a great opportunity is rarely, if ever, reflected in a manager's performance. Consequently, "staying the course" is often the rational choice for most people in large organizations. Traditional reward systems are supposed to create equality, stability, and security. As company after company announces massive layoffs, the "security" and other supposed advantages of such systems must be seriously questioned.

In an internal market organization, a greater range of incentives is incorporated into the performance measurement and reward system to provide motivation and a sense of equity. This typically produces larger differences between the compensation of people at the same "level" in the organization, depending on their own performances and that of their units. There may also be a greater variability in the same individual's compensation from year to year. Such differentiating reward systems are probably more widespread than may seem at first sight. The concept of "pay for performance," for example, is now at the core of most new compensation systems, and sales organizations in every industry have been utilizing it for years. It is not uncommon to find salespeople who make more money than their managers, and a few who make more money, in some years, than the CEO.

No formula can guarantee the right balance between stability and performance-based incentive systems. Every organization must develop its own design based on the level of variability best suited to the needs of current and potential employees. Over time, however, internal market companies will attract a significantly different population of employees (those who value entrepreneurship more than stability and have higher levels of tolerance for unpredictability and risk) from traditional bureaucracies.

Question 8: Why Wouldn't Internal Enterprises Leave the System?

If each unit is an autonomous enterprise managed by entrepreneurs, why should these people want to remain within the corporation at all? What makes this collection of small companies different from those in the external market?

Internal units that do not find net benefits in belonging to an organization should not be forced to, nor expected to, stay. In traditional organizations, the evaluation of advantages of belonging are unidirectional: Does the unit add value to the corporation? Internal market organizations also ask whether the corporation adds any value to the units. They encourage their internal units to continually evaluate their membership in the organization. If an internal unit has a better long-term future outside the corporation than inside, why should it be forced to remain part of the corporation? A corporation that can confidently grant this "right of secession" to its units will never worry about lack of synergy among them.

The responsibility of top management in an internal market is to create a nurturing business environment that will encourage creative people to do a better job within the corporation than they could outside it. The office of the CEO must carry out this role efficiently to make membership more attractive. That is, the CEO must minimize the costs and maximize the gains of membership to compete against other parent corporations. In fact, as some chapters in this book make clear, the office of the CEO should become a profit center in its own right, evaluated on how well it performs this function.

Traditional organizations use the same logic to justify their management of numerous business units. Unfortunately, their record in capitalizing on the synergy among their different business units has been rather poor.[11] As corporate managers diversified and manipulated their portfolios in search of synergies that never materialized, they exposed their corporations to the dangers of hostile takeovers based on a simple analysis of breakup value. Any corporation whose total value is less than the sum of the value of its businesses is subject to a takeover threat. Internal markets that grant their participating units the freedom to leave essentially internalize the takeover threat as a way of evaluating their managers.

Corporate executives who believe they do indeed add value to the operation of their internal units should welcome an internal market approach because it explicitly recognizes their contributions and the advantages of belonging to their organization. The more that corporations adopt this concept, the less of a threat corporate raiders will pose to U.S. industry.

In the final analysis, what makes the collection of units in an internal market different from a group of independent companies in the external environment is the synergy they can create together. This synergy, or positive net benefits of belonging to an organization, may come from reduction of risk, more efficient allocation of capital, economies of scale, a shared vision of the future they want to create, the value system they all embrace, and other factors that make this collection a system larger than the sum of its parts. These are the same reasons that justify keeping units together in a traditional hierarchical organization. The difference is that in internal markets, evaluation of the contribution of the whole to the parts is an ongoing and explicit process.

Question 9: How Can Organizations Make the Required Cultural Transformation?

The internal market environment puts new demands on the skills of managers and employees. How can this profound cultural change to an enterprise system be managed?

Lack of a well-designed transition plan is probably the single most common reason for failure of internal market applications. Some managers tend to regard the concept only as a new accounting system or a new performance-measurement system. Therefore, they often focus on technical details and miss the larger significance of the transition: The internal market organization presents a profound cultural change.

Members of the organization must have both the *ability* and the *desire* to function in the new entrepreneurial system. Most transition plans focus on the first requirement and overlook the second. Although the details vary from organization to organization, developing the needed abilities usually requires training and education in general management because internal market organizations rely on general managers rather than functional managers. Sales and marketing skills are also crucial because all managers need to understand the importance of hearing the voice of the customer, and of selling their services.

Desire to change results both from aspiring to create a better work environment and from appreciating the shortcomings of the traditional organizations in meeting today's challenges. All members of the organization must understand the need for change, be convinced that internal markets are a good solution, and be given a chance to design their own version of it. Therefore, they must be part of the process from the beginning to the end. Once they have been inspired by a vision of their desired future, their creativity will take care of the rest.

Question 10: Why Would Top Managers Give Up Their Power?

This all sounds fine for the internal units, but why would any CEO choose to diminish his or her control?

The internal market approach does not seek to reduce the power of top managers; they simply need to exercise a different type of power. Managers in traditional organizations have come to view their role as synonymous with supervision; that is, controlling the work of those who report to them. They have learned to manage downward. Managers in internal markets, by contrast, need to manage upward. They must manage the interactions of their units with other units in the internal market and with their containing organization. Even the CEO of an internal market organization would focus his or her attention on managing the interactions of the organization with its external environment, rather than managing the internal operations.

The changes that internal markets require from top managers are in their own best interest. Authoritarian power is no longer an effective way to run any organization, be it a small business enterprise or a large public institution. This is particularly true when those who are managed are educated professionals, and when the rate of change in the environment places a premium on local initiative and responsiveness. Corporate executives who have not yet internalized this change will feel increasing pressure both from above and from below: Corporate boards demand results showing little patience for ineffective management practices, and employees demand more involvement in decisions affecting their lives.

Today's environment requires managers who are leaders, designers, and educators. Those corporate managers who have adopted this philosophy almost always gain more power, respect, and personal satisfaction by performing their roles better. The new demands on CEOs created by the internal market perspective replace the outmoded authoritarian form of power with the far greater power that is accorded leaders.

CONCLUSIONS

The internal market paradigm is a powerful new idea especially well suited to today's environment because it keeps a company agile, responsive, and customer focused. Such a company relies on the force of competition as the engine for its vitality and dynamic evolution, replacing destructive internal conflicts with constructive competition.

To be successful, however, internal markets must be thought of as total systems. An organization cannot adopt only a few parts of the concept leaving others out. The result would be chaos. As Boulding has noted, exchange (buying and selling of goods and services in the marketplace) is only one of three organizers of social systems: A role structure and a threat system must also be present.[12] Each unit within the organization must help define and understand its role within the larger system, and each unit must understand the conditions under which it may lose its membership in the group. All three organizing systems must be designed.

The need for design of this total system cannot be overemphasized. There are no simple recipes for success. Integration processes, performance measurement and reward systems, management's intervention in imperfect markets, and the transition process must all be designed.

Perhaps the most important transformation in internal market companies is the change in the roles of "management" and "employees." There is no need for supervision in internal markets. Management's role is to create a supportive environment that respects freedom of action and nurtures the creative energies of organizational members, and to manage the relationship of the unit as a whole with its environment. The whole organization is biased toward action because members enjoy unprecedented freedom to act. Along with this freedom comes accountability and responsibility. Survival of each internal unit, like that of the organization as a whole, depends on its performance.

The internal market approach is still a very young concept. While some of its basic ideas have been discussed for some time, the practice of internal markets is only now being invented. Pioneering managers are experimenting with a variety of different approaches to designing internal markets. They are inventing the field as they go. Our hope is that this chapter and this book will inspire other executives and scholars to join us in helping organizations realize the full potential of this powerful new perspective.

PART TWO

FROM CORPORATE BUREAUCRACY TO INTERNAL ENTERPRISE

7 Principles That Make MCI a Dynamic Organization

Bert C. Roberts, Jr. and John H. Zimmerman

It has become increasingly obvious that only dynamic organizations can stand up to the business challenges of the 1990s. From the globalization of markets, to technological advances, to shifting political influences, today's business world faces new challenges every day. To survive in this new climate and take advantage of the opportunities it presents, a successful company must be lean, agile, and responsive. Most important, it must emphasize the demands of its customers over its own needs.

The concept of internal markets proposed by Halal and Ackoff—the creation of a market economy within the company itself—is a good description of the way MCI always has operated. At MCI, we rely on a few key principles to create a dynamic, entrepreneurial organization: individual autonomy to foster innovation, informal management systems that avoid bureaucracy, an ability and willingness to change, a responsive environment for employees, and constant communications.

These principles have helped us shape a unique MCI culture in which entrepreneurship is the norm and restrictions are few. MCI

Bert C. Roberts, Jr. is CEO and chairman and **John H. Zimmerman** is senior vice president for Human Resources of MCI Communications Corporation.

employees are encouraged to consider new ideas, and they are given the freedom and resources to make things happen. Our people don't work well amid layers of management, or by having to present extensive plans to a host of superiors before taking action. They don't want tidy, well-defined jobs. They are risk takers, entrepreneurs eager to go beyond the limits of their jobs to achieve success.

Our approach to management fits closely with the internal market concept, but it achieves the creative interplay of a market economy more by shaping a flexible, dynamic MCI culture that supports this type of behavior, rather than by relying on the nuts and bolts of complex management systems. This MCI culture has been the driving force behind MCI's evolution long before today's business environment made entrepreneurship such a widely understood imperative for success. When MCI started out in 1968, it was essential to be entrepreneurial. Our early years were spent fighting for the right to compete with what was then the largest and most entrenched monopoly in the world.

We could not compete with AT&T on their terms. However, we knew we could succeed both by anticipating the needs of telecommunications users and by driving change and competition, not only in the industry, but in our own organization as well. Yet, as our company grew, we realized how easily the bureaucratic layers could pile on and hinder this competitive flexibility. So we made it a primary goal to avoid becoming bound by bureaucracy, as our competitors were.

Once an underdog, we are now a $10.5 billion worldwide telecommunications service provider. We doubled our revenue five times in 10 years, and we have made strategic acquisitions and alliances that have helped us grow into an international corporation with 35,000 employees.

But in spite of our increasing size, we work hard to preserve our scrappy and nimble persona. A good example is the way we managed the acquisition of Satellite Business Systems (SBS) from IBM. Before this acquisition, we had 12,500 employees, and the acquisition was about to expand this number by another 1,800. The newcomers hailed from a significantly different working environment. At that time, IBM was still a highly traditional company with a complex, formal organization and a bureaucratic culture. In shepherding the merger of the two systems, we carefully planned the need to maintain the MCI culture, to communicate its values to SBS employees, and to facilitate their adjustment to our decentralized, unstructured environment.

To accomplish this, we held numerous orientation programs to discuss the different cultures with both our existing MCI employees and the new ones from SBS. The values we associate with the MCI culture were sharply identified and clearly defined for the first time in our history during these sessions. This concerted effort to communicate cultural values helped smooth the transition, and, more important, it also helped us to better understand and preserve the very thing that made MCI such a creative, rewarding, and responsive place to work.

Today, MCI remains deeply committed to these key "principles of dynamic organization" in order to keep our corporate environment as flexible and close to the constantly shifting market realities as possible. The following sections describe these interrelated principles, which are the driving forces that allow MCI to retain its position on the cutting edge of the highly competitive telecommunications industry.

PROMOTE INDIVIDUALISM

Rather than simply supervise employees, we empower them to take risks and to come up with new and better ways of doing things. Our overriding goal is to foster a spirit of entrepreneurship. We want our employees to view themselves as decision makers personally accountable for the company's success. This power of individualism has served as a propelling force in the growth of the company and is the key to staying ahead of our aggressive competition.

For example, a short time ago, a U.S. congressman called to report that he could not use his MCI calling card from pay phones at National Airport. Because the congressman and his staff are frequent card users, the employee responsible for his account wanted to clear the problem up immediately. She made a snap decision to go to the airport and personally investigate. It turned out that unclear instructions in the pay phones were causing people to dial the wrong access number. The salesperson then went to the congressman's office to explain and to train his staff in avoiding future mistakes. There are not many companies where an employee is free to dash around solving problems like this. At MCI, we give our people the flexibility to take this kind of initiative, and it pays off.

But commitment to individualism puts the onus on MCI to hire people who will accept this type of empowerment and who will be effective in an environment that encourages employees to handle autonomy, to take risks, to be aggressive, flexible, and comfortable with constant change. In such an atmosphere, people occasionally will make mistakes. A truly dynamic company, however, has to be ready to forgive and forget—or else risk dampening its employees' willingness to offer their ideas. At MCI, we view the odd mistake as a learning experience. In fact, an article about MCI in the *Washingtonian* magazine bore the headline, "Make Some Damn Mistakes."

Mistakes are the exception, fortunately, because we make a point of using extensive training, constant communications, and other means to keep MCI employees fully informed about their jobs and the corporation, as we will show in the remaining principles to be discussed. Our surveys show that the vast majority of MCI people clearly understand the company's mission, the roles of various units, their own responsibilities, and, above all, the guiding principles of the MCI culture. As a result, we feel confident that MCI employees have the skill and knowledge to decide what will best serve both MCI and its customers.

Having firmly channeled the power of individualism through these concepts and values, we have little hesitation in according MCI employees the freedom to go out and do things on their own. This allows us to manage MCI with a true entrepreneurial spirit that minimizes bureaucracy, which leads to Principle Number Two . . .

STAMP OUT BUREAUCRACY

A company enmeshed in bureaucratic rules and red tape is like a ship at anchor. The waves hit, it bobs up and down, but it goes nowhere. Bureaucracy hampers a company's ability to progress and compete, just as it impedes the individual employee's freedom. In large bureaucracies, managers are judged by the number of staff they supervise. The result is empire building, inefficiency, and employee frustration. Because of this threat, our employees are constantly encouraged to perpetuate our entrepreneurial spirit and fight bureaucratic strangulation.

We use many of the market mechanisms described in this book to operate a decentralized market economy. For instance, costs are always driven down into operating units so as to create local accountability for performance while minimizing overhead. The converse is that this allows operating units the entrepreneurial freedom to run their own businesses, so they are able to choose their own suppliers for most needs and to work with their customers their own way. We even allow internal competition. For instance, training is often purchased competitively from other MCI units or outside vendors.

But the main weapon we use in this fight against bureaucracy is to keep our formal management systems to an absolute minimum. We struggle to avoid encrusting the MCI organizational structure with unnecessary rules, procedures, and reporting relationships. Our experience has shown that these are the seeds of bureaucracy.

Instead, we rely on our MCI culture to define how the organization works to such an extent that it could be called a "virtual organization"—an organization that exists primarily in our MCI principles, values, and other cultural artifacts. This type of virtual organization minimizes the need for complex management structures and processes. It is not defined by anything so cumbersome and restrictive as organizational charts, job descriptions, written policies, or other formal systems. Rather, it is a far more flexible, living thing because it resides in the common understanding that all MCI employees hold as they go about their daily tasks. The MCI management system is a *shared idea.*

With this type of virtual organization, we do not worry too much about devising clever management systems that direct employee behavior toward serving the company in some mechanical way. The essence of the virtual organization concept is that the organization lives in the collective minds of its members; MCI employees *are* the company. The MCI culture, its employees, and the organization are one and the same.

The advantages are enormous. This sense of mutual identity is essential for helping us undertake entrepreneurial ventures quickly and successfully. Whether it is a new acquisition, an entry into a new market, or a reorganization, new projects aren't formidable challenges that the company plans extensively or has to sell to its people. Since the employees are the company, the entire system can almost react spontaneously.

Perhaps the best example of this entrepreneurial flexibility can be seen in the way we reorganized nearly the entire corporation in 1990 and again in 1992. Before that, MCI was structured into seven divisions, each with the responsibility for a particular geographic region. In 1990 as the economy softened and AT&T intensified its effort in the residential/small business market segment, we responded by pulling together our technical, customer service, and telemarketing capabilities from all seven divisions to create a nationwide market segment unit that could meet this challenge.

The new unit proved very successful, and it propelled MCI's drive ahead. Our share of the market increased, while AT&T's share dropped. This division launched some of our most exciting new products such as

"Friends & Family," which have proved smashing successes. Soon, we saw the possibility of using this basic organizational concept as a model for the other market segments.

In the summer of 1992, we restructured the rest of our company along these lines almost overnight. When the dust settled in less than six months, MCI assumed its present configuration of four customer-centered business units, each sharply focused on a major segment of our market: (1) The "Consumer Markets" unit serves individual households, (2) "Business Services" handles small and mid-sized companies, (3) "National Accounts" serves large corporate accounts, and (4) "International" deals with the global market. A fifth business unit was established to manage the network. In spite of this radical restructuring and a continuing soft economy, momentum never slowed and our 1992 performance broke all records.

This ability to operate in an informal, flexible manner also explains why MCI managers are intuitively hands-on team leaders, judged by their ability to produce with a minimum of staff. We can easily delegate responsibility and authority downward and set well-understood goals for quality, efficiency, and value. How units or projects achieve these goals is up to them. Just as we give our individual employees flexibility to do their jobs, as a large corporation we remain innovative and competitive through functional and structural flexibility.

In short, our concept of a virtual organization serves as a natural deterrent to bureaucracy and permits a continual evolution of the company's structure and systems. This allows us to continually reinvent ourselves, changing not only the way we do things but the shape of the company itself. We can also change by growing our company through strategic acquisitions and joint alliances that extend our reach in the marketplace. The result is a constantly shifting, dynamic mix of new people, new business units, new responsibilities, new products, and new capabilities.

MCI's special capability for remaining flexible has enabled us to take advantage of the many opportunities that constantly appear as the highly competitive telecommunications industry changes at lightning speed today, which leads to our Third Principle . . .

SEEK CHANGE AS AN OPPORTUNITY FOR SUCCESS

MCI was born of change. Before MCI, there was no competition in the U.S. telecommunications services industry. We literally created it. This heritage has left its mark on everything we do. We embrace change as a competitive weapon. Rather than simply selling what we have, we see our mission as helping customers benefit from technological advances. We accept, welcome, and initiate new directions to keep ahead of our competition.

Some of our most exciting products were introduced by seeking out opportunities for radical change. A good example is the development of MCI Fax, the world's first fax network. Previously, facsimile transmission was viewed as a dead technology that was going nowhere. In the mid-1980s, our technical people noted the development of a new generation of fax that promised to become indispensable in today's fast-paced business world. MCI organized network specialists, customer service, and sales teams to roll out a new fax service in six months, and placed national ads inviting customers to fax in requests for information. The morning the ads appeared, our fax center was knee-deep in requests.

Another example is the development of our most famous product, "Friends & Family," which offers discounts for calls made within a defined "circle" of family members and friends. We had known that the majority of personal calls are directed among people who are close to one another, but none of our competitors were able to provide the high levels of network intelligence required to track and bill calls for this purpose. MCI developed this sophisticated capability, and eight months after the program was launched, we enrolled five million customers to make it the most successful product introduction in the history of long-distance telephone service. Friends & Family now serves 10 million people.

These examples show that MCI regards change as an opportunity to secure a competitive advantage. We are always ready to change ourselves and the industry. This does not mean that change is an easy process at MCI. On the contrary, dramatic, entrepreneurial undertakings of the type described here are always fraught with risk and uncertainty, so they are controversial. Rather than avoid controversy, MCI embraces it as a stimulant for critical thought. We sometimes call it "constructive dissonance." In plain words, we often engage in heated debates among ourselves over tough issues in order to discover a solid course of action that we can support with confidence. A new idea like MCI Fax or Friends & Family will usually be proposed by sales, engineering, or some other group, and then tested through the crucible of constructive controversy until a decision emerges.

For a dynamic company to maximize growth opportunities through change, however, it must guard against change degenerating into chaos, a condition dominated by too many individual agendas. To maintain consistency in both the company's culture and its direction, change must be based on what MCI terms "bedrocks." These bedrocks comprise our models, concepts, and values, which serve as reference points and guides for what we need to accomplish. They are not inviolable rules, but they exist as a constant foundation to guide change.

Thus, our basic guideline to creating successful change is to recognize and foster what *doesn't change*—the principles and values that make up the MCI culture. Communication of these bedrocks is vital. The bedrocks are augmented with a set of strategic objectives developed through our informal strategic planning, which we think of as a "corporate roadmap" showing where the company is heading. Communicating clearly both the bedrocks and objectives to employees is a must at MCI because together they form a powerful but controlled force for driving successful change.

To take charge of change and make it work to competitive advantage, however, a company must hire and train the right people, then foster an environment where the "penchant for change" thrives and is rewarded. Fostering this environment is MCI's Fourth Principle . . .

SHAPE THE ENVIRONMENT TO ENCOURAGE SUCCESS

The starting point for observing this principle lies in recognizing that the employment environment doesn't just happen. It has to be created, it has to be nurtured, and at times it has to be changed. The stewardship of this environment rests with every MCI employee, but the accountability to pull it all together rests with our Human Resources Department. This is their primary role.

A key aspect of MCI's culture is that we expect a great deal from our employees. We set high goals that demand maximum effort and promise maximum reward if achieved. Because MCI employees are encouraged to be decision makers and entrepreneurial risk takers, they also will face times of uncertainty, stress, and confusion. These demanding responsibilities are matched, however, by the level and amount of attention we give to their needs, their goals, and their expectations. If any organization wants its people to behave creatively, it must encourage that type of behavior with sound personnel policies that temper tough demands and risk taking with a supportive environment.

Our extensive employee development program gives employees the tools and skills they need and the opportunity to hone those they already possess. To accomplish this, we work hard at understanding our employees, at knowing how they perceive the company and their place in it, their personal concerns, and what they find most conducive to success.

Our cornerstone of this effort is the MCI All-Employee Survey conducted roughly every 24 months. The survey helps senior management evaluate how well MCI creates an environment where employees feel encouraged to contribute. More importantly, we want to evaluate the extent to which they feel we are responding to their concerns. Managers who do not respond are not fulfilling their commitment to MCI.

Another important feedback tool is MCI's Performance Management System. This provides managers the opportunity to review an employee's past performance with thought and care, and to set meaningful goals for improving future performance. It is a sort of personal roadmap that tracks each individual's career and attempts to fit it into the corporate roadmap. In other words, it links the individual employee's goals with the strategic objectives of MCI, thus ensuring that individual efforts and aspirations are connected directly to the company's collective success.

In addition, our compensation system rewards entrepreneurial behavior and outstanding individual performance. The process by which each employee's pay is determined is totally open to personal review. There are no secrets as to how compensation, grade levels, and salary increases are arrived at. The system is augmented by a myriad of programs for recognizing special achievements, including recognition conferences that acknowledge outstanding employees, a commission system for sales representatives and technical support personnel, and annual incentives for over 400 MCI managers and executives.

People are supported in reaching their potential by an extensive employee training program. During 1992, we conducted more than one million hours of formal training reaching three out of every four employees. This training covered everything from technology to management, sales to customer service, and higher education to remedial skills. Our future plans are even more ambitious because we estimate that 75 percent of our work force will be retrained to meet new demands during the 1990s: technological advances, more complex and varied jobs, and professional advancement.

This varied approach to shaping the employee environment also is related to the Fifth—and perhaps the most important—MCI Principle . . .

THE OVERPOWERING IMPORTANCE OF COMMUNICATION

Communication is the lifeblood of a dynamic organization. An environment where employees take risks and seize opportunity is in danger of becoming sheer anarchy without two-way, in-depth communication. Just as senior management depends on the employee survey to hear from our people, the employees want to hear everything they need to do their jobs. We tell our employees that, if we err, it will be on the side of *too much* information. "Overcommunication" simply isn't possible.

To present company news and major issues, we use a wide range of media, both print and electronic, including internal publications, audiovisual messages, and face-to-face meetings. And, since we're a telecommunications company, naturally we take advantage of our own technology—particularly our electronic mail system, MCI Mail. Our employees send an estimated one million MCI Mail messages a week because it is an indispensable part of conducting business at MCI.

Another exciting communications tool is MCI-TV, a wideband internal television network that reaches every major concentration of employees in the country. MCI-TV carries regular news and information programs on both a national and regional basis. It's also interactive, so viewers can call in to ask questions and offer opinions. This capability makes MCI-TV invaluable as a training and development medium.

We make these investments in communicating with our employees because, when all is said and done, MCI people have made our company what it is today. Its success is their success. Back in the early days, we told our employees that we, a tiny upstart company, intended to take on the world's largest monopoly, one that was going to fight us at every turn. Yet, we expected our people to win. And they did.

CONCLUSIONS

These principles comprise an interrelated set of values and guidelines at the heart of the MCI culture that we use to shape the company and give it strategic direction. Looking back at MCI's evolution, what we have learned is that you cannot let the organization drive the people—the people have to drive the organization. Our obligation as the leaders of MCI is to create and maintain this dynamic organizational culture so that each employee can maximize his or her contribution to the company.

This belief goes to the heart of what MCI is all about: promoting individualism, fighting bureaucracy, embracing change, creating an entrepreneurial environment, and maintaining effective communications. We may not consciously think of this as an internal market because our approach relies heavily on cultural factors, but the concept and MCI management are the same.

What does the MCI experience have to offer other companies? All managers have to find the solutions that work for them in their organizations. However, no solution can create a dynamic organization unless it is solidly based on a strong entrepreneurial culture. We hope this account of MCI's principles can help others to develop a management system for their needs that is as effective as our system has been for us.

8 Reintroducing Alcoa to Economic Reality

Corporate Parenting of Indulged Departments

John P. Starr

Since the dawn of time, parents have had an irrepressible instinct to protect their young. It may sound a bit strange, but those of us who are corporate managers often suffer from this same instinct. We carefully insulate our "babies"—the various departments that support any organization—from the harsh realities of the outside world.

In the past, when national boundaries limited competition, we could afford this protective behavior. We often used our collective strength to support weak departments that might not be able to stand on their own. For many years, U.S. auto companies supported subsidiaries that utilized outdated technology and production processes, and

John P. Starr was president of Alcoa Separations Technology, a division of Alcoa Corporation, at the time of the reorganization described in this chapter.

produced inferior quality. Under the pressure of global competition, however, other manufacturers such as the Japanese required their suppliers to grow and compete vigorously. The result was that these firms set today's high standards of productivity and quality, which in turn enabled them to dominate their industries.

In a different sense, these fierce competitors were really better parents because they required their youngsters to grow up into responsible adults. Protecting departments in organizations can lead to the same problems confronting any parent who is overprotective of its young. Sooner or later, the child must face the world, and, if unprepared, some aggressor is likely to threaten when the child is out of the parent's sight. To avoid the business equivalent of being eaten alive, we must require all our units to become fully capable, mature enterprises that can survive and prosper in the real world against tough competition.

WEANING SUPPORT UNITS AT ALCOA
SEPARATIONS TECHNOLOGY

Alcoa, like so many other corporations in U.S. industry, was once comfortably ensconced in its cozy, protected world. We were in a growing industry, and we had strong technical and commercial positions that allowed ample opportunities to make money. Not surprisingly, whenever operating costs would rise, sales and marketing teams were dispatched to "raise prices." Things were looking pretty good.

However, the outside world started to change. Competitors became more skillful, and technical gaps began to close. Perhaps of greatest importance, our past success had brought growth, and this growth caused some of the large departments to lose contact with their customers. Many of these departments had become more driven by their own bureaucratic internal processes, than by the need to deliver solutions to demanding customers.

Within this envelope of Alcoa Corporation, Alcoa Separations was a $100-million-plus subsidiary that had been assembled by adding several acquired businesses to an existing base within the company. Its primary business was making engineered equipment and systems, particularly for the water and waste treatment industries. This equipment frequently consists of large tanks connected by complex piping arrangements, with numerous valves and fittings scattered throughout to control flow.

This is also roughly the way our organization worked—like a cumbersome, mechanical plumbing system. Figure 8–1 shows a slightly exaggerated, but nonetheless fairly accurate, depiction of the way departments communicated with each other and our customers. Groups functioned as "towers of power." Communications between units were highly formal, much like the flow of liquid through pipes in the equipment they made—limited to a few tightly controlled, precise directions. There was little room for creativity and considerable filtering of customer input at many stages in the process. As a result, many individual departments were far more interested in what went on inside their own "tank" than in what happened to the customer at the output end of the process.

As a result, groups were optimizing their own activities at the cost of suboptimizing results for the whole system. In comparing the performance of our departments against competitive standards, we found that a number of units were seriously falling behind. They were losing the

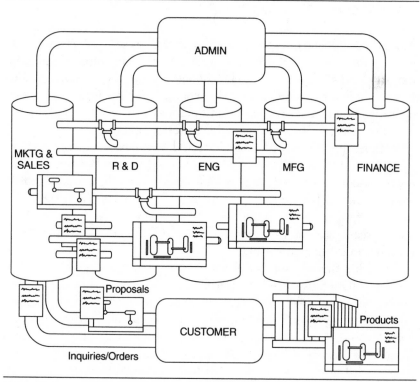

FIGURE 8–1.   **Organizational towers of power.**

advantages of speed, flexibility, and customer contact that had driven success in their smaller, more entrepreneurial days.

Growth, compartmentalization, and fuzzy competitive drivers had begun to insulate departments from reality. Like all good parents who wish the best for their children's future, we had to wean these indulged youngsters if they were to survive in a harsh competitive world.

SWITCHING TO A THREE-DIMENSIONAL INTERNAL MARKET SYSTEM

This unflattering portrait of our unwieldy structure led to a decision to recapture the customer- and market-driven forces that had created the group's success in the first place. We saw a strong need to refocus our efforts through a system that would require each unit to constantly examine its activities and goals against competitive benchmarks of quality, cost, and customer satisfaction. After much reflection, the model that we decided to follow was the Three-Dimensional (3-D) Internal Market System introduced to us by INTERACT.

In this 3-D System, the "input" units of manufacturing, engineering, and R&D are viewed as suppliers to the business units, which are then treated as their customers. The business units in turn serve *their* internal customers—the sales units, which provide the final "output" to the environment. The idea is that everyone in the organization has a customer and a supplier, and in turn is itself a customer or a supplier. Just as in real-world situations, suppliers must develop sound working relationships with their customers and raise the quality of their goods and services to compete with other vendors. Customers are free to choose among possible suppliers, both internal and external, so internal vendors who do not perform could be replaced by external suppliers, the equivalent of contracting out an operation. The flip side is that the internal suppliers also have the opportunity to seek outside clients for their goods and services.

If your organization is like ours, however, achieving this perfect system is easier said than done. When we originally discussed the 3-D concept, all our people who were in the customer role literally licked their chops. At long last, they said, they would have the freedom to dump those rascals down the hall who were really causing all their problems. And those in a supplier mode said, Aha! Just let our internal customers try finding an outside vendor who will put up with the same pitifully poor information we've been dealing with. Maybe, just maybe, this could make our salespeople shape up and give us what we really need to perform well.

Obviously, we could not tolerate a situation where all parts of the organization were allowed to jump ship, which would have allowed chaos to reign supreme. To make the transition in orderly fashion, we agreed to establish transfer prices based on the previous year's costs. Each unit would use these prices for a specified period without having their customers move to external suppliers, or having their suppliers abandon them for better customers. During this warm-up period, suppliers would be expected to take whatever actions were necessary to bring their costs and quality up to competitive standards, while customers would be expected to clean up their act by collaborating with supplier groups to help lower their costs.

As this process proceeded, we found that some of our units apparently could not compete with costs quoted from outside vendors. I say apparently because our cost system had never been designed to give accurate breakdowns by department, with overhead properly applied as if each department were a company in its own right. Quite often, the costs for a given unit did not delineate fixed corporate expenses that would not go away if a particular piece of business were given to an outside supplier.

The hidden effect of these "membership" costs is nicely illustrated by a story about a chain of food stores. Several of the stores were not profitable, so the company decided to close them. After doing so, they reallocated corporate overhead to the remaining stores, which increased *their* costs and made a few more stores unprofitable. They then closed these additional stores and reallocated again, without seeing where all this was heading. It took a while to realize how important such membership costs can be if not addressed in a meaningful context.

This problem was especially acute in our case because we were moving to an internal market system. We had to spend a considerable amount of time and effort to reclassify these fixed overhead costs so that comparisons to outside vendors would be accurate. This is a crucial task in the transition to a market economy. Without a workable, responsive cost analysis system, inappropriate competitive comparisons are likely. If this happens, the market approach will not work well. The process bogs down and comparisons become meaningless.

Other difficulties arose after costs were refigured along these lines. A lot of effort was wasted by managers arguing about the relative fairness of cost figures, rather than addressing the underlying competitive issues that were being raised. People also complained vigorously about the level of the transfer prices in general, which pointed to other problems.

These were transient issues, however, because they occurred directly out of our decision to curtail complete market freedom somewhat during the transition phase. When fully implemented, we expect to simply allow the price offerings of competitors to guide internal transactions. In the final analysis, there is nothing to argue about in a market system. If you don't like the terms offered, it is always possible to take your business elsewhere.

It took us far longer than we had hoped to proceed down this path, primarily because our financial system was weaker than many of us had suspected. We had to relearn the first rule of management—you can only manage something if you can measure it. Unfortunately, we found ourselves woefully short on our capability of measuring various operations to the level that a market economy requires. As a result, our ability to capture many of the benefits of the concept were delayed.

We know now that these financial measurement problems existed long before we embarked on the market economy approach. One of the unexpected benefits of the internal market system was to make this shortcoming visible. After improving our information systems, we were then able to take the corrective actions needed to make each unit more competitive and to optimize overall results for the entire company. I cannot too strongly emphasize how critical solid financial analysis is early in the process to make an internal market system work.

EVOLUTION OF THE INTERNAL MARKET STRUCTURE

Our experience with the internal market system produced both successes and failures. Perhaps our most dramatic success has come from, of all places, our research and development department. Under the old system, the only way the R&D group could fund projects was to convince a business unit that they had a great idea. As a result, the battles between R&D and business units became legendary. R&D always complained that the marketing groups were too short-term-oriented and did not understand the complexities of long-term development. Business units complained that R&D could never finish anything, was prohibitively expensive, and was always off working on some harebrained

idea rather than accomplishing projects that would yield revenue sometime in this century.

After the internal market was working, R&D was forced to do
some serious reflection. Realizing that their internal customers had limited funds and desires for long-term work, they decided to reorient
themselves to focus on various hot projects emerging from the business
units. This did not satisfy their interests in more creative and challenging projects, so they also decided to search outside for funding from various clients that valued their special expertise. Certain boundaries were
placed on this pursuit, primarily that any work they obtained must be
linked to the strategic direction of the company.

As a result of these efforts, almost 35 percent of R&D's budget is
now being funded via external sources. They have done an exceptional
job of finding funding for projects that contribute to our strategic goals,
and even the business units have been pleasantly surprised by the new
possibilities that have been introduced. This contact with outside
clients has also shown that R&D costs were not as far out of line with
competitive pricing as we had thought.

There have been other success stories as well. Our manufacturing
organization decided to subcontract several operations that could be
performed better and more cheaply by outside vendors, at great savings
in time and money. The European sales division moved aggressively to
represent additional product lines from other divisions and suppliers
where they could add value. And our engineering unit created several
subcontractor relationships to help meet customer schedules during
peak periods.

But we also had to struggle in some areas. The most crucial problem occurred where it was least expected—our business units, which
package and market our products. They envisioned the new system as
their personal nirvana, an ideal world in which they were the "customer
supreme" and could force their internal suppliers to meet every whim.
These demands were enforced by the threat of taking their business
elsewhere if they did not get action.

The business units could possibly have prevailed in their demands
if they had been able to meet outside competition by serving their
clients' needs effectively. Unfortunately, some marketing managers took
a myopic view and forced outdated policies and procedures on their
captive internal suppliers, blocking many of the quality and cost improvements that might have been possible.

With 20-20 hindsight, we can now see that the move to an internal market revealed the wastefulness of these antiquated processes, just as it showed the truth about our financial system. We did not realize how uncompetitive we were until the new demand for accountability forced the problem to surface. To use my earlier analogy of a manager as a parent, we had left an unprotected child in a dangerous situation.

Ironically, the very units that were used to dealing with external customers disavowed the checks and balances of internal competition. That development truly caught us off guard, and highlights how crucial market forces are for keeping every part of the organization alert.

Ultimately, we were able to address this flaw by focusing on external customer satisfaction as the common measure driving performance throughout the company. This was accomplished by forcing all units to benchmark their own processes and to bring them up to leading standards. This, in turn, drove the need to restructure operations and retrain people; but even with ample training opportunities, we lost some people who could not adapt to a competitive environment. Now, however, the organization has a solid base of knowledge and tools to upgrade our marketing by linking improvements across the organization to the customer.

REVITALIZATION

A sense of revitalization grew as the internal market system drove accountability for performance into all layers and units of the organization. This accountability can be viewed as a chain linking all successive internal customer dealings to the ultimate needs of the final customer. It also relies heavily on monitoring and measuring performance, by the performer, at each step in this chain. The net effect is a continuous striving for improvement and excellence in all we do.

We have had particular success where this process has been pushed all the way to the factory floor. In several work centers, we gave teams the freedom to rearrange their equipment to gain better work flow of material. Later, we also allowed them the authority to control their own work-in-process inventory.

One of the most far-reaching changes was to have workers receive orders directly from their customers via computers that we installed in the work centers. Previously, supervisors were needed to transfer this planning information to work centers and to provide instructions at the beginning of each workday. The supervisor would then check back during the day to see if people were working on the proper jobs at the proper pace. Under the new system, the work team takes this planning information directly and schedules its own work to meet customer demands.

With this new flexibility, a direct link to their customers, and feedback on the profitability of their units, members of the work centers became highly interested, and even excited, about their jobs in a way they never had been before. Having their destiny in their own hands, work teams could directly see the result of their actions on costs and on how quickly a product moved out the door. As a result, lead times for moving products through one work center were reduced from 12–14 weeks to 2–5 days. The team is confident they can further reduce this to 4 hours as they totally close the loop with their customers and suppliers.

One major result of this self-organizing approach is that far fewer supervisors are needed, permitting layers to be removed from the organizational hierarchy. Those supervisors remaining now act more like a coach and a champion of continuous improvement. The company is clearly heading toward self-managed teams that are driven directly by customer demands, and who are accountable for final performance. In short, an autonomous work team model that behaves as a small business enterprise in its own right.

During the past year, many additional units have continued to implement the internal market concept, thereby driving accountability, competitiveness, and rigorous financial discipline within each operating unit, and leading to significant gains in productivity and performance. Most notably, output per worker in the water treatment and environmental segments has nearly doubled. Also, lead times were cut by up to 80 percent in the water treatment segment, resulting in a more profitable and dynamic business.

Today, this business is a successful part of the rapidly growing U.S. Filter Corporation, which acquired it from Alcoa in 1992. U.S. Filter is one of the country's largest companies dedicated to fluid processing equipment and technology, contributing a further customer focus on critical items for success within this business. Meanwhile, Alcoa continues to refocus on its core aluminum business, and is attempting to drive the same concepts of accountability, quality, and customer satisfaction throughout all of its businesses.

HOPES FOR THE FUTURE

Improvements of this type represent only a small start to what is possible. We have all either had the opportunity to visit or read about what seems like a never-ending stream of success stories coming out of Japan. It is quite interesting that most such successes, regardless of where they occur in the world, are based on the same principles. Give people the freedom to pursue their own good ideas in an environment of trust and cooperation, with timely measurement and feedback on how they are doing, and progress is sure to be made. We may not make quantum leaps, but the results nonetheless produce impressive, constant gains.

Going back to my analogy between parents and managers again, seldom does a baby move directly from his or her first spoken words to delivering the State of the Union Address before Congress. What we experience in life, and what we should attempt to emulate in business, is a series of incremental steps that keep improving our capability to tackle ever more challenging tasks by a never-ending process of learning.

The best way to bring learning alive in our organizations is to introduce market-based concepts into each and every job and group in the corporation. If we desire to have our organizations function at higher levels of performance, we must gradually expose them to an environment of free enterprise. There is a lot of discretionary effort out there in capable people who want to perform. It is just waiting to be tapped by managers with vision.

A market-based economy operating on competition allows organizations and people to grow and mature. Just as we marvel at how nature can transform weak, helpless children into powerful adults able to protect their parents, so can small business units become strong internal enterprises able to strengthen the parent corporation as a whole. Our challenge as managers is to harness people's great reserves of dormant energy by turning them loose in a market-based enterprise system.

Alcoa's experience in moving to an internal market system has proven to be a valuable lesson in good corporate parenting. It has forcefully driven home the need to stop protecting indulged units, and instead to teach them how to cope in the real world. Only by learning to survive in a competitive environment can we hope to produce stable, productive, long-term business relationships. Insulating individuals from such hard but unavoidable realities inevitably produces unproductive, unstable situations that cannot long endure, whether in nature or in business.

9 The Executive Office Should Also Be a Profit Center

Highlights from a Career at General Motors and Clark Equipment

James R. Rinehart

Peter Drucker has observed that the decline of large American corporations has reached alarmingly low levels, and that this decline is largely caused by an outmoded philosophy of management which now threatens the American standard of living. By inference, therefore, the problem deserves our best efforts.

My own thinking about this issue is rooted in 30 years of experience at General Motors and Clark Equipment Company. This chapter is an attempt to share the valuable lessons I gained from this experience.

James R. Rinehart was CEO of Clark Equipment Company. Prior to that, he served in a variety of positions at General Motors, including general manager of the Packard Electric Division and president of GM Canada.

There is no substitute for the discipline of the marketplace, and we often insulate our large corporations from that discipline at our peril. I am not only speaking about line business units, or even staff units, but all operations, including the office of the CEO.

The title I have chosen for this chapter is intended to drive this point home as forcefully as possible: The chief executive's office can, and should, also be a profit center.

First, I would like to recall an ironic bit of history in management science that I was a witness to during my business career at General Motors.

THE DECLINE OF GENERAL MOTORS AND AMERICAN COMPETITIVENESS

As World War II was drawing to a close, Alfred Sloan invited Peter Drucker to make a study of General Motors (GM), and to provide the organization with his observations and recommendations. When the study was submitted, GM leaders felt betrayed. They saw the study as a criticism because it called for reevaluating Sloan's basic principles of management. The relationship was abruptly terminated, and "the book was burned" as far as GM was concerned.

In 1946, Mr. Drucker published his GM study in a book titled *Concept of the Corporation.* Ironically, the rest of the world thought Mr. Drucker had "praised Caesar" and used the book as a how-to manual for organizing many of the world's large manufacturing companies in GM's image.

Thus, the seeds of today's decline of U.S. corporations can be traced back to those seminal years after World War II. Successful, centrally controlled corporations such as GM served as a model for the organization of American industry. When the success of that model ended during the past decade or two with the onset of a more competitive global economy, it was hard to abandon this deeply entrenched, outmoded philosophy. The reluctance of GM's management to consider Peter Drucker's recommendations was only the beginning of the still-persistent resistance to the massive changes now haunting this great enterprise that is failing so badly.

I joined the Packard Electric Division of General Motors in 1953 as an industrial engineer. At that time, our studies showed that Packard Electric's costs and quality were competitive domestically.

Twenty-two years later in 1975 as Packard Electric's General Manager, I already knew that our little piece of GM was far from being competitive in world markets. In fact, our internal costs were double those of competitive levels, and a similar situation had developed in most other GM divisions.

How was it possible in just 22 years for GM to have lost so much ground? It is worth a few minutes to identify the culprits. The root of the problem was that transfer prices from divisions such as Packard Electric were kept above competitive levels by a deliberate policy of GM management. The result was enormous slack that was soon filled by rising costs, leading to the non-competitive situation in 1975.

Let me explain. It was Mr. Sloan's conviction that profits in "supply divisions" such as Packard Electric flowed through undiluted to the corporation, whereas profits in "end-product divisions," such as the major auto lines, were subject to erosion as they bore the massive expenditures needed to maintain market share. Adoption of this idea also helped allay GM's constant concern about a government antitrust suit. For the same reason, a policy of keeping internal profitability a secret was firmly in place. We knew, however, that it was not unusual for the profit margins of supply divisions to exceed those of car divisions by as much as a factor of 10. You can imagine the massaging of results that this required to operate a corporatewide bonus plan.

To maintain this system, a company policy prevented the end-product divisions from outsourcing any product made by a supplying division without securing permission from the corporate financial staff. Their analysis compared outside price to inside *variable cost.* Today such a policy is almost inconceivable. But remember that this policy was made before the onset of tough foreign competition, when the supply divisions were still cost and quality competitive.

It didn't take long for the end-product divisions to assign their least able buyers to work with their allied suppliers who, of course, assigned their sharpest sales engineers to the GM accounts. The result of 20 years of this unequal interaction was not only a loss of overall product cost competitiveness but, even worse, a lack of knowledge of what domestic competitive levels actually were and, beyond this, what was going on in Japan. In 1953, the fact that GM internally supplied 65 percent of its components, as opposed to 50 percent at Ford and 35 percent at Chrysler, was seen as a competitive advantage since it was viewed as greater "added value." But because the 65 percent "value added" actually consisted of inflated costs, by 1975 this supposed advantage had been transformed into a millstone around GM's neck in the eyes of price-conscious buyers and auto industry observers.

The corporate staffs required to control this complex internal pricing policy were by no means insignificant, and the demands of World War II had caused the staffs to bloat even further. These factors were all overlooked when the conversion to peacetime production roared ahead. New staff activities such as labor relations, real estate management, and research were added, and before we knew it, the era of the "bean counter CEOs" had begun with an inevitable slide toward corporate operating controls. The challenges posed by the oil embargo and the resultant fuel efficiency goals added even higher layers of bureaucracy to this growing corporate monster.

By 1975, General Motors had become a battle of wits between the operating division executives who were constantly trying to beat this archaic system, and the staff executives who were continually increasing corporate control even further. Almost no one within GM was focused on the massive changes required to meet the twin challenges posed by Japan and OPEC. Today, some real understanding of the extent of these grave problems seems to have developed, but I wonder whether there is an equivalent understanding of what an appropriate response might be.

In contrast, the Packard Electric Division of General Motors put itself firmly on the road to world cost and quality competitiveness during the five years from 1975 to 1980, and this success continued with the incredible gains the division made in the decade of the 1980s. What I took with me from that five-year experience as general manager may be relevant to the needs of American management today.

I learned that employees know more about their own jobs than anyone else, and that they will support decisions, programs, and products which they help create. However, people need the opportunities, accountability, and incentives provided by an internal market economy to do so. Respect for employees and their active participation are the taps to an almost limitless stream of development potential when harnessed to a market-driven corporate structure guided by a planning system that designs an ideal future and invents ways to make it happen. We didn't know it at the time, but we had stumbled onto our version of Professor Ackoff's social systems science. Bert Olson, my mentor and predecessor at Packard, never tired of reminding me that it is easier to secure forgiveness than permission. That's been quite useful to me from time to time.

RESTRUCTURING THE CEO'S OFFICE AT CLARK EQUIPMENT

I joined Clark Equipment as CEO in 1981. The first two weeks in my new job were spent in budget reviews from which I learned two things: If Clark followed the proposed 1982 operating plan, we would be in Chapter 11 in six months; and Clark Equipment was designed as a pocket-size GM with all the same bureaucratic problems. To avoid bankruptcy, we reduced inventories by 50 percent, put a freeze on hiring, closed half our worldwide manufacturing capacity, and established new credit lines to ensure sufficient funds. These moves bought time for turning the company around and reduced our break-even point by 33 percent.

An entire family of plans and actions was required over the next 10 years to take Clark Equipment from the brink of bankruptcy to world competitiveness, which mainly consisted of reintroducing the company to economic realities that had been ignored for years. However, I want to focus this discussion on our approach to managing the corporate executive office. As I suggested at the onset of this chapter, the role we developed for the chief executive's office exemplifies the type of change that is needed in prevailing U.S. management philosophy.

On January 1982, when I came aboard, the number of people working within corporate headquarters was a shade under 500—burdening Clark Equipment with unneeded administrative overhead. Our first step was to identify possible freestanding businesses within the corporate office. The list included a law firm, an accounting firm, a data processing/telecommunications company, a trucking company, and a printing and graphics company. These units were given two years to become self-supporting by accomplishing two goals:

1. Develop 50 percent of their business outside Clark.
2. Earn their cost of capital.

After one year, Clark's operating companies were no longer required to use these internal services. An internal service unit that met the two preceding objectives had three options:

1. Become a Clark operating company.
2. Undertake an employee buyout.
3. Find themselves a new owner.

If a service unit failed to meet the two objectives, option 1 would not be available to it. The result was three buyouts, one sale, and one new Clark operating company. Some people thought we took a rather extreme position, but it is always interesting that people will support drastic action when they understand the reasons and are involved in finding the solution.

The second step was to announce that the corporate personnel and purchasing staffs would be phased out in one year as the new operating companies assumed these responsibilities. My experience has been that these two functions atrophy at the operating level when overlaid by corporate staffs. This can be and often is disastrous because people and purchases constitute the lion's share of manageable costs. Operating companies must perform these functions in a decentralized manner, thereby subjecting costs to the accountability of local performance controls and minimizing complex corporate controls and overhead.

Needless to say, the people on these corporate staffs had a different view. A few of them accepted offers from the operating companies, and the majority left under one or another of our voluntary separation plans. These two steps reduced the corporate office to less than 100, which resulted in a huge decrease in overhead costs by eliminating 400 staff jobs, most of which had been filled by well-paid professionals and managers.

The third step was to redesign the working relationships between business units and the corporate office to minimize bureaucratic controls. For example, we developed a decentralized cost system that required no central office intervention and a corporate consolidation program that required only one corporate office person. This step proved harder than expected, and so the new cost accounting system was not debugged and in place until early 1985. At this point, the corporate staff dropped to less than 75, and we began examining what might be considered the ideal future for the corporate office of a market-driven organization.

Three concepts had emerged by the time I left Clark. These differing versions of the corporate management system I will call the "Buffett" model, the "Volvo" model, and the "Ackoff" model.[1] The salient features of each are summarized in Table 9–1.

These three models represent increasing levels of involvement between the company's business units and corporate headquarters. The Buffett model offers the most minimal relationship, with the CEO's role limited to holding an annual review and planning meeting with each

TABLE 9–1.   Three Models of a Corporate (Executive) Office

Design Parameters	Models		
	The Buffett Model	The Volvo Model	The Ackoff Model
Corporate Office Size	10	20	30
Corporate Contact with Operating Companies	Annual planning meeting plus one-on-one consultation as requested	Buffett model plus quarterly meetings of board of directors of operating companies including corporate officers and outside directors	Buffett model plus quarterly board meetings with directors from corporate office, operating companies, and outside directors
Responsibility for Banking Relationships	Operating companies	Operating companies	Corporate office functions as both the commercial and investment bank for the operating companies
Corporate Dividends	None	Tax levied quarterly on operating companies to pay dividends	Tax levied quarterly on operating companies to pay dividends
Management of Free Cash	Added to corporate acquisition capital	Added to corporate acquisition capital	Added to corporate acquisition capital
Value Added by Corporate Management	Relieves operating companies of stockholder relations and free cash investment	Buffett model reduced by the cost of servicing a board of directors—no small matter	Volvo model plus a favorable spread on cost of capital

operating company, and retrieving surplus cash for other investments; the corporation pays no dividends, and operating companies manage their own banking relationships. The Volvo model adds quarterly review meetings, a board of directors for operating companies, and a tax levy on operating companies to pay corporate dividends. The Ackoff model further requires the CEO to act as an investment banker to operating companies, providing risk capital for new ventures in the expectation of realizing an attractive return. The Ackoff model also proposes that the executive office itself should be a profit center. As shown in the table, the corporate staff increases from 10, to 20, to 30 people respectively for the three models because of these added responsibilities.

Today, corporate managers face a critical dilemma. The law courts continue to rule that the sole responsibility of management is to maximize shareholder value. Management, meanwhile, has learned the hard way that it must satisfy five other stakeholders in addition to its investors—employees, customers, suppliers, community, and government. All three models direct operating managers to maximize the long-term value of their companies by optimizing the interests of all six stakeholders—a necessity if large corporations are to be world cost and quality competitive. The corporate office assumes the responsibility for relationships with stockholders, financial analysts, and the business press.

The role of the corporate office in managing investment capital is especially important in an internal market system. The time of greatest risk in an operating company occurs when it has a significant surplus of cash over and beyond the foreseeable needs of the business. This condition can bring on unfortunate and impulsive management decisions, such as indulging in unjustified acquisitions. To avoid this, each of the models assumes that the first requisite of corporate management is to have superior investment skills that can put the reserves generated by operating companies to better use. The "value saved" by avoiding one disastrous acquisition a decade is justification enough for a corporate office under any of the three models.

Clark Equipment chose to implement the Ackoff model, largely out of a conviction that the CEO's office should be a profit center.

CONCLUSIONS

The ranks of corporate offices that do not subtract value from the enterprise are, at best, thin. One of the greatest contributions a CEO can make is to be a bureaucracy buster 24 hours a day. To promote long-term development of the corporation, the CEO's task must be to empower, not control, the operating companies. The internal market economy concept provides a sound basis for accomplishing these objectives because it offers a conceptual framework that defines each unit in the corporation as an autonomous profit center, like a business in its own right.

From this viewpoint, even the CEO's office should be a profit center, with the CEO's performance based on his or her own costs and revenues, as in any business unit. Revenue is derived from a "tax" charged to operating units for the services provided by the CEO, and from the return generated by corporate capital invested in operating companies. Since operating companies are the CEO's clients, however, they must find this a useful relationship that enhances their own profitability or they will be tempted to go elsewhere. Thus, the main test in this model is the CEO's ability to make participation in the enterprise attractive to operating managers by maximizing the value offered while also minimizing the costs they must pay. Ultimately, then, the performance of the CEO's function is measured by the extent to which the executive is successful in creating a corporate system that enhances the value created by all operating units.

The internal market concept offers the practical advantage of providing a bottom line for the corporate office that reflects the value it creates for the enterprise as whole but is separately identifiable from the performance of operating companies. In addition to aligning the performance of the CEO's office with the company's operating units, this concept requires the CEO to set an example for his or her managers. If CEOs are to be perceived as leaders who contribute value to the enterprise, they must share in meeting the same profit responsibility they ask of their operating executives. So I am led to the final conclusion: Why, indeed, shouldn't the chief executive's office also be a profit center?

10

Lessons in Converting Corporate Staff Units into Profit Centers

The Control Data Business Advisors Story

David M. Noer

This chapter is a retrospective look at Control Data's attempt to place a number of staff units into what it called "a profit and loss environment." A fundamental organizational change that we would today call a "socio-technical intervention" caused a "paradigm shift" resulting in the creation of "an internal market economy." While these concepts provide useful models, the translation of theory into reality is never smooth or predictable. What unfolded was somewhat different from either the

David M. Noer was the president and CEO of Control Data Business Advisors, a wholly owned subsidiary of Control Data Corporation, during the experiences he describes in this chapter. He is now vice president for Training and Education at the Center for Creative Leadership, Greensboro, North Carolina.

models or the initial intentions of the organization. Our attempt can be best understood as a case study occurring within its own unique phenomenological situation.

The Control Data experience is a useful case study for those interested in creating market economies within organizational boundaries. Placing the life span of such innovations into a "success/failure" frame of reference is much too binary and confining, but we can always learn from efforts that go awry as they ride the bumpy back roads of reality in different directions than shown on the smooth maps of intent.

This chapter outlines the development, maturation, and death of this experiment, highlighting what we learned along the way. Although our attempt to create a new form of entrepreneurial staff function was unique and somewhat unsuccessful, others who may follow our example can learn many valuable principles from our experience. The description that follows represents one perspective—mine—and thus is subject to other interpretations.

OVERVIEW

From 1982 to 1988, Control Data Corporation moved many of its corporate staff units into a "profit and loss environment." These units were folded into a wholly owned subsidiary, moved into a separate facility, and expected to sell products and services back to the parent organization and to external customers. At its peak, this new subsidiary encompassed the functions of strategic planning, market research, human resource development, training, labor relations, compensation and benefits, business strategy, productivity, quality, health care services, temporary staffing, and other "corporate staff" functions.

The new organization created for this purpose was called Control Data Business Advisors. It also included some nonstaff functions: small business development and venture capital, human-resource-oriented computer products, and an outplacement and recruiting function. I was initially the president of the human resource component, and eventually of the entire operation.

Business Advisors grew, floundered, evolved a strategy, and was eventually divested. Some functions then moved back to the parent organization; others closed, were sold, or were spun off as independent businesses.

ROOTS

The roots of what eventually became Control Data Business Advisors were deeply embedded in the values and vision of the organization's founder and chairman, William Norris. These values were shared by his successor, who was then president of Control Data, Robert Price. As will be discussed later in this chapter, these values were not shared by other executives.

Mr. Norris's views were formed when he grow up on a farm in Nebraska during the depression. He was suspicious of the stultifying effects of largeness, believed in personal responsibility, and based his business philosophy on the creative power of market forces. He was an early advocate of developing business relations between the United States and Russia. Although often criticized by both the private and public sector, he strongly advocated business involvement in the solving of societal problems such as education, health care, and transportation. Market economies, in his view, would do a far better job than noncompetitive government bureaucracy.

Control Data's strategy flowed from Norris's vision of fostering innovation by creating small, market-driven work units. This strategy was developed in an intuitive fashion by Norris and a few key executives, and therefore, it was not clearly articulated or deeply shared among others on the executive team. Nonetheless, it drove the organization toward a novel practice of allowing employees to "spin off" their own businesses in partnership with the parent organization. This entrepreneurial culture laid the foundation for creating the internal market orientation that became a large part of Business Advisors. Some general rules were applied to these spin-offs:

1. The business spin-off should be consistent with, but not identical to, the company's own goals.
2. The company should take an equity position in the new business, thus participating in both the risk and reward.
3. The individual should also take a well-defined risk; for example, a salary reduction that would apply toward his or her own equity position.
4. The entrepreneur should also have a well-defined reward, based on the development of the business.
5. Since the business was to be independent, there had to be rules facilitating the buildup of capital.

This spin-off philosophy raised a number of questions and problems. How many employee entrepreneurs could the company work with, and how did it choose them? How should the organization structure the benefits to the entrepreneur, and how much should the company invest in a given project? What support would the corporation give in terms of flexible scheduling, in-kind services, and relief from other responsibilities? And what about the managers who had worked long, hard, and loyally, and now saw new people getting corporate support to go out on their own?

Although most of the early spin-offs were "line" as opposed to "staff" functions, the momentum created by this new culture soon made staff spin-offs an interesting additional possibility. In the early 1980s, some executives developed a vision of extending the spin-off strategy to staff units. To paraphrase a comment by an executive in the early 1980s, "Suppose for a minute you could spin-off these G&A [general and administrative] functions, and use them only on an as-needed basis. No benefits expense, no facilities expense, no salaries. Instead, we could have a roster of closely aligned independent contractors, with all the advantages that brings: responsiveness, competitive pricing, and so on. . . ."

CREATING STAFF SPIN-OFFS

A number of staff units, particularly those in human resources, had developed products and services—employee opinion surveys, job evaluation systems, and training programs—that were in demand by outside organizations. The professionals working in these units also had a desire to expand their horizons, and they welcomed an opportunity to utilize their skills for solving problems in diverse organizational environments. At the same time, they had neither the desire nor the venture capital to strike out on their own as independent consultants.

Another environmental factor was the sheer cost of corporate staff operations. As is the case with many organizations, Control Data maintained a staff of highly educated and talented professionals who continued to refine, develop, and market their services within the organization—year after year. Each year, the cost of maintaining this professional staff would rise, while the incremental value of their efforts approached a point of diminishing returns.

If the staff could maintain their professional edge, pass on much of the expense base and costs to external customers, and at the same time provide a reduced but nonetheless substantial degree of internal service, everyone would win. The external customers would get the benefit of proven products and services with much of the developmental costs already paid by Control Data. Control Data would realize a significant reduction in its costs, and the members of the corporate staff would have the best of both worlds—the freedom and entrepreneurial spirit of an independent business, coupled with the security and stability of a large organization.

Control Data set up a "shell"—a wholly owned subsidiary to provide venture capital and other helpful services to the spin-offs. The first large unit to be added to this shell was the human resource development (HRD) staff. Most of the HRD staff woke up one morning and found that they were no longer corporate resources buried in the cocoon of a large company, but were now revenue producers, measured on a profit and loss statement. Many employees found themselves in a situation not of their own making. Later, many other corporate staff units were spun off as well. Most were drafted, and very few had a choice.

To maintain physical and psychological distance from the parent organization, employees were relocated from the corporate staff complex to a leased facility approximately "five miles down the freeway."

ORGANIZATIONAL LEARNINGS

We learned a number of important lessons along the way. The following stand out.

The Perils of an All-Draftee Army

A major issue was choice. Most of the initial staff found themselves forced into a very different and frightening environment. Many had chosen careers in technical or developmental staff roles. The idea of "selling" their services, or of attempting to define their contribution in a commercial context was not only philosophically alien and difficult but often terrifying. Although these units were subsidized and not expected to be self-sustaining for a grace period of one year while Control Data weaned them gradually from central funding, many people felt that if they didn't get a 100 percent response to their sales activities, their paychecks would suffer.

Changing Skills and Attitudes

We learned that implementing a successful market-driven business required a variety of new abilities, and that customer-relation skills were among the most crucial. We also learned that the necessary skills and attitudes could, indeed, be taught. But back in the early days, many employees—even the most skilled—feared rejection from the external market and were embarrassed and reluctant to sell their services to their former colleagues. This attitude did not help in making the adjustment.

The Importance of Training

Not surprisingly, we found that we needed one of our own products—training. Any organization attempting to do what we did needs to commit a major investment in training people to handle sales, customer service, and business systems. Desire, enthusiasm, and dedication can move mountains. But it is unrealistic to assume that successful staff executives can immediately make the adjustments necessary to understand business concepts. It is one thing to manage a large and sophisticated training and development staff function. It is another to manage a business that sells these services, and requires funding, pricing decisions, and financial analysis. Thus, our leaders, too, had to undergo training and orientation.

Pay Attention to Those Who Stay Behind

Some staff functions remained with the parent organization, which led to interesting issues. The most bothersome to the new consultants was that many of their former peers no longer behaved collegially. Those who remained with the parent began treating the new consultants as costs to be minimized—not as fellow staff members or human assets to be nurtured. Worse, some corporate managers were jealous that the consultants would "have fun" bringing products to the outside market while they had to stay home and mind the store. This illustrates that joint planning and organization development activities are essential. From the consultant's perspective, it is difficult to be both a vendor and a colleague. From the parent administrator's perspective, it is psychologically difficult to pay for something once perceived as free.

Make a Long-Term Commitment

Putting an internal staff function into a market-driven environment is expensive; it requires a change in culture and an extensive commitment to training. Before any organization makes the decision to transform a staff function to a market system, these costs need to be weighed carefully, and top management must be committed for the long term.

Have Good Products and Excellent People

No amount of planning or commitment can gain marketplace acceptance (internal or external) for mediocre staff or second-rate products. Before putting a staff function in a market economy, the people must have skills that are valued and the products must be relevant and meet real customer needs.

Embed Your Efforts in a Strategy

The marketplace (internal and external) is large, complex, and fluid. If you have excellent people and products that meet customer needs, someone will buy them. The risk is in getting spread too thin, trying to serve too many masters, and failing for lack of focus. Agree on a strategy and force yourself to adhere to it.

Define a Pricing Policy

Our pricing strategy evolved in many different directions. The articulated strategy was to have "one price" for the internal and external customers. In reality, almost every internal sale was negotiated. Some units priced for an immediate profit and "burden" recovery, while others, for fear of losing the business, negotiated long-term retainers at a loss.

WHY IT DIED

There were also a variety of reasons why this experiment did not make it.

Recession in the Industry

"You can't go home—the old house has been sold and the new one has no room," was a telling metaphor that was heard in the hallways. The development of Business Advisors took place at a time of unprecedented decline in the U.S. computer business, and unfortunately, Control Data suffered severely as an industry leader. Among other things, this meant a great reduction in the need for staff services for the parent, and the inability to meet negotiated commitments for services from the new enterprise. This also reduced the means for fluid transfers back and forth into the consulting organization.

Incompatible Market Niches

It proved very difficult to leverage the variety of staff functions into a coherent external business. They were just too diverse. Although many functions did extremely well on their own externally, they were often unable to create the leverage of cross-functional synergy.

Worst of Both Worlds Model

Since the consulting company was part of a larger organization, it had to deal with the bureaucracy and inflexibility of a corporation. At the same time, the consultants were expected and encouraged to engage in risk-taking behavior. This placed them in a double bind. In effect, we had not succeeded in creating an organization that truly operated as an internal market economy.

Top Management Ferment

As discussed earlier, the vision of Bill Norris and his successor, Bob Price, to create market-driven staff functions was not shared by other executives. When Control Data began to decline, new executives were recruited from outside the organization, and existing executives moved into more influential roles, negating the original commitment to an internal market strategy. A generalized negative reaction to what was perceived as the "old" strategy and a fervor of cost cutting and organizational downsizing eroded the former support for subsidizing and nurturing the consulting business.

Consulting—Not a Core Business

As the computer business declined, there was a move to focus only on core activities. Since the core business of a computer company was not consulting, Control Data Business Advisors, along with a number of other "noncore" units, was divested. The advantages of internal market economies were overlooked in the rush to divest entire business units.

BENEFITS REALIZED

Control Data implemented an innovative effort that would have succeeded despite many tactical errors if the parent organization had not been in such a period of decline. Many of the staff units succeeded in building profitable external businesses. A number of these exist today, either as independent organizations or as parts of other consulting organizations.

The initial mission of reducing corporate expenses through offsetting external revenue was, indeed, accomplished. Another consequence was a much crisper and sharper appreciation of the true cost of staff expenses. Finally, there was the unintended, but nonetheless significant advantage of developing staff executives into more entrepreneurial individuals who better understood the need to create value.

Were these rewards worth the risk and trauma we undertook? I think the majority of our employees would respond with a resounding yes! Our external sales grew beyond our projections, and our products and services were valued in the marketplace. Our employees developed self-esteem and were proud to be profit contributors, as opposed to staff spenders. These gains convinced many people that they prefer to work in an entrepreneurial environment.[1]

THE PAIN AND NECESSITY OF CULTURE-BUSTING

As time and distance have provided a degree of perspective on the Control Data Business Advisors experiment, two related truths have emerged for me. The first is the difficulty of changing a collaborative culture into a competitive one. The second is the necessity of going through the pain of making this transition. I am also convinced that this change is needed, not only for economic efficiency, although that is very important, but also for the mental adjustment of employees in a new age that is experiencing a shifting employment contract.

An area that was never adequately resolved at Control Data was the deep-seated tension between employees who were attempting to interact in a commercial rather than a collegial relationship. These interactions were often clumsy, contrived, and painful. One Business Advisor employee who was attempting to negotiate a retainer with a former colleague captured the essence of the issue: "It's like trying to sell my time to my family—it just doesn't feel right!"

Control Data, like many organizations, put a great deal of effort into building loyalty, identity, and trust with our relationships to the corporation as a whole, rather than with individual units. This sense of community was reflected in all aspects of culture building: the communications strategy, the compensation and reward structure, our common myths and folklore, and rituals such as celebrating five-year increments of tenure by passing out culture-building artifacts such as tie bars and key chains. The messages were clear: "You are a valued member of this community. We are all in the same boat together. Work with your colleagues, trust them, beat the competition. Competition is not inside, it is outside. We don't relate commercially to one another, we relate collegially."

To implement an internal market system was, indeed, to move in a direction counter to this carefully constructed culture. Little wonder that it was so difficult. What was needed was a process to reshape the culture-building scripts and artifacts. This would have involved reframing the paradigm to legitimize the development of an internal market system, making it acceptable to interact in a competitive mode under the umbrella of the Control Data culture.

It is possible and desirable to make these cultural shifts. However, those of us involved in changing organizational cultures recognize the time and effort needed. The problems faced by Control Data were not unique. They are shared by many organizations with strong central values desiring to move to a more market-driven culture. It requires a systemwide effort to unfreeze the old culture. Letting go of a strong culture is painful, and the energy needed for this effort is almost always underestimated.

Organizations like Control Data, with strong, collaborative, central cultures, find themselves in an especially difficult bind. It is because of their strong central culture that they most need to change, yet because of this culture they have the most difficulty making the transition. For such organizations today, this change is mandatory to adjust to a more competitive global economy, and they need to struggle through the pain.

There are two reasons organizations must move in the direction of internal market economies to assure survival. The first and most obvious is that market economies are more efficient than hierarchical controls; they allocate resources more effectively and allow organizations to meet their competition more quickly and creatively in world markets. From a staff perspective, this shift allows staff functions to be clear on both their value added and their customer focus.

The second, and not so obvious reason, concerns the psychological damage that is occurring as the "old" employment contract continues to unravel. It is consistent with an emerging body of research, including mine, on what I have called "layoff survivor sickness." Under the old psychological employment contract that was formed after World War II, an employee performing at an acceptable level in a viable, large organization could count on a job until she or he chose to leave or retire. This created a long-term dependency relationship that was undermined in the 1980s when organizations found themselves with bloated payrolls and employees blindly trusting the old contract.

When organizations downsized and terminated huge numbers of employees, many employees experienced a wrenching violation of this psychological contract. Research indicates that many organizations are attempting to compete in the world market with employees who are suffering the effects of this perceived violation. They are angry, anxious, and risk averse, and report lowered productivity. They are not very healthy people, and they are not doing themselves or their organizations much good.

The creation of market economies within organizations is perhaps the best antidote to the sense of violation underlying layoff survivor symptoms because it gets at the root cause: unhealthy dependency. When employees are clear about their value and the value of the service they provide to other parts of their organizations, dependency evaporates and is replaced with self-esteem and a sense of purpose. The "old" contract was about organizational codependence. The "new" contract is about self-reliance, services rendered, and value received.

CONCLUSIONS

The creation of internal market economies is a primary strategy both for developing dynamic organizations and creating autonomous, empowered employees. The pioneering efforts of Control Data to establish an internal market relationship between staff and line units represents an important milestone in the evolution of market economies within organizational systems.

11 Corporate Integrity and Internal Market Economies

Experiences with Armco in Latin America

Julio R. Bartol and Ali Geranmayeh

The internal market approach brings the principles of the free-market system inside what is traditionally thought of as a single indivisible firm. In an internal market system, every organizational unit is a business in its own right, having its own customers, suppliers, competitors, and responsibility for the profitability of its operations. Success or failure of the unit will depend on how well it serves its customers' needs. Such an organization is more likely to result in a dynamic, effective enterprise

Julio R. Bartol was president of Armco's Latin American Division until February 1993. **Ali Geranmayeh** is a senior partner at INTERACT and was a consultant to Armco. The authors wish to acknowledge the invaluable help of Julio Freyre in preparing this chapter.

than is a traditionally organized bureaucracy comprising numerous cost centers.

The interest in internal markets is building up so rapidly that it promises to become a new wave in the practice of management. As with other new waves in management, however, there is a tendency to apply these concepts indiscriminately to any business activity and under any set of circumstances. In particular, a danger exists that the integrity and competitiveness of the enterprise as a whole may be sacrificed if the ideas of internal markets are not implemented with prudence.

In this chapter we will draw on our experience in Armco's Latin American Division (ALAD) to recommend an approach for application of internal market concepts that avoids typical pitfalls.

BACKGROUND

Companies in Latin America face special problems in utilizing the principles of strategic planning. The environment is so volatile that any forecast of key variables affecting the enterprise is certain to be wrong. Hence, the traditional approaches to planning have all been discredited in Latin America. Consequently, most managers are resigned to a posture of "maximum flexibility," ready to react to opportunities as they arise, whatever they may be.

This kind of "drifting along" seemed rather inadequate to us in ALAD. We found the concepts of *interactive planning* as developed by Ackoff and his colleagues much more inspiring and challenging. At the time we embarked on this planning process, the division had manufacturing and marketing operations in eight countries in Latin America, and it employed about 3,600 people in its core business of steel processing and fabrication.

The basic tenet of interactive planning is to design a desirable future for the business and to invent ways to approximate it as closely as possible. Our idealized redesign for ALAD incorporated internal markets as a way to nurture responsiveness and efficiency throughout the division. In the detailed design phase of our planning, we faced the following three questions:

1. Which units should be kept within the division and converted into autonomous internal enterprises competing for both internal and external business?

2. Which units should be divested and their services obtained from external sources?

3. Which units should be kept within the division but not treated as autonomous enterprises competing freely in internal and external markets?

Our experience taught us that these questions can be answered only in the context of an overall plan and strategy. This requires a three-step process:

1. A Design for a Desirable Future. The first step is to develop an overall vision and a strategic intent for the company as a whole. In interactive planning, this vision is developed as a "design" that defines the role each part is expected to play in the system. In this way not only is a strategic intent articulated for the organization, but a design is also developed for actualizing the intent.

An important aspect of our design for ALAD was a desire to offer unique solutions to customer problems that could not be easily copied by our competitors.[1] This has important implications for our approach to internal markets that will become clear later in this chapter.

2. Critical Business Processes. This step involves identifying and developing support services and business processes that maintain the integrity of the system as a whole. These provide the infrastructure that keeps the various units of the company together. Examples of such processes include our strategic planning process, information network, performance measurement and reward systems, and hiring and training policies.

3. Requirements for the Success of the Design. Lastly, the designers must identify essential and nonessential attributes of the system:

Essential attributes are those components that contribute to the integrity and uniqueness of the system as a whole, and are central to the delivery of its mission. These are the areas that the company must excel in if it is to succeed in realizing its strategic intent.

Nonessential attributes are nonstrategic components of the system that are necessary for its proper functioning but do not contribute to its uniqueness in the markets served.

Essential attributes are unique to each system; what is an essential attribute of one system may be a nonessential one of another. In ALAD, for example, we considered *product design* (especially adaptation of products to Latin American environments) to be essential to our success. Most of our staff functions, on the other hand, were considered nonessential except for our financial unit, which we regarded as essential.

ORGANIZATIONAL UNITS IN INTERNAL MARKETS

Once this phase of planning is completed and the essential attributes are identified, it will be relatively easy to determine which units ought to participate in internal markets. Those units not providing an essential attribute of the system should be converted into business enterprises, operating freely in both the internal and external markets. Our information services unit was the first to go this route. Following soon thereafter were manufacturing, distribution, maintenance, and many functions of the human resources department.

Each unit competing in an internal market should be required to prepare a business plan. Those without a credible plan for becoming a viable business are to be divested. Those that have a convincing business plan will compete for investment capital with other units. In addition, in companies having different legal entities in different countries, such as ALAD does, it is possible to allow such units to finance their capital needs outside the corporate structure (by borrowing independently, for example) if their potential is deemed to be otherwise impeded.

As a general rule, the dominant criteria for the sourcing or selling of nonessential attributes are economic: cost, quality, reliability, and delivery. Each unit, acting as an independent buyer or seller, is free to make its own decisions. Internal suppliers and customers have an "arm's-length" commercial relationship. It does not particularly matter to the company as a whole whether the services are provided internally or externally. The impact on the rest of the units is minimal.[2]

Sourcing and selling of functions or components that make up the essential attributes of the system, on the other hand, should be based primarily on strategic criteria. Economic considerations are important but are secondary to the strategic ones. The organization as a whole simply cannot afford to have its internal suppliers of strategic components fail, nor can it sell away its strategic advantages. Therefore, a classical laissez-faire market approach to essential attributes would be imprudent. For instance, a company cannot remain indifferent to the sourcing decisions of internal units when they concern strategic components of the company's products. And it simply cannot rely on outside suppliers for development and provision of its core technologies. It is possible to secure such requirements through joint ventures with other suppliers or by contracting proprietary research, but to rely completely on independent suppliers for such technologies would not be wise.

This does not mean that internal suppliers of strategic components should operate as cost-plus units shielded from market pressures and discipline. Such an approach would only result in complacency on the part of the protected units. Rather, it means that management should play a strategic role in mediating the short-term supply and demand pressures to ensure the competitiveness of such units in the long run. This is particularly true in the case of core technologies and components where, more often than not, the organization does not find a properly functioning and efficient market. The market structure for such goods is often oligopolistic, and typically the alternative suppliers are themselves direct competitors of the parent company in the end-product market.

In summary, both essential and nonessential attributes benefit from the rigor of free markets, but different management processes are required for each. Sourcing and selling decisions for nonessential functions and components should be left to free markets with minimum intervention by upper management. Essential attributes, however, because of their strategic implications and systemic impact, require the involvement of higher management in a "managed competition" structure.

This view of the firm, developed to its logical limit, conceives a corporation as a network of organizational units: At the core of the network are the strategic units that create the essential attributes of the corporation. Transactions of these units are governed by strategic management of market mechanisms. The outlying nodes of the network constitute all other organizational units. The relationships of these outer nodes with the core, with each other, and with the external market are governed by autonomous decisions of managers operating in free markets.[3]

CRITERIA APPLIED IN ALAD

The following example from our experience in ALAD illustrates these concepts. In turbulent economies such as those in Latin America, highly developed financial management skills are an essential requirement for success. The short, violent cycles that characterize these economies, the lack of available funds even to the most creditworthy businesses, and the unpredictable fluctuations in inflation and currency values, in effect, place the finance function at the heart of any competitive strategy. In ALAD, which is dominated by engineers, we were used to thinking of technology and products as the only sources of competitive advantage. It took us over five years to appreciate the role of finance in our competitive strategy. Had we reacted earlier, we could have become even more profitable.

We have developed quite an advanced capability to use our financial expertise to enhance our overall strategy. A preliminary survey confirmed a strong external demand for such financial services. The problem we confronted was whether we should convert our finance department into an enterprise that would compete for external business. And conversely, would we allow our operating companies to obtain financial services from external sources of their choice? We answered no to both questions, despite the strong likelihood of attractive returns for a financial services business and the unlikelihood that any operating company would find better service from an outside source. What helped us in making this decision was our idealized design, and the determination that finance was a core competency for us. We did not want to enter the financial services business because it simply did not fit within the design we had created for our company, and pursuing outside sales only on an opportunistic basis would be distracting to our core businesses.

When internal markets are implemented in a company that hasn't explicitly formulated its desired future and arrived at a clear understanding of what is essential to achieving this future, many managers are tempted by the lure of short-term profits. The long-term strategic impact to the business as a whole is likely to be ignored.

Many examples illustrate this danger, but one strikes close to home: After World War II, some U.S. steel producers helped rebuild the steel industry in Europe and in Japan. They made a handsome profit for a while. But they had to trade away their technology to do so. Each U.S. company justified its action by arguing that if it had refused to sell its technology, another competitor would have provided it. They could not resist the opportunity to make an immediate impact on profits.

Shortly thereafter, the licensees invaded the United States with products made with the same technology they had bought from American firms. The result has been a continued decline of the U. S. steel industry and the initiation of import quotas to protect what was, until a few years ago, the most efficient and creative steel industry in the world.

To be sure, the decline of the U.S. steel industry involved factors other than licensing core technologies. But the sole focus on economic factors prevented these companies from properly assessing their strategic vulnerabilities when they were so eager to help put formidable competitors in business. They treated their technology as a nonessential attribute.

CONCLUSIONS

A business organization is a complex social and economic system. The job of management is to optimize the performance of the system as a whole, not its component parts. Therefore, management's challenge is to design an environment that encourages cooperation and synergy among organizational units while minimizing constraints on each unit's ability to respond to, and to serve, its customer needs.

Internal markets can meet this challenge, but they need to be applied prudently. Successful implementation of the concept requires a deep understanding of the essential and nonessential attributes of the company that the designers want to create.

Such understanding can result only from (1) articulation of a clear vision—a design—of a desirable future and a strategic intent for the company as a whole, (2) development of support services and business processes necessary to maintain the integrity of the total system, and (3) identification and development of core capabilities and the competencies that are required to realize the design.

12 Decentralizing the Canadian Imperial Bank of Commerce

The Metamorphosis of a Sleeping Giant into a Nimble Enterprise

John MacLean

In the early 1980s, the Canadian Imperial Bank of Commerce (CIBC) was, according to one observer, a "sleeping giant." Although CIBC ranked second in size among Canada's major banks, our performance lagged behind our competitors. Complacency and easy, predictable competition had lulled the bank into inertia. When deregulation of the financial services industry and fierce competition appeared, the bank's centralized, hierarchical structure rendered us too sluggish to respond swiftly and effectively to changes in the marketplace.

In 1985, a new chairman initiated CIBC's metamorphosis from a sleeping giant to a nimble, innovative enterprise by decentralizing

John MacLean was executive vice president of the Canadian Imperial Bank of Commerce until 1992. CIBC has continued to evolve since this article was written in May 1991.

decision-making power away from his office. We decided to introduce market discipline on all our organizational units to enable their quick adaptation to changes and opportunities.

We implemented this strategy by reorganizing the company into a decentralized structure of market-oriented business units. Disentangling our operations from an outmoded bureaucratic system enabled us to reshape the company into a group of streamlined, distinct, and entrepreneurial entities. We were also able to refocus on responsive customer service and sound lending practices—the fundamental values on which our organization was originally built.

This chapter describes the rationale for this change and the results of our efforts to turn a hierarchical institution into a vigorous market economy. Our transformation to a market system was not on the same scale as the upheaval within the former Soviet Union and Eastern Europe. But in banking, an industry that traditionally resisted change, our reorganization amounted to a revolution.

ORIGINS OF THE DECENTRALIZATION STRATEGY

Both Canadian and United States banks are presently being forced to change by passing through the crucible of recession. The downturn has caused major failings in loan portfolios, real estate has been battered, and business and personal bankruptcies are at record levels.

There are substantial differences between the Canadian and the U.S. banking systems. More than half of Canada's banking business is controlled by six commercial banks. Our banking system is national in scope. The United States, by comparison, has approximately 14,000 banks, giving its system a regional character.

Despite our differences, however, Canadian and U.S. banks share the same conundrum. Deregulation and globalization have led to a decline in our dominance of finance. The banking industry is experiencing the same rationalization and restructuring that has transformed the airline and steel industries.

Annual net income for U.S. banks stood at US $14.3 billion at the end of the 1980s, virtually flat when compared with net income of $13.9 billion at the start of that decade. And American banks no longer rank among the world's top 10. These spots are reserved by 8 Japanese and 2 French banks. In fact, the assets of Japan's 12 commercial banks are almost equal to the total assets of the entire U.S. banking system.

The decline of Canadian banks has been almost as severe. In 1978, four Canadian banks—including CIBC—ranked in the top 50 banks in the world by assets. In 1988, there was one. Today, not a single Canadian bank is included in this group.

While the competitive position of Canada's major banks has weakened, we are not lacking in muscle. CIBC, for example ranks fifth in North America in terms of assets and deposits. The bank has more than 48,000 employees and over 1,600 branches and offices in Canada and 23 other countries.

CIBC may be big, but we came to see that our greatest need was to use this power to achieve greater market penetration across a diverse geographic region thus strengthening the bank's competitive position. This strategic goal was in keeping with the general trend among other Canadian banks, which are also looking to diversify and expand their lines of business.

To attract a wider customer base, Canadian banks are entering less traditional businesses such as technology products, mutual funds, mortgage-backed securities, and debit cards. During the past few years, four of the five major Canadian banks, including CIBC, have acquired an investment dealer. These banks are also adding discount brokerage and home insurance to their product lines, and they are exploring opportunities in merchant banking, trusts, and life and health insurance.

But to move outward and seize these new opportunities, we also knew that we had to look inward to streamline the organization, improve efficiency, and increase profitability. We had to expand our operations, but not be encumbered by them. We needed a more entrepreneurial form of organization.

IMPLEMENTING THE NEW STRUCTURE

This decentralization strategy led to our decision in 1985 to restructure the bank. The purpose of CIBC's reorganization was to create an entrepreneurial internal market system that could keep step with changing competitive conditions and bring specialized skills and resources to bear on new and expanding opportunities.

CIBC's highly centralized structure was replaced with five relatively self-contained strategic business units (SBUs): Individual, Corporate, Investment, Administrative, and Development. Each SBU is headed by a president who is responsible for that unit's strategy, customer focus, and bottom-line results:

- The Individual Bank, the retail arm of CIBC, serves individual customers, independent businesses, and the farming community in Canada.
- The Corporate Bank serves commercial, corporate, and government clients.
- The Investment Bank is active in treasury products, foreign exchange, precious metals, and investment banking products and services.
- The Administrative Bank provides support services to the SBUs.
- In 1989, a fifth unit—CIBC Development Corporation—was created to manage CIBC's real estate holdings.

Obviously, releasing the operations of a major institution from its formerly entrenched hierarchy was not a simple task. Our goal, however, was to have the entire organization realigned by the start of our next fiscal year.

How did we determine which functions should be decentralized and which should remain centralized? We were guided by our key objective of becoming more market driven. Those parts of the bank dealing directly with customers were realigned according to our designated client groups. Other functions not directly related to sales and service— such as systems, accounting, and legal—have remained centralized. We believed this approach was more cost-effective and would also free up the business units to concentrate on their customers and increase market share. However, we also considered the possibility of decentralizing these support units after the initial change was working well.

Managing this transition turned out to be a demanding, but, nevertheless, relatively simple operation. Once the implementation plan was developed, the next step was to appoint a president to head each business unit. This sent an indisputable signal throughout CIBC. Our centralized structure was so ingrained that some people were skeptical of whether we were sincere about change. These appointments quelled any "I'll-believe-it-when-I-see-it" attitudes.

The next steps followed in rapid succession. We divided our customer base into more precisely defined groups. We examined the bricks and mortar of our organization—our physical premises—to determine how CIBC could run most efficiently. We considered the allocation of capital among the business units. And we began the recruiting and selection process for the management groups that would run the four strategic business units.

As these step-by-step changes progressed across CIBC, interest in the reorganization mushroomed. New career paths opened. Enthusiasm and morale were buoyant. Middle management and staff, who often considered themselves small cogs in a big wheel, realized they were expected to assume more responsibility and initiative.

Not everyone, however, was able to adjust to the new environment. For some people who had been with the organization for most of their working life, the changes were difficult. But the overwhelming number of employees responded wholeheartedly. Few employees could fail to notice that improved financial results were not only anticipated, they were expected.

RESULTS

How successful have we been with the new decentralized market structure? Here are some of the results. This strategy strengthened CIBC in four areas:

1. Profitability and market share.
2. Organizational flexibility.
3. Employee motivation.
4. Customer service.

First, profitability and market share: The steady improvement in CIBC's financial performance over the past few years has convinced us that the strategy was effective. Ten years ago, CIBC trailed its competitors by virtually every financial measurement. With reorganization, the bank not only caught up, in many instances it has surpassed its competitors.

In 1990, the average net income of the four other major Canadian banks decreased 8 percent. CIBC's earnings, on the other hand, increased 6 percent, for a total gain over the other banks of 14 percent.

Our market share also increased. In retail banking, CIBC controls over 20 percent of the personal deposit, residential mortgage, and Visa card market. It is also the largest private banker in the country, controlling 30 percent of the market.

Our competitive position strengthened so dramatically that most Canadian financial analysts recommend CIBC for financial institutions. In Canada, as in the United States, the opinion of financial analysts and the market value of the organization's stock are usually reliable indicators of the firm's condition.

The second area of improvement was in our organizational flexibility. Deregulation, as mentioned earlier, has brought unparalleled change to the banking industry. But at a time when some lines of our business have diminished in importance and when CIBC had to abandon others altogether, our organization was still able to achieve overall growth. Although CIBC is large, I think it has the same agility as a small company because it can get in and get out of lines of business swiftly.

For example, we readily discontinued some operations in the United States, Australia, and the United Kingdom that were not proving successful. By the same token, the new structure enabled us to enter new lines of business with equal ease. We bought a controlling interest in Wood Gundy, an investment dealer, at a time when the value of brokerage houses was relatively low. Merging a brokerage culture with a banking culture was not a painless exercise. But because we had a business unit engaged in investment banking, we were able to absorb this operation quickly.

A third area of improvement was in the performance of our employees. When decision making became decentralized to the SBUs, we began drawing more strongly on the abilities and energies of our people. Management became less paternalistic and more demanding of staff performance. We eliminated layers of management so that more decisions could be made at lower levels of the organization. Line staff have been given more flexibility in their jobs to solve customer problems quickly and efficiently.

These changes also led us to provide staff with the means to make better decisions. For example, each lending officer in the bank now has a computerized workstation. Artificial intelligence, including a technology known as automated credit-scoring, enhances the analytical skills of our lending officers—in addition to improving the quality of loans they make.

CIBC employees are also better trained than they were yesterday. Banks used to be known as "the industry that puts its least qualified people on the front line." Because the CIBC bank staff is now more involved, they are also more knowledgeable about a wider, more complex array of financial products. Since the mid-1980s, our annual training budget has doubled every year. Since approximately 20 percent of our operating expenses in retail banking had been the direct result of correcting errors made by customers and staff, anything that could be done to complete tasks correctly the first time had the potential of gradually reducing operating expenses by 20 percent.

A market system also encourages employees to be more accountable for their decisions. In our retail bank, for example, we made branch staff more responsible for their lending decisions. Loans that have to be written off are now charged directly to the branch where they were booked and not to the bank as a whole.

We improved responsibility, too, by linking pay more closely with performance. The CIBC profit-sharing plan rewards the performance of employees who meet individual and corporate targets. In 1990, well over two-thirds of CIBC employees received a payout. The fund they shared was over US $26 million.

The fourth, and perhaps most important, area of improvement has been in customer service. Until a couple of years ago, few banks were known for their service. Now every financial institution seems to be focused on providing customer care and value. Like other industries, banks are discovering that their existing customers are the most profitable ones. Estimated costs for securing new customers range between 5 to 11 times more than retaining an existing one. So it's not surprising that banks are becoming more customer driven.

CIBC's decentralization set the stage for improving service delivery by bringing us closer to the market and our customers. We conducted extensive studies to help us define our customers more precisely and to determine their requirements and expectations. The studies also identified the geographic areas meriting our involvement. And they revealed that our customers, as well as our products and services, are not equally profitable.

CONCLUSIONS

Decentralizing into a market-driven system enabled us to examine critically every element of our business and to make some important distinctions among approximately six million CIBC customers. I am not suggesting that decentralization resolved all our problems. We didn't think for a moment that our new structure was perfect.

A major challenge has been that this type of structure demands a new culture to replace the one that developed over many years. Although decentralization rallied some 48,000 employees to become more performance oriented and we put programs in place to reward that performance, it will probably take another five years to change the bank's culture completely. It is a great challenge to change an entire organization's culture.

Another challenge is that we encouraged the SBUs to operate as independent, self-standing businesses. Each has its own unique priorities. In some cases, that has meant creating separate information technology, human resources, marketing areas, and other support staffs. Some duplication has been necessary, and operating costs for CIBC as a whole have risen. CIBC spends more, on a percentage basis, than its competitors, so it is working vigorously to bring expenses in line with industry averages.

Prior to CIBC's decentralization, we had a core support group performing various human resource functions. Five years later, the number swelled to three times the size, too high even for an organization as large as CIBC. As we anticipated, the company is now in the process of reorganizing this function to a more appropriate level. It seems likely that we could gain better control over these staff units by including them in the market system as well.

Another challenge stems from our success at focusing each of the SBUs on their bottom line. For an organization as diverse as CIBC, it is unrealistic to expect all the business units to move in lockstep on all issues. They sometimes push in inconsistent directions, which is unavoidable and natural. But while CIBC needs to maintain its diversity, it can't overlook the common purpose. The bank is now examining areas it feels it is too narrowly focused. Through a little redirection, CIBC wants to achieve its specific goals while contributing to the good of the larger corporation.

So decentralization has not been perfect. But the advantages outweigh the disadvantages. CIBC continues to adapt and adjust its systems to meet these diverse needs. The bank, for example, is finding that although the SBUs offer different products and services, they often deal with the same market segments. CIBC's Individual Bank, Investment Bank, and Corporate Bank are all active in the upscale market, with each having specific products and services for this group. What CIBC should do eventually is set up sales units that would combine the delivery of these products in a more integrated and cohesive way. These units might form the equivalent of internal distributorships. They would help to serve customers without running into the internal impediments and demarcations of SBU boundaries. The boundaries would still be there but they would be more transparent.

The nature of the new organization allows CIBC to make these kinds of modifications easily and quickly. It doesn't require a major reorganization. Similarly, the structure permits keeping up with shifting competitive conditions and changing business opportunities. The marketplace will always move faster than organizations, but CIBC is in a position to continue to evolve.

Another key variable is the way in which technology is radically altering the banking industry. Electronic transactions are expected to grow at a compound rate of 40 percent each year. Cash and currency will be replaced with cash information stored on plastic cards. Products and services will multiply so rapidly that they will exceed the current support capabilities of banks. In short, banking will change more dramatically during this decade than it has in the past 50 years. The criterion for success will be a flexible organizational infrastructure. CIBC's decentralized market system is perfect for this.

New opportunities are also unfolding because of the reregulation of financial services in Canada. The new structure provides the framework for CIBC to enter new lines of business swiftly and smoothly. In addition, CIBC may want to increase its presence in the United States. It now has the framework to integrate an acquisition into its distribution network easily.

One of the key lessons bankers have learned during the past decade is that long-term planning is becoming an impossible and impractical exercise. Events such as Black Monday, the Canada–U.S. Free Trade Agreement, Europe 1992, and Hong Kong 1997 require that we constantly reevaluate our position in various markets and adapt our organizational structure accordingly.

It's been said that the problem with strategic planning is that it's too much like a ritual rain dance. It has no effect on the weather, but it makes the dancers feel in control. Unfortunately, when planning is too long-term, the dancing improves, but not the weather.

The new organizational structure at CIBC, however, acts as an umbrella, shielding us against the unforeseen, the unanticipated, and the unplanned. CIBC bears little resemblance to the organization it was 10 years ago. It will continue to evolve. CIBC's decentralized structure will permit adapting delivery and business lines to provide products and services that meet the needs of our customers.

Ten years ago, the chairman dominated CIBC. Back then, the bank's critical endeavors were handled by his office. The same individual who called CIBC a sleeping giant in the early 1980s also said, "The title of chairman and chief executive officer [at CIBC] is the only title that matters." Today, the bank is dramatically different. CIBC's chairman would be the first to acknowledge that the bank's employees and customers matter most because, in the new internal market system, they determine CIBC's success.

13

How Independent Subsidiaries Tried to Jump-Start Blue Cross/Blue Shield

Benefits and Problems of an Internal Market Strategy

Joseph Gamble, Michael Sheehan, and Seton Shields

Group Hospitalization and Medical Services, Inc. (GHMSI), is the corporate name of the Blue Cross and Blue Shield Plan serving the Washington, DC, metropolitan area. During its 40-year history, GHMSI was a small, regional insurance company providing health insurance to groups and individuals. Health insurance was an accepted employee benefit at most of our client organizations, usually chosen by the personnel manager from among HMOs or an indemnity plan such as Blue Cross/Blue

Joseph Gamble was CEO of Group Hospitalization and Medical Services, Inc. (GHMSI), the parent of the Blue Cross/Blue Shield Plan in the Washington, DC, area during the time of this reorganization. **Michael Sheehan** is the GHMSI corporate planning officer, and **Seton Shields** is president of Health Management Strategies, Inc., one of the subsidiaries of GHMSI.

Shield. We had a narrow product line, low premiums, and limited profit potential.

In the early 1980s, we adopted an internal market strategy that transformed our small, placid insurance company into a diversified, entrepreneurial, international corporation that showed great potential for continued robust growth. However, we did not contain the creative energy that was released by this strategy in a sufficiently careful manner, allowing temporary but serious losses to threaten the company's survival. This chapter describes how we developed and implemented this strategy, focusing on the benefits and problems that resulted. We also offer some suggestions that may help others who choose to follow this difficult but promising path.

THE INTERNAL MARKET STRATEGY

During the early 1980s, the health care industry was racked by a complex new economic environment that traditional health insurance companies were ill equipped to handle. The number and type of benefit plans multiplied, new competitors entered the market, the price of health insurance rose so rapidly that decisions moved from the client's personnel department to higher levels, including the CEO, and there was increasing scrutiny by state insurance departments and legislatures.

We soon realized that GHMSI had to change quickly. The primary problem was that the firm was almost totally dependent on the cyclical performance that characterized its largest division, Blue Cross and Blue Shield of the National Capital Area (BCBSNCA). We were also concerned because BCBSNCA's overall performance trend was steadily eroding as the entire health insurance industry entered a crisis. Costs were rising even as political pressures were demanding lower premiums. The problem was especially severe for us because BCBS plans are committed to remaining the insurer of last resort, and so BCBSNCA was being left with the high-risk policies other companies would not take. To make matters worse, BCBSNCA was a traditional, bureaucratic organization, unable to adjust to the great upheaval in medical care that lay ahead.

After considerable study and thought, it became clear that we needed to inject a healthy dose of invigorating enterprise into this lumbering old corporate body to help it meet the challenges of today's revolution in medicine. Corporate management decided to create an entrepreneurial system that could spin off large numbers of independent subsidiaries to serve the vast range of new needs that were emerging in health care. In short, we chose to pursue an internal market strategy to jump-start the company. This strategy consisted of the following three initiatives:

1. Revamp the entire organization of our main division, BCB-SNCA, by improving its flexibility and effectiveness, in order to introduce the many new product variations that the marketplace was demanding.
2. Form independent subsidiaries to expand the product and market capabilities of GHMSI both within and outside the local area. (BCBSNCA was only allowed to offer products within Washington, DC, two Maryland counties, and part of northern Virginia.)
3. Establish an international division to introduce new products for various overseas markets.

BENEFITS OF THE REORGANIZATION

All these initiatives were implemented in about a three- to four-year period. This would be a tremendous amount of change for any company, but for a traditional, bureaucratic company like ours, it was a massive and somewhat traumatic reorganization.

GHMSI's primary goal in setting up subsidiaries was to quickly build sales and market share in a variety of business areas in order to become less dependent on BCBSNCA and to be able to survive in a complex, turbulent economic environment. The rapid growth of subsidiaries was impressive. Their collective revenue went from $20 million in 1986 to more than $350 million in 1991, increasing the proportion of GHMSI's revenue generated by subsidiaries from 3 percent in 1986 to 22 percent in 1991 (see Figure 13–1).

There were eight divisions within GHMSI, including BCBSNCA, which collectively operated a total of 35 individual subsidiaries. Figure 13–2 shows some of the more prominent subsidiaries.

Some of our divisions established enviable positions in their fields. The Assistance Division was the market leader in credit card protection programs and one of the leading marketers of travel insurance. Health

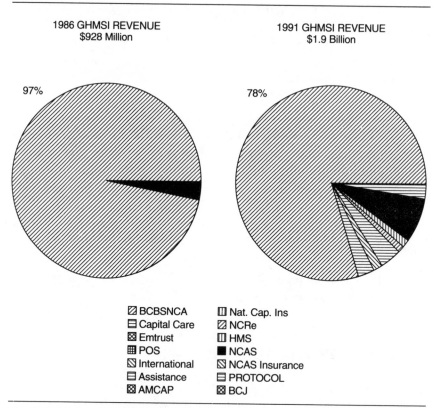

1986 GHMSI REVENUE
$928 Million

1991 GHMSI REVENUE
$1.9 Billion

97%

78%

☑ BCBSNCA   ▥ Nat. Cap. Ins
🮑 Capital Care   ☒ NCRe
⊠ Emtrust   ▥ HMS
⊞ POS   ■ NCAS
🮖 International   🮖 NCAS Insurance
🮑 Assistance   🮑 PROTOCOL
⊠ AMCAP   ⊠ BCJ

FIGURE 13–1.   GHMSI revenue growth.

Management Strategies was one of the top three utilization review companies in the country. The International Division was a major player
in providing foreign insurance companies with out-of-country coverage
in more than 50 countries. GHMSI had offices in France, Ireland,
Canada, Singapore, Australia, Virgin Islands, and Jamaica.

While the subsidiaries were growing so vigorously, however,
BCBSNCA's performance was only fair in terms of revenue, and the
number of people covered by contracts continued to decline each year.
Thus corporate management's decision to diversify into independent
subsidiaries was proven correct since GHMSI became less dependent
on the cyclical ups and downs of its main division, and solid growth was
started in promising new areas.

A beneficial effect of the reorganization was that the subsidiaries
interjected a vital new entrepreneurial spirit into GHMSI which was

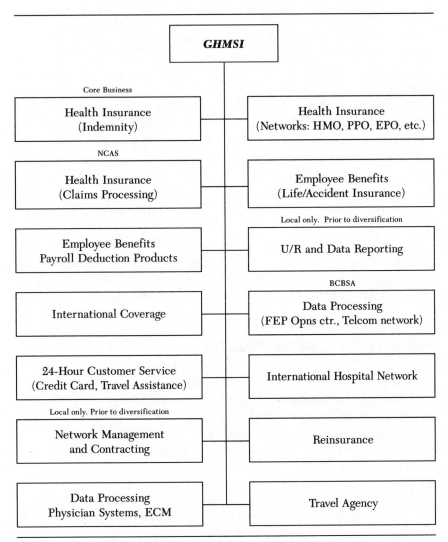

FIGURE 13–2.   Product diversification.

starting to change BCBSNCA as well. Subsidiaries forced BCBSNCA to improve bureaucratic staff services and management systems; they encouraged taking risks and reacting more quickly to market changes; and they even introduced new people and new ideas that were slowly improving BCBSNCA's openness to new ideas and change.

For instance, there were early signs that BCBSNCA was going through an organizational change process intended to reorient its support departments toward serving "internal customers" in a more responsive manner. Resentment arose when BCBSNCA managers first realized that the subsidiaries were free to go elsewhere for support services. Some staff departments soon recognized the need to become more responsive to these internal client groups, especially since the subsidiaries continued to reinforce this need by exercising their option to use or not use BCBSNCA's services. But this process was still in its initial stages of development, and there was a long way to go before the idea that staff departments should serve internal customers could became accepted as the normal way to conduct business at GHMSI.

BCBSNCA was also trying to become a more flexible organization that was responsive to changes in its markets. This can be attributed at least partly to the example set by subsidiaries as they were visibly seen operating in a new entrepreneurial mode. They moved in and out of markets and implemented various products and systems in a fraction of the time that BCBSNCA once did, so a new dynamic standard of entrepreneurial action was established within GHMSI.

PROBLEMS OF THE REORGANIZATION

These benefits were not gained easily, however, as we struggled with several formidable problems. The major strategic issue faced in this reorganization was that the introduction of subsidiaries radically changed the corporate culture by challenging the existing structures and policies of the entire corporation. Time and time again, corporate management was forced to deal with problems caused by the subsidiaries' independence.

For example, subsidiaries were running into conflicts with each other in the marketplace as they submitted competing bids for the same projects, which confused our customers and divided our efforts. Also, the independence enjoyed by subsidiaries created legal risks for the parent corporation, particularly in critical areas such as corporate reports and legal regulations. In addition, there was a new need to establish equitable transfer prices; we often wondered about the duplication of some resources; and there was an acute need for coordinating financial/regulatory reports for multiple organizations.

All these concerns led to the unavoidable challenge of designing corporatewide systems that encouraged cooperative behavior to benefit the entire company, without stifling the entrepreneurial spirit that helped the subsidiaries grow so quickly. Corporate management, working with operating units, introduced policies for financial reporting, strategic planning, operating procedures, and compensation to create a new corporate structure that could coordinate the activities of a large number of autonomous internal enterprises:

1. A standard monthly financial reporting system for all units in the corporation.
2. A series of status meetings for all division heads held on a bimonthly basis.
3. A common planning process that included the exchange and discussion of each division's business plan.
4. Quarterly board meetings for each subsidiary with the boards consisting either entirely or primarily of senior GHMSI officers.
5. The addition of two GHMSI vice presidents who coordinated marketing and network development at the corporate level, in addition to our existing Corporate Planning and Internal Audit staff.
6. An enterprise compensation program based on both corporate and individual results.

We also learned that the systems we put in place often had an unintended effect on the behavior of various subsidiaries, and conversely, that decisions made at the subsidiary level often had unanticipated effects at the corporate level. This led us to examine our policies from a systems perspective. Although these changes helped contain the turmoil raised by the internal market structure, it was very hard to retain the entrepreneurial behavior of market-driven subsidiaries while creating an advantageous synergy among them that would benefit the parent corporation.

The most damaging problem, however, was that starting up all these subsidiaries was costly, particularly since several troublesome ventures resulted in significant losses. Many subsidiaries did become profitable, and we expected their contribution to the total profit performance of the parent company would equal or surpass that of BCBSNCA in a few years. But the unfortunate combination of a major economic recession and growing losses in our main division did not allow the time needed to fully develop these subsidiaries.

Learning how to handle the risk of start-ups was especially difficult because GHMSI had no experience in starting new ventures. The problem was also allowed to grow because our primary goal was to generate new sources of revenue, perhaps without sufficient regard for ensuring that this was profitable growth. We did move firmly to require all units to become self-supporting, and we began to cut losses if the potential for a start-up no longer looked promising. In hindsight, these decisions were probably implemented later than prudence would have suggested. However, these were tactical problems in implementing the internal market structure; the basic strategy was sound.

AN EXAMPLE OF THE NEW SUBSIDIARIES

Ms. Seton Shields, a long-time Blue Cross employee, was chosen to start up one of the subsidiaries, Health Management Strategies, Inc. (HMS), which was formed to provide utilization management and cost containment services to Blue Cross and other clients. The following personal account by Ms. Shields describes the founding of HMS, which serves as a good example of the challenges presented in moving to the new internal market structure.

Example _____

HEALTH MANAGEMENT STRATEGIES, INC. (HMS)

During the mid-1980s, a number of companies began providing solutions to the increasing costs of health care, including second medical opinions, review of hospital charges and length of stay, and so on. Blue Cross performed many of these functions on its own operations internally; however, it seemed to me and other GHMSI managers that customers preferred an outside company to "audit" their insurance company. I was asked to launch HMS into this promising new market in cost containment/review services.

HMS started slowly as I and a few other employees spent several months developing a business plan. After corporate management reviewed and approved the plan, we rented office space in a separate building and began to build our staff. HMS proved successful in serving Blue Cross accounts, but the market for independent utilization review firms was much harder to penetrate than we had originally envisioned. HMS, by now a company with 15 employees, struggled to find a product that could be sold outside of Blue Cross at a profit.

We finally identified mental health as an area that offered significant opportunities since it was the fastest growing element of medical costs and only a few companies were involved in the field. HMS moved aggressively into mental health review, developing proprietary standards and demonstrating a capability to reduce costs while delivering high-quality service.

Our first market was other Blue Cross and Blue Shield Plans. They usually had their own internal cost containment firms or functions, but they had no experience in mental health. Blue Cross Plans signed up with us in large numbers very quickly, which began to build into a very attractive and profitable niche market. By 1987, HMS had expanded its operations into 10 states.

Once HMS had established itself as a legitimate player in the mental health review market, our management team began to look for ways to build on this success. We became aware that CHAMPUS, the Defense Department's civilian health insurance program, was seeking bids on their mental health review contract. CHAMPUS is one of the largest contractors in the United States with approximately six million beneficiaries nationwide. After a careful review, HMS management spent almost a year putting the proposal together, and in 1989, we won the contract.

Overnight, HMS went from being a company with $4 million in revenue and 80 employees to one with more than $18 million and 230 employees. We successfully implemented the program, and CHAMPUS renewed the contract for 1991 and 1992. Recently, we developed a major new product in this area—a managed mental health network—that should position HMS to compete more effectively on CHAMPUS contracts and other related work.

HMS faced a number of difficulties in achieving its current success that illustrate the strategic issues GHMSI noted in developing an internal market economy.

The first problem was the shift from a large, safe, home organization to a small, independent, highly volatile firm with few of the support mechanisms that BCBSNCA provided. We decided to move away from BCBSNCA and set up our own offices in another part of the city as did most of the subsidiaries. This was one of the most visible signs that the subsidiaries were independent entities. The separation allowed each subsidiary to establish its own culture but also caused resentment and mistrust within the parent company.

One of the most difficult problems was that, in an internal market system, HMS functioned as both a vendor and customer to BCBSNCA. As a vendor to BCBSNCA, we were faced with the attitude that their internal staff could do the job better than HMS. On the customer side, BCBSNCA staff departments were not used to meeting our requirements as a client. Naturally, they seemed intent on providing the services their way and on their schedule, and they were not particularly interested in trying to change to meet the needs of a smaller organization that had to react quickly. Many of the subsidiaries, including ours, decided not to use all BCBSNCA support services, and this in turn caused additional animosity between BCBSNCA and the subsidiaries.

Another significant problem was the issue of transfer pricing. HMS was required to price their services to Blue Cross at cost because this was required by federal purchasing guidelines and because it has been traditionally done this way at BCBSNCA. There have been constant battles between BCBSNCA and HMS over what these costs really amount to, and BCBSNCA has made various attempts to take over certain functions in the belief that it could do the job cheaper. This argument is confused somewhat because the cost accounting system of BCBSNCA does not allocate all costs to the appropriate product line, so the actual costs for the organization would be significantly higher if all overhead were allocated.

This tension between BCBSNCA and HMS had to be continuously managed, and I spent a great deal of my time at Blue Cross trying to mediate between HMS staff and the BCBSNCA staff. Although the problem has improved to some extent, the difficulties have not yet been resolved.

Another challenge that HMS had to deal with was managing its explosive growth. Many employees put their personal lives on hold and worked around the clock to put together the CHAMPUS bid and the subsequent move to our new offices. It was not unusual to see many staff members working nights, holidays, and weekends to move the program forward. Some women were so dedicated that they came back to work on parts of the CHAMPUS proposal within days of having children. Many times, I walked into the conference room to find a group of my people working late at night with their children and spouses at the other end of the room. Often, babies would be sleeping on the conference table.

This problem affected many of us personally, but it also illustrates one of the advantages of an internal market structure. Such dedication is priceless and not often found in large companies, yet it seems to be common among small internal enterprises like ours.

CONCLUSIONS AND SUGGESTIONS

There is little question that independent subsidiaries were highly successful in transforming our company into a dramatically different enterprise system that produced new revenue sources and business opportunities. GHMSI management's decision to implement an internal market system quickly drove a radical change that was apparent to all as the rapid growth of a diverse range of independent subsidiaries inspired a strikingly new entrepreneurial spirit that could cut through the old bureaucracy and decision layers. In retrospect, the idea seems an intuitively reasonable way to develop a dynamic organization that can enter exploding market opportunities quickly and effectively.

The internal market concept made so much sense that we contemplated other applications, such as the development of marketing units that would handle the full line of GHMSI products in particular regions. This would have the effect of setting up "internal distributors," operating as profit centers, which could provide our clients with one-stop service.

The major drawback to the internal market strategy was that the problem of integrating a host of independent entrepreneurs into a coherent, working whole was not fully anticipated so it did not get the attention it deserved until problems became evident. There is a very fine line between allowing individuals the freedom to build their business and respond to market changes, and also maintaining enough central control to avoid internal conflicts and exposing the parent company to regulatory/legal problems.

It is necessary to design and build an appropriate corporate infrastructure to contain this entrepreneurial turbulence, but the problem involves more than having the right management systems, communication channels, planning reviews, and other technical features. The old GHMSI culture that managed BCBSNCA in a stable, mechanistic mode was such a powerful force during the firm's past history that it continued to live on as a deeply ingrained way of thought hindering our collective response to the difficult new issues that were raised by the internal market system.

A more basic solution to the difficulty of getting various units to work together involves learning how to live in a dramatically different corporate environment that requires people to cooperate and compete with one another at the same time. There does not seem to be a way to avoid this new reality of the business world, so it is important to help managers and employees adjust to this new ethic. Training programs are useful, as well as organizational development programs in which personal issues can be explored to develop more appropriate forms of behavior. Competition is a fact of life, and we think it is possible to handle it constructively without hindering our ability to work together as a corporate community.

Another needed shift in the corporate culture involves redefining the working relationship between operating units and corporate management. Although the natural inclination of subsidiaries toward entrepreneurial action is wonderful, they also tend to avoid fully accepting their responsibilities to other units and to the general health of the corporation. Thus, top management found itself in the difficult position of struggling alone to figure out what was going wrong, to devise clever solutions, and then to implement them, sometimes over the opposition of subsidiary managers.

Accurate, tight accountability is required in which subsidiaries operate as independent financial entities with their own profit and loss statements and balance sheets, but more than this is needed. Corporate management has to make a critical shift from its present role of monitoring and controlling operating units, which simply reinforces their dependence. A redefinition of roles is needed in which operating managers accept responsibility for their own performance, which would then allow corporate executives to serve more as internal consultants helping managers find their own solutions.

The difficulty we experienced in controlling some of our more serious financial losses produced a backlash within parts of the company and from external constituencies, so GHMSI came under pressure to move back toward a more tightly controlled system. This is understandable, and it highlights the need to channel the raw energy released by a market system more carefully.

These financial losses were seriously aggravated by the economic downturn of 1991–1992 that affected other Blue Cross and Blue Shield Plans in New York State, New Jersey, West Virginia, New Hampshire, Vermont, Maryland, and other regions of the nation.[1] As a result of this economic decline, GHMSI suffered losses in its real estate holdings and in our major division, BCBSNCA—the very scenario we had long feared. The resulting financial crisis then forced us to explore various ways to obtain financial support. At the time of this writing, we have been selling some of our less attractive divisions and considering a possible merger with another Blue Cross/Blue Shield organization.

Looking back on our implementation of the internal market strategy, we can now see that we could have managed these problems better if we had the benefits of the learning experiences reported here, but that is always true of hindsight. Our hope is that others can now gain these benefits more easily by virtue of this chapter. The unfortunate timing of the 1991–1992 recession also magnified our tactical errors. In a more robust economy, most losses would have soon converted to profitable ventures.

However, the main lesson of this experience is the need to balance entrepreneurship with strong accountability measures. Both are necessary. If GHMSI had not taken the difficult step of moving toward an internal market system, we would now be nursing a tired, bureaucratic insurance company into old age, as the recent losses of BCBSNCA make manifestly clear. The internal market strategy did transform GHMSI into a dynamic global enterprise with new opportunities that were only limited by our collective abilities and vision, but the transition was made without adequate preparation and controls, so we suffered the opposite fate—excessive conflict, losses from new ventures, and other challenges we had not yet learned to manage very well.

The unavoidable challenge facing all business today is to ensure that organizational structures are solidly based on the two main foundations of any sound economic system—entrepreneurial freedom and accountability for performance. Since these are the features which Halal and Ackoff stress as comprising the twin benefits of an internal market economy, the key to implementing this concept is balance. Risk and responsibility are simply the two inevitable sides of creative enterprise, and for better or for worse, our experience has convinced us that the future can only be managed as a creative enterprise.

14 Creating Customer-Focused Research and Development

A Plan for Esso Petroleum Canada

John Charlton

Our experience with internal markets at Esso Petroleum differs from other contributions in this volume in that ours is mostly a report on "work-in-progress." So I cannot provide a testimonial of the success of this concept nor a postmortem on its failure, but rather will present an

John Charlton is a manager of strategic planning at Esso Petroleum of Canada (EPC). The author wishes to acknowledge the invaluable help of Ali Geranmayeh in preparing this chapter. Bill Innes, president, and Clarke Henry, director of research, sponsored the internal market project at EPC. Research managers Len Carey and George Cranton helped design and implement the project in the R&D unit. Russell Ackoff, Ali Geranmayeh, and John Pourdehnad of INTERACT helped us with the conceptual development and the overall transformation of our parent corporation, Imperial Oil Limited.

interim report on our attempts to experiment with a promising new concept that could be of long-term value to our corporation.

This chapter describes the background of our company, why we are attracted to the concept of an internal market economy, and how we have gone about implementing the concept in a pilot project with our research and development (R&D) organization. I will then summarize where we are today, and what outcomes we expect.

BACKGROUND

Esso Petroleum Canada (EPC) constitutes what is known in the oil business as the "downstream" division of Imperial Oil Limited (IOL). That is, EPC is concerned with the refining, distribution, and marketing of petroleum products. Our parent corporation, IOL, is a Canadian company with majority ownership by Exxon Corporation. IOL has been in business for 110 years and has been among the most successful companies in Canada.

Ironically, this very history of success has presented a formidable challenge to implementing new concepts such as the internal market economy. Our history of success fights against the recognition of the need for change and the urgency with which it has to come about. After all, we had been successful by doing things in a certain way for a hundred years!

In 1989, Imperial Oil Limited made a major acquisition of Texaco Canada roughly increasing the size of our company by 40 percent. Part of the merger process was to look for the "best practices" that might be available for our use in the new merged entity. This global search involved not only practices in Canada and the United States, but also in other countries around the world. The search for a strategic planning methodology led us to Russell Ackoff and his colleagues at INTERACT, who introduced us to the concept of an internal market economy.

WHY AN INTERNAL MARKET?

Our reasons for becoming excited about the idea of an internal market were numerous. First, although the concept was new to us, it was consistent with other initiatives that we had undertaken. In particular, it was highly supportive of our decision to provide more autonomy to our profit centers, and to push decision making lower in the organization. Second, we were interested in understanding what parts of the business were contributing to our success and what parts needed further improvement, which was by no means clear to us. But what really sold us on the concept was its fit with our strategic initiatives defined in the idealized design of our division.[1] The most important of these initiatives were customer orientation, decentralization, effective resource allocation, and individual responsibility and contribution. I will discuss each of these in detail.

Customer Orientation

The cornerstone of our strategic direction was market responsiveness. We wanted a greater customer orientation because we realized that the world has changed, and customers have a greater choice of suppliers. We can no longer expect them to take our products simply because *we* believe that they are the best available. We must find out what *customers* want and deliver it to them. We have to be very finely tuned to the voice of the market. This is not a simple task for a business that has been traditionally supply driven.

What is true for external customers is equally true of internal customers. The internal market economy takes the imperative of "customer focus" one step further and internalizes it throughout the company. In effect, it is a mechanism for forcing internal suppliers of goods and services to listen to their customers and to give them what they expect to receive at a competitive price. We felt from that point of view it would create a discipline of becoming more customer oriented.

Decentralization

Our senior management believed that the degree of vertical integration in our company had become excessive over the years. Such integration attracts more staff people and requires more intervention on the part of senior management in the day-to-day activities of the business. As Miles and Snow point out (Chapter 4), you reach a point where the coordination efforts necessary to manage such an integrated business exceed the benefits of vertical integration. We felt we were at that point.

In addition, the growth of staff forces management to periodically pare down the "head count" to control spiraling costs. Such measures have a large negative impact on morale, so we were looking for a system that would automatically regulate the size and scale of our internal operations.

The internal market economy takes many fundamental decisions—evaluation of cost-competitiveness, affordability, and make-or-buy decisions—from the support staff and diffuses them out to the line. Such decisions flow down to where the rubber hits the road, causing managers of these divisions to continuously evaluate and improve their operations.

Allocation of Resources

We were also concerned about the optimum use of our resources, especially the use of capital. It was unclear which cost centers across the company were yielding an adequate return on investment. Should we invest more or less in each of them? Should we divest any of them? Our traditional measures looked only at cost. But costs do not necessarily reflect the value of products and services produced. Profitability looks at both sides of the equation and is a uniform and unambiguous measurement system. The internal market makes profit the key focus for each unit, and the main yardstick for comparison.

Individual Responsibility and Contribution

A common theme of corporate reorganization these days is "commitment and accountability." We want every member of our company to know how he or she can make the company more successful, and we want each person to act on that knowledge. The profit orientation of the internal market facilitates this by providing alignment with the company's goal and permitting measurement of the impact of each unit's performance on the bottom line. This measurement can and should be extended down through the corporation low enough for individuals to understand their own contribution.

IMPLEMENTATION

Being a successful company, we did not need to introduce a major change all at once. We were implementing the concept for its long-term benefits and were willing to invest some time in doing it right.* We developed a six-step process of implementation:

1. Evaluate the experiences of other companies who had tried various versions of the internal market concept.
2. Develop appropriate criteria for selecting a candidate pilot unit within our company.
3. Plan implementation of the project in conjunction with the members of the pilot unit. We did this in the belief that commitment is needed about issues that affect people, and you get that commitment through participation. The understanding must be shared, and the processes designed to fit the work unit.
4. Implement the plan at the pilot unit.
5. Assess the experience and the modify the plans accordingly.
6. Finally, make a decision about moving this concept out into other units of the corporation.

We learned a great deal from the experiences of other companies. We visited many companies and conducted interviews with many people, including some whose stories also appear in this volume.

We came to a few key conclusions quickly that made us feel a little bolder. The first was that an internal market was a viable concept. The basic idea had proven sound and robust in practice. A number of companies had put it into practice and had achieved success. Also, the benefits we were seeking were realistic. We found out, however, that there was no single design that fit every corporation. Each company had its own variation.

Our second conclusion was that we had to plan the transition carefully. All the unsuccessful cases suffered from hasty execution. The lack of preparation resulted in chaos and inefficiency because people were confused about what was expected of them, and they didn't have the competence to execute their new roles and responsibilities. Fear, insecurity, and incompetence defeated the new system.

---

* *Editor's Note:* In retrospect, this sentiment proved to be too optimistic. IOL reported a quarterly loss for the first time in its history in fiscal year 1992. The company went through major and painful downsizing programs throughout 1992 resulting in a reduction of about 30 percent in the work force.

The third conclusion was that there is nothing worse than treating this change merely as an accounting issue. This is not a numbers game, it is a completely different way of operating. Different accounting systems are required, but that is only a small part of it. You are really after a change in mind-set, and so you should try to educate people about the impact of these changes, not buffer them from it.

Fourth, even if the concept is implemented correctly, the consequences may be difficult to accept in some corporate cultures. Initially, there will be many demands on management time. Units will challenge the status quo to do things differently. There will be a flurry of activity for a while as people stretch the system to find out what they can and cannot do. They will test the managers' commitment to the idea by confronting them with every conceivable difficulty all at once. There will be a number of people in the organization who won't fit in this operating mode. The old culture will resist it. The attrition rate may well go up. There will be a natural process of adjustment during which some individuals adapt and others leave. The new employees will be those who feel more comfortable executing this kind of role. This is a major change of culture.

CRITERIA FOR SELECTION OF A PILOT UNIT

Although our research had prepared us for what we were getting into, we wanted to experiment with the concept ourselves to test the impact in our own environment. We established some criteria to select a part of our company where we could try it out.

The pilot would be one of the internal service units, primarily because of their large size and cost of operation. We wanted a significant size so that the results would be meaningful and the learnings would be transferable to other service groups. We looked for a unit that had a reasonable degree of complexity in its operations with significant interactions with other units in the company. It had to have marketable products and services, and sufficient spare capacity to sell externally. If possible, the unit was to be physically separate so we could introduce a new culture independent of the influence of the old. As we wanted to work out the problems of implementation, we sought a place where the immediate impact on the business results would be low. Lastly, and most importantly, we wanted people who were willing to do this.

We had about five or six potential candidates including engineering, information systems, research, controllers, and human resources. Research satisfied all the criteria, especially the willingness to embrace change.

RESEARCH AND DEVELOPMENT AS THE PILOT CASE

We have had a very successful research operation in Sarnia, Ontario, for 67 years with an impressive record of achievement. Many of our competitors license processes that were developed by this research unit. Despite this long history of success, however, the future of our R&D organization was far from certain. The petroleum business today is perceived as mature to slowly declining. This perception drives the industry to try and operate at the lowest possible cost. Research budgets are under increasing scrutiny as a discretionary expenditure that can be reduced to improve cost competitiveness. This tendency is exacerbated because R&D's value has been difficult to quantify.

The internal market economy offered R&D the opportunity to represent their contribution to the success of the company more explicitly. They would be able to demonstrate that they were making a solid financial contribution. Also, the chance to sell services outside the company constituted a potential growth opportunity in an industry that was flat. So Research had a genuine interest in the concept. The people in the R&D organization were quite willing to undertake the experiment and work with us to make it a success.

As we began to work with Research on an implementation plan, four elements emerged based on the experiences of other companies. First, we had to work with the people in the organization to create a shared vision of what it would be like to operate in an internal market economy. This was done by redesigning the entire unit to operate in the new mode. Detailed business plans were drawn up for each of the units with specific performance targets and essential activities required for success. This process provided answers to the key questions on people's minds: what does it mean to have an internal market economy? What do we do differently? What are the expected outcomes? And what are the expectations from us?

Second, we involved our training department to address skill shortfalls, particularly in the area of business literacy. Third, we set up an operating framework for the internal market economy that included establishing formal contracts for all services so as to create a clear understanding of what would be expected to be done for what price between the suppliers of services and their customers. We created timely reporting of results so there was quick feedback on performance. We also bridged the internal market system to the corporate accounting system, although we had underestimated the level of effort involved. Fourth, we encouraged bottom-line results by providing recognition and reward for people when they did the right things.

We are now in the middle of all this change, finishing the business plans, developing the training, and still working with people in Research very closely. I will explicitly state our expectations because it is important to keep in mind what you want at the end of the road. If the results turn out better than expected, you will be pleasantly surprised; and if they are worse, you will notice in time to work on improving them.

Our Research Department should continue to provide top-quality research predominantly to its existing clients: Esso Petroleum, Exxon, and other affiliated companies. The growth of external business will augment our internal requirements and allow us both to support existing investments and to make future investments more attractive by leveraging a larger shared base. It will also ensure that our research is cost competitive because we will be continuously offering services to outside customers. Internal customers should become more discriminating; research programs should be more sharply focused on value-driven activities; projects should become more clearly defined; and administration should be reduced. These are the expected results. The researchers expect their contribution to the success of the company to become more explicit and to have opportunities for growth in a nongrowth industry. Finally, we are trying to execute this pilot in such a way that we can transfer all that we learn to the other business units.

CONCLUSIONS

I will conclude this chapter by responding to some of the concerns that often appear when the concept of an internal market economy is discussed for the first time.

There is a common perception that an internal market economy will decrease cooperation among business units, causing the organization to degenerate into an aggregation of people who do everything solely on the basis of their own interests.

This perception is based on two assumptions that, to quote Russell Ackoff, are *"completely false."* The first false assumption is that cooperation exists in your organization today. If you look around, you may find that cooperation is really minimal in many functionally oriented companies. Functions are rewarded for functional excellence as opposed to their contribution to the goals of the larger organization. As a result, each unit is a fiefdom in its own right. This is a serious problem today when many of the challenges facing major organizations involve inter-functional issues requiring alignment with the company mission.

The second false assumption is that a commercial relationship is not a cooperative venture but a win–lose proposition. This is a limited and outdated perception of what selling and buying is all about. Most professionals who are involved in marketing and selling today know that successful selling has become a win–win venture. It is common for both parties to have considerable choice in whom they sell to and whom they buy from. Any party trying to take advantage of the other will find itself without a contract. Win–lose relationships thrive in situations of unequal power (monopolistic internal suppliers). By breaking up monopolistic situations, internal markets can result in better cooperation not worse.

Another common theme regards profit as having an intrinsic short-term orientation. Profit is only a measurement of some attribute of a system. A person can choose to take this measurement at every instant, or at longer intervals. An organization may choose to measure the performance of the system by averaging the profits over an extended period, use rolling averages, or use projections of expected future profits. In and of itself, profit as a measure does not have any intrinsic property of time, short term or long term. You decide how to use it for your purposes. Therefore if your organization is afflicted with short-term thinking today, it will continue that way in an internal market economy. And if it has long-term thinking, the internal market economy will not change that at all. Whether you have a few people at the top of the organization thinking short term and driving the whole company that way, or you have a hundred people in different parts of the organization thinking short term, you are likely to be equally dissatisfied. You should not look at an internal market economy as a solution to short- or long-term thinking. It doesn't address that issue.

Furthermore, profit is not the only answer to all performance evaluation questions. When evaluating the performance of a company, financial analysts do not look at profit by itself. They consider many variables including profitability. The same will be true in internal markets.

An internal market economy offers a new system of organization that performs better than a traditional hierarchical bureaucracy. This does not mean that it will solve every management problem. It certainly is not a panacea. But it is an exciting concept that offers great potential for creating a dynamic, entrepreneurial, accountable, and customer-focused organization that is needed in today's environment.

PART THREE

ENTERPRISE IN THE PUBLIC SECTOR

15 The New Paradigm of Government

Passing the Torch to a New Administration

James P. Pinkerton

Although I was an advisor to President Bush during his administration, the policies I helped develop for revitalizing government remain equally relevant for President Clinton. A change of administrations does not change the major issues facing our nation, nor does it change the historic forces that are affecting the world.

James P. Pinkerton was Deputy Assistant to the President for Policy Planning during the Bush Administration. He is now the John Locke Foundation Fellow in Residence at the Manhattan Institute, Washington, DC.

THE SHIFT FROM AN OLD PARADIGM TO A NEW PARADIGM

A "New Paradigm" of government is spreading around the entire globe. This redefinition of how the public sector works brings a new form of government organization based on competition and choice rather than hierarchical, centralized controls. It presents a powerful but unsettling new perspective that has already cracked the Berlin Wall, dismantled the Soviet Union, liberated Eastern Europe, and is now integrating the world into a single market economy offering a better life for everyone.

After decades of collectivization, we have seen the truth about an ideology whose central premise is a war against human nature, the basic human impulse for voluntary economic exchange and political freedom. Socialism, or central planning, doesn't work, no matter what name it goes by or where it is practiced. These failures were apparent to insightful scholars like Frederick Hayek a half century ago; many are simply more manifest in today's rapid world.

The same idea has failed here at home in its lesser manifestations. The "Old Paradigm" of centralized government has been a well-intentioned but dismal failure because it assumes that experts, bureaucrats, and politicians can somehow administer supply and demand from within their offices far away. That's why our citizens are so cynical about the federal government. Bureaucracies such as Health and Human Services, the Postal Service, and Congress are in disrepute because they cannot possibly anticipate and serve effectively the complex, changing needs of people today. The crises in our economy, cities, and schools are all symptoms of a larger crisis, which I suggest is really the terminal crisis of the Old Paradigm. House Republican Whip Newt Gingrich described the current problem in government this way:

> Today we have two standards of time. One is the time you use when going into a private business, and the other is the time you use when walking into a government office. The first is [measured] in minutes, the second in hours. There is also one level of customer service you expect in a private business, and there is a vastly different level of customer service you expect when going into a government office. If any private enterprise in America treated people the way they are treated by government, it would be out of business quickly.

Private sector bureaucracies can be just as bad. Ross Perot built Electronic Data Systems (EDS) from nothing into a billion-dollar company and then sold it to General Motors (GM). Now GM is taking EDS down with it as the parent company spirals into decline. Perot illustrated the cause of this failure by pointing out that it takes GM seven years to design a car, whereas we won World War II in only three and a half years.

Even IBM, one of the greatest companies in the United States until a few years ago, is also failing because it is still trying to be Big Brother to its clients while the PC revolution has allowed people to become their own Gutenberg. Fortunately, companies in a free economic system face the ultimate test of the market where such inefficiencies cannot continue for long.

But we should put the issue of bureaucracy versus markets in perspective. Modern bureaucracy was a great idea when our ancestors invented it 100 years ago because it solved social problems in an era of heavy industry and low educational levels. That explains why both the industrial age and bureaucracy were created at about the same time: the "means of production" for bureaucracy and industry were cognates. Bureaucracy has the rhythm of mass production—assembly lines, interchangeable parts, standardized work rules. Let's give credit where credit is due: In the past, bureaucracy helped to make our lives less nasty, brutish, and short.

The federal government as we know it today was also largely constructed along these same principles of bureaucracy between 1883—when the civil service was created—and a half century later when the New Deal began. That made sense at the time. Now the question is what structure, what paradigm, will enable us to move ahead? The contours of the new American political reality are being shaped by two areas in which a fairly clear national consensus exists:

1. Most people agree on the goals this country should achieve. Whether Democrats or Republicans, black or white, male or female, all of us want an educated young generation, economic prosperity, racial and sexual equality, and a clean environment.
2. There is a consensus that these goals cannot be achieved through the old form of government control. That type of government produced today's federal budget deficit and gridlock. Most Americans and politicians agree that the federal government may provide leadership in solving problems, as President Clinton is trying to do, but the old big government programs and controls should be modified in a qualitative sense.

The New Paradigm emerging out of this consensus is an attempt to cut through the prevailing cynicism about Washington, DC, by offering a different type of entrepreneurial government. If Americans can grasp this new vision and make it a reality, we can restructure today's monopolistic bureaucracies into a more powerful type of government that harnesses the power of markets. And so, I hope in this chapter to pass on to President Clinton the key policy ideas I helped develop for President Bush. Like all patriotic Americans, I want to pass the torch of freedom to the new administration.

PRINCIPLES OF THE NEW PARADIGM

I adapted the term "New Paradigm" from Thomas S. Kuhn's classic work *The Structure of Scientific Revolutions* as a way of understanding today's social transformation. Kuhn argues that all scientific work is based on working assumptions that he calls "paradigms." Scientific "revolutions" occur when old, discredited paradigms are overturned by new and more useful paradigms.

For example, in the third century A.D., the astronomer Ptolemy outlined the theory, or "paradigm," that the sun revolved around the earth. This "geocentric" paradigm dominated astronomy for over a thousand years, until it was overturned by the "heliocentric" paradigm of Copernicus and Galileo.

Kuhn's insight into the evolution of science applies to society as well. In the eighteenth century, mercantilism—capitalism without freedom or competition—was the dominant paradigm. In 1776, Adam Smith's *Wealth of Nations* articulated a new paradigm calling for economic freedom. Smith's paradigm was widely applied during the next two centuries, and the result has been the greatest period of progress and prosperity in human history.

As Galileo discovered, new ideas are not always welcomed. But despite the best efforts of the Inquisition, people have since become used to the idea that the earth revolves around the sun. In economics, however, even today not everybody understands that choice and competition—freedom—works best.

Fortunately, most Americans today see that the Old Paradigm is failing. The search for an alternative has led to a wave of freedom and markets sweeping through the world. This same vital, energizing electricity of change is flowing here at home to jolt the status quo and introduce a remarkably different concept of government. The New Paradigm has five characteristic features or principles:

1. Governments are now subject to market forces as never before.
2. The New Paradigm is energized by personal choice.
3. The New Paradigm empowers people to control their lives.
4. The New Paradigm is based on decentralization.
5. The New Paradigm emphasizes what works.

The following sections discuss these concepts in detail.

Governments Are Subject to Market Forces

The place to begin describing the New Paradigm is to recognize the changing reality that national economies today are now driven almost instantaneously by global market forces.

I've used the metaphor of energy and electricity to describe the power of the New Paradigm. But it isn't just a metaphor, it's a literal description. Prices are signals. And nowadays, these signals are carried at the speed of light. The financial circuits that control the international economy can switch in seconds when responding to new information.

For instance, when President Mitterand vowed to make France socialist after being elected in 1981, he inadvertently pushed the wrong policy button, producing an almost immediate outflow of investment capital from France to other nations across entire continents and oceans. It did not take long for the Mitterand government to reverse its socialist stance in favor of free market policies.

This aspect of the New Paradigm is a function of *feedback* and the increasing sensitivity of the global market. Today's electronically managed markets are self-monitoring and self-correcting systems that leave little room for failed social and economic experiments, as during the 1960s. The North American Free Trade Agreement is the key test for President Clinton. He should know that if politicians fail to address the new economic realities, other people will.

The New Paradigm Is Energized by Choice

One of the most conspicuous failures of the Old Paradigm is found in public education.

During the 1980s, real spending per student rose nearly 30 percent, and is now about $5,500 for each public school student. Imagine a class of 20 to 25 students. Multiply that by $5,500. The result is $110,000 to $137,500 in expenditures per classroom. If the teacher is paid an average of $35,000, where is the rest of the money going? Into a black hole of bureaucracy, that's where! Not only is public education costly, SAT scores are still sinking, and the United States typically ranks in the second decile internationally. In big cities, where spending is even higher than these average levels, students routinely graduate from high school without being able to read. We must face the fact that our public schools are failing to educate students properly.

Meanwhile, parochial schools can teach us something about educating children. In New York City, the Catholic schools do a better job for one-fourth the cost of public schools. The reason is simple; they have less than a tenth of the administrative overhead, and they never forget about rigor and discipline.

Instead of pouring more money into today's failing structure of public education, we must change that structure. In a changing world, schools cannot be exempted from changing as well. The biggest problem in education is that we have not held schools accountable for their performance. Parents and children have simply accepted education as it was presented, while the educational bureaucracy decided how to manage public schools for us.

The key to successful reform in education is to grant parents the power to choose the public school their children will attend. The New Paradigm gives parents a choice in deciding what school their children attend, thereby requiring schools to find better ways to serve their clients—students and parents—by improving education. Of course, there are other needs as well, primarily developing these superior forms of education. However, the concept of choice in education is so fundamental that it has been embraced in 20 states by Democrats and Republicans, liberals and conservatives.

A good example is provided by a former welfare mother. Polly Williams, now a Democratic state representative, has led a grass-roots movement of poor parents in Milwaukee, Wisconsin. They have gained the freedom to choose the schools, public or private, that their children will attend.

If President Clinton's Education Department makes good on its threat to limit complete school choice, he will succeed only in heightening the internal contradictions of the Old Paradigm, accelerating its ultimate replacement by a model more in keeping with contemporary reality.

The New Paradigm Empowers People

This is the age of empowerment. *Empowerment* is the flip side of *choice*. The choice side provides options, the empowerment side enables people to exercise those options. By contrast, the Old Paradigm was bureaucracy, one-size-fits-all. It is the ultimate in trickle-down economics; tax money floods into Washington to irrigate the bureaucratic gardens, whether or not people are satisfied with the government services they receive.

The fault in this approach is its focus on the quantity of *inputs*—the amount of money spent on any program was considered a measure of the benefits to be derived. Often, these tax dollars were spent in ways that only made things worse. To get out of the mess that government is now in, we will have to focus on *outputs,* rather than inputs. In other words, if we hope to improve government, it is essential to begin by accurately evaluating the performance, or "outcomes," of government programs. People can only exercise their freedom to act wisely in a market system if they have accurate information about the outcomes of their choices.

Fortunately, today the information age empowers everyone with more sophisticated information. Knowledge is power, so a more discriminating awareness has emerged that is very broadly distributed.

In 1993, a bipartisan Empowerment Caucus was established in the U.S. Congress. Representative Rob Andrews (Dem. NJ) and his cochair Curt Weldon (Rep. PA) are serious about bringing choice and autonomy to the poor, confident that with more freedom will come a greater sense of responsibility. Agriculture Secretary Mike Espry is expected to spearhead the Clinton Administration's empowerment efforts.

Once people are empowered by knowledge, top-down government loses its authority. Communism was destroyed fundamentally by the flow of information into the USSR, making its subject people aware of the alternatives. Even Uncle Sam finds that he is being watched closely by a citizenry made more alert by their Apples and IBM PCs.

The New Paradigm Is Based on Decentralization

Authority is dispersing around the world. Former socialist governments abroad, stodgy corporations on Park Avenue, and sclerotic city halls here at home are all changing. Let's look particularly at the Third World, where the Old Paradigm has been particularly damaging.

Social scientists who subscribe to the Old Paradigm often presumed that the Third World was too "backward" to develop modern market economies. There was a common belief that socialism was needed to protect these people from the rigors of the marketplace. This type of help turned out to be devastating because it is impossible to avoid the demands of the global market. In contrast, consider the central insight of the great Peruvian economist Hernando de Soto, who described the reality in undeveloped countries as follows:

> By walking the streets of Lima, not analyzing official statistics, I found that the poor of Latin America—who have never read Jefferson or Adam Smith—ran their affairs democratically outside the formal economy, organizing their private, parallel economy in a free and unregulated manner. . . . People everywhere want the same things. And when left alone by government, people everywhere organize their lives in remarkably similar ways.

In a like manner, the New Paradigm is not based on the wisdom of centrally controlled institutions, whether in business or government. Instead, it relies on diversity and innovation in a decentralized intellectual and economic marketplace. As Frederick Hayek pointed out, the best approaches for solving problems usually arise spontaneously and are confirmed by the results of millions of individual decisions.

A particularly vivid example is telecommuting—working from home. No government programs encouraged millions of people to work via their telephones and computers, but that is exactly what is happening. The common estimate from several studies is that one out of five Americans now works from home at least part of the time. Aside from the obvious environmental benefits, telecommuting allows people to work where and how they want, increasing productivity, decreasing traffic congestion, and saving time and money. Telecommuting is merely a simple example of a new wave of decentralization that is just beginning to sweep over our economy.

President Clinton is taking these ideas into the 1990s. Vice President Gore, with the help of able thinkers such as David Osborne and others, will be heading a "Reinventing Government" Commission.

The New Paradigm Emphasizes What Works

Once we agree on the goal of a decent life for every American, the debate shifts to achieving this goal, as opposed to merely spending money on government bureaucracies. In New York City, the Old Paradigm holds such sway that three different agencies have responsibility for building safety. Yet there was a tragic fire at the Happy Land Disco at which 87 people lost their lives.

The point is that in crucial areas of public safety, we don't necessarily need more government or less government. We need capable government, and the Old Paradigm structures have proven themselves incapable of working very effectively, largely because they were immune from common sense. Consider how one local police force ran its promotion system:

> Amazingly, the department has a promotion system in which effectiveness at a patrolman's job has nothing to do with promotion. Who makes sergeant is based on an exam and a brief interview with two police officials and a citizen who are all unacquainted with the officer being evaluated.

This defies reason. Bureaucracy elevates standard operating procedures above the practical. As people discover that government does not know best, they refuse to turn their decision-making power over to officials, and instead learn to decide for themselves. Popular opinion now converges around the notion that a major social restructuring is needed to put government in tune with a society that has changed enormously in recent years.

RECLAIMING AMERICAN CREATIVITY

The 1992 presidential election may have changed from a Republican to a Democratic administration, but Bill Clinton must utilize many of the same principles of Jack Kemp and other empowerment Republicans because the dominant issue in government today—qualitative restructuring—cuts across political parties. The form of government that worked well in the past is no longer appropriate for a vastly different new era. That path can only lead to more government monopoly, which strangulates initiative, creativity, and freedom.

Ross Perot, who was the strongest third-party candidate since Bob LaFollette in 1924, epitomizes this new bottom-line pragmatism. It only seems radical when compared to the Brezhnevian status quo.

The future of the United States depends on our ability to encourage the free thinkers and iconoclasts who are the engine of progress. But we are all being buried in a morass of bureaucratic mediocrity that chokes upward mobility for everyone. As James Fallows argues, we will never be able to compete with the Japanese or the Germans if the game is discipline and following orders. The future of our country can't depend on becoming more like them. Our future depends on becoming what Fallows calls *More Like Us*—reclaiming the tradition of creativity and common sense that is the heritage of Americans.

The New Paradigm is not limited to the United States, nor should it be. The lessons of the New Paradigm are universal, and many around the world are applying them to create more intense competition in a global economy. However, history reminds us that opportunity is all that Americans have ever needed to succeed.

16 Ten Ways to Turn DC Around

David Osborne

Editors' Note: The government of Washington, DC, was poised for change in 1990 when Sharon Pratt Dixon (now Kelly) was elected to replace the former mayor, Marion Barry. Because the election seemed a crucial turning point in the nation's capital, David Osborne wrote an open letter to the new mayor suggesting policies based on an entrepreneurial concept of government that would revitalize the city. That letter is reprinted in this chapter to offer an insightful example of how internal market principles can be applied in the public sector. Progress in this direction has been slow for various reasons, but there is a general sense that this path is badly needed. Mayor Kelly's spokesperson commented in 1992, "We've got to [undertake] more innovation in the District government as a means of our future survival."

David Osborne is an independent author and consultant to city, state, and federal governments. His recent book with Ted Gaebler, *Reinventing Government: How the Entrepreneurial Spirit is Transforming the Public Sector* (Reading, MA: Addison-Wesley, 1992), has become a bible for restructuring government. This chapter is reprinted with permission from the *Washington Post* (December 9, 1990).

To: **Sharon Pratt Dixon**
From: **David Osborne**
Re: **How to really make the city work**

Congratulations. You promised to clean out the DC bureaucracy, fire 2,000 managers and hold the line on taxes. The good news is that you have a mandate. The bad news is that people expect you to deliver.

You're not the first candidate to make such promises, of course. Many a politician has swept into office on the same basic platform, then departed 4 or 8 or 12 years later with little changed. The problem is hardly limited to mayors. Ronald Reagan ran a campaign much like yours in 1980. Michael Dukakis was elected governor of Massachusetts in 1974 on a pledge to clean up state government and hold the line on taxes. Sixteen years later, as the battered Dukakis made his exit, William Weld was elected on the same pledge.

Politicians come and go, in other words, but the bureaucracy remains.

We all know that the DC government is bloated. We know that it could shed 2,000 managers without skipping a beat. But firing 2,000 middle managers is not going to solve the District's problems. In fact, it could make them worse. Under the city's archaic civil service system, those managers can just bump lower-level employees who have less seniority; those employees will bump still others; and you could wind up eliminating the fresh faces but keeping the deadwood—in jobs for which they have little training and less desire.

So as you sweep clean the bureaucracy, you need to keep one thing uppermost in your mind: The people are not the problem. The system is the problem.

The DC government, like most governments, operates with a set of incentives that reward sloth, waste, and inefficiency. You have a budget system that *encourages* managers to waste money. You have a personnel system that *encourages* managers to live with mediocrity. You have a salary system that *encourages* managers to build empires. You have an accounting system that *encourages* people to scrutinize how much is spent but ignores the results of that spending. These systems have created a culture that rewards the very behavior you want to eliminate.

You've probably read Peter Drucker, the management sage. He puts it well: "Critics of bureaucracy blame the resistance of public-service institutions to entrepreneurship and innovation on 'timid bureaucrats,' on time-servers who 'have never met a payroll,' or on 'power-hungry politicians.' It is a very old litany—in fact, it was already hoary when Machiavelli chanted it almost five hundred years ago. . . . Alas, things are not that simple, and "better people"—that perennial panacea of reformists—are a mirage. The most entrepreneurial, innovative people behave like the worst time-serving bureaucrat or power-hungry politician six months after they have taken over the management of a public-service institution, particularly if it is a government institution.

Your basic challenge is this: You have inherited a government designed for the 1940s, and you need a government designed for the 1990s.

The kind of governments that developed during the 1930s, 1940s, and 1950s, with their sluggish, centralized bureaucracies, their preoccupation with rules and regulations, and their hierarchical chains of command, no longer work very well. They accomplished great things in their time. They professionalized government, built safety net programs like Social Security and Medicaid, and won a world war. But somewhere along the line they got away from us. They became bloated, wasteful, ineffective. More important, the environment changed, and they failed to change with it. Hierarchical, centralized bureaucracies simply do not function well in the rapidly changing, information-rich, knowledge-intensive society and economy of the 1990s. They are like luxury ocean liners in an age of supersonic jets: big, cumbersome, expensive, and extremely difficult to turn around.

Not surprisingly, new kinds of public sector organizations are beginning to take their place. They are flexible, adaptable, quick to adjust when conditions change. They are lean, decentralized and innovative. They use competition, customer choice and a variety of other nonbureaucratic mechanisms to get things done as flexibly, creatively, and effectively as possible. They contract with private firms and nonprofit organizations to provide services. And they change the basic incentive systems that drive public employees behavior: budget systems, personnel systems, pay systems.

These are *entrepreneurial* governments, not *bureaucratic* governments. Your experience in the private sector—and your campaign rhetoric—suggests that you have an intuitive understanding of the difference. But to turn around a luxury ocean liner with 48,000 employees, you will need more than intuition. You will need a clear understanding of what makes entrepreneurial governments tick.

I've spent five years studying such governments, trying to understand what drives their employees to behave so differently. I have boiled the answer down into 10 principles—10 sometimes-overlapping pieces of what is really a coherent whole, a new way to operate public institutions. Think of them, if you will, as 10 lessons drawn from the experience of others who have gone before you in the task of reinventing government.

LESSON 1: USE GOVERNMENT MORE TO STEER THAN TO ROW

Entrepreneurial leaders understand that communities are healthy when their families, neighborhoods, schools, voluntary organizations and businesses are healthy—and that government's most profound role is to steer these institutions to health. Hence entrepreneurial governments act more as catalysts, brokers, and facilitators than traditional governments do.

Nobody embodied this philosophy more than George Latimer, mayor of St. Paul, Minnesota, from 1976 through 1989. Latimer cut the city's staff by 12 percent, kept budget and property tax growth below the rate of inflation and reduced the city's debt—but he dramatically *increased* the activism of St. Paul government. He did it by catalyzing private sector activity: He used nonprofit, voluntary organizations to manage parks and perform energy audits and operate recycling programs; he set up nonprofit corporations to redevelop downtown, invest in low-income housing and organize the nation's first downtown-wide hot water heating system; and he created more partnerships with foundations than any mayor in American history.

E.S. Savas, a veteran of the Lindsay administration in New York City and the Reagan administration in Washington, introduced the metaphor of steering versus rowing. The word "govern," he pointed out, comes from a Greek word that means "to steer." Most of us understand that government's primary role is to steer. What we fail to understand is that when government also rows, it can lose the flexibility it needs to steer effectively, particularly in times of rapid change.

To vary the metaphor: If policy makers can "buy" services only from their own bureaucracy, they become captives of sole-source, monopoly suppliers. This becomes a problem as soon as they decide to change their strategies. When they want to move their welfare departments into the business of training, educating and placing people in jobs, for instance, they are stuck with caseworkers who have the wrong skills. The solution is to keep policy decisions within public hands but contract with or empower separate organizations (public, private, nonprofit or voluntary) to deliver services, depending on who can best do the job.

LESSON 2: WHENEVER POSSIBLE, INJECT COMPETITION INTO PUBLIC SERVICE

During your campaign you suggested that you wanted to see more competitive bidding on existing city contracts. Think bigger: Think about injecting competition into *every* city service. Entrepreneurial governments have discovered that when organizations must compete for funding, they keep their costs down, respond quickly to changing demands, and strive mightily to satisfy their customers. This is particularly important in cities where contracting has been a seedbed for corruption. True competition makes it very hard to award contracts to political cronies.

Phoenix, a city of almost a million people, is a compelling model. The city government there uses competitive bidding in garbage collection, street repair, landfill operation, custodial services, security in city buildings, and a variety of other areas.

Phoenix first decided to contract out garbage collection in 1978, during a fiscal crisis. It divided the city into five districts and bid out one district at a time, on a long-term contract. Surprisingly, the Public Works Department—the agency then collecting the garbage—decided to compete. Three times it submitted bids, and three times it lost a district. But the losses forced its managers and employees to get serious about improving their operations. Management let the drivers redesign their own routes and work schedules. Together, they refined their trucks and became a technology leader in the industry. Together they created labor-management committees to work out better ways to do things. And gradually they got their costs down.

In 1984, Public Works finally won a contract. By 1988, it had won back all the districts. "Over a 10-year period you see the costs for all the other city programs going up," says Ron Jensen, who runs the department. "Solid waste costs have gone down by 4.5 percent a year, in real, inflation-adjusted dollars."

Charles Fanniel, president of the union local, would prefer the comfort of guaranteed jobs for his employees. But he acknowledges that working conditions, pay, and morale are all better than they were before 1978. "What happens with this bidding system," he says, "is you cut out all the fat."

To make sure the bidders are all competing on a level playing field, the city auditor's office examines each bid, public or private. (The city auditor is the watchdog, a vital role in any contracting process—especially when corruption is a problem.) Phoenix City Auditor Jim Flanagan says he has discovered there is no truth in the old saw that business is always more efficient than government. The important distinction is not public versus private, it is monopoly versus competition: "Where there's competition, you get better results, more cost-consciousness, and superior service delivery."

This is simple common sense. We all know that monopolies protect inefficiency and resist change. And yet, to this day we deride competition within government as "waste and duplication." We still assume that each neighborhood should have one school, each city should have one organization picking up its garbage or managing its public housing, each public service should have one provider. It is one of the enduring paradoxes of American politics that we attack monopoly so fervently when it appears in the private sector but embrace it so warmly in government.

LESSON 3: TIE SPENDING TO RESULTS

Unlike businesses, government agencies normally face no market test. The results of their work are secondary; their ultimate test is political—who gets elected. For an appointed manager, that means the bottom line is pleasing the politicians, not achieving any particular outcomes. And elected politicians normally care about voters' and interest groups' perceptions more than about the performance of public agencies—many of which they barely understand. So public managers quickly learn that their value and clout flow not from how well their agencies perform, but from how the politicians view them. Because politicians often judge their worth by looking at the size of their budgets and staffs, managers assiduously build their empires. Because politicians make obeisance to organized constituencies, managers become extremely sensitive to interest groups. Because politicians need friends and campaign contributors, managers are sometimes pressured to show favoritism when contracts are let.

The way out of this trap is to tie funding and managers' pay to the results of their work. Bureaucratic governments fund according to *inputs:* how many full-time positions are allotted, how many students enroll, how many people are poor enough to qualify. Entrepreneurial governments try to fund according to *outcomes:* how much children learn, how many people find jobs and get off welfare, how clean the streets are. They know that when institutions are funded according to inputs, they have little reason to strive for better performance. But when they are funded according to outcomes, they become obsessive about performance. Again, this is particularly important in dealing with corruption: When contractors are not paid until they produce documented, measurable results, corruption becomes far more difficult.

New York City is often written off as beyond hope. But these principles work just as well in a city of 7 million as in a town of 5,000, as the following story shows.

During New York's fiscal crisis in the 1970s, an independent foundation developed a method called "Scorecard" to measure the cleanliness of streets. It then sent out volunteers every month to rate each of 6,000 streets.

The Sanitation Department had always focused on inputs: How many trucks were assigned to each district? How many men were needed on each truck? Now it began to look at the Scorecard information, which rated outcomes: How clean was each street? Using this information, it reassigned its street cleaners and began to reward crews that made the greatest improvements. By 1986, the percentage of streets rated "filthy" had declined from 43 to less than 4 percent. Nearly 75 percent were rated "acceptably clean."

The foundation, called the Fund for the City of New York, went on to develop outcome measures for parks maintenance, job training and placement, foster care, home care services, school maintenance, and other programs. For example, the Department of Housing Preservation and Development contracts with community organizations to manage, renovate, and sell so-called "In Rem" apartment buildings—those the city has seized from tax-delinquent owners. The Fund for the City of New York developed standards for rent collection, vacancy rates, and expense levels, which the department built into the performance contracts it signs with these community organizations. The In Rem program is one of the city's most successful.

LESSON 4: LET PEOPLE CHOOSE AMONG MANY SERVICE PROVIDERS

The best way to tie funding to performance is to think of citizens as *customers* of government. Most businesses get their revenues directly from their customers: If they please the customers, sales increase; if someone else pleases the customers more, sales decline. So businesses in competitive environments learn very quickly to pay enormous attention to their customers. But city agencies get most of their funding from taxpayers, via city councils. And most of their "customers" are captive: Short of moving, they have few alternatives to city services. So managers in the public sector learn very quickly to ignore them. Instead, the managers respond to the mayor and city council—because that's where they get their funding.

The most entrepreneurial governments understand that the best way to force a bureaucracy to get close to its customers is to make it dependent on them for its very livelihood. This takes competition a step further: Rather than government managers choosing service providers in a competitive bidding process, it lets each *citizen choose* his or her service provider.

How does it work? Consider Community School District 4, in East Harlem. New York City has 32 school districts. Twenty years ago District 4 was at the bottom of the barrel: 32nd out of 32 in test scores.

"It was totally out of control," says Michael Friedman, a teacher who now directs a junior high. "The schools were chaotic, they were overcrowded. There was a lot of violence, gangs roaming the streets. It was sink or swim as a classroom teacher. They closed the door: 'That's your class, do what you can.' And it seemed like nobody could or would try to do anything about it. You had a lot of people who had been there a long time, and they were just punching that clock."

In 1974, out of sheer desperation, district leaders decided they had to get the worst kids out of the schools so other kids could learn. So they created an alternative junior high for troubled students. The task was so daunting, they told the teachers to do whatever it took to get results. Not surprisingly, the result was a very nontraditional school. It worked, so they created another one. Soon teachers began proposing alternative schools for other children: a performing arts school, a traditional school in which children wore uniforms, a marine sciences school, a school that specialized in creative expression, a career preparation school. Each provided a basic core of instruction in math, English, and social sciences, but each also had a distinct focus.

Today District 4 boasts 23 junior high schools, all of them schools of choice. (Six grade schools are also schools of choice.) Rather than being assigned to a school and offered the same kind of education as every other child, students are allowed to choose the style of education they prefer. (In other words, they are treated as customers.) They can choose traditional schools or open classrooms; reading institutes for those behind grade level or advanced schools for gifted students; a computer-oriented school; or a school run in conjunction with the Big Apple Circus. Schools are small—from 50 to 300 students.

"Kids need to be dealt with personally, not impersonally," says John Falco, who administers the choice program. "They need to be recognized for what they are, what they could do, and what they could accomplish—and then you need to figure out how to help them accomplish that."

Obviously, Falco is not describing the normal attitude of an inner city teacher or administrator. Why do people in East Harlem think that way? Because they have to. "If you're not operating a program that kids want to come to, you're out of business," says

Falco. "That's happened in a couple of cases. You just can't rest on your laurels. You have to continually strive for ways to meet the needs of these kids."

The results speak for themselves. In 1973, 15 percent of District 4 junior high students read at grade level: by 1989, 64 percent did. In the mid-1970s, only a handful of the district's graduates were admitted annually to New York's elite public high schools, like Bronx Science and Brooklyn Technical. In 1987, 139 were— 10 percent of district graduates, almost double the rate for the rest of New York City. Thirty-six other graduates went to selective private schools, including Andover and the Hill School.

LESSON 5: DON'T JUST SPEND MONEY; INVEST IT AND MEASURE YOUR RETURN

When George Latimer became mayor, in 1976, downtown St. Paul was hemorrhaging. It had lost 41 percent of its retail volume over the previous 18 years. The worst section was known as Lowertown, a depressed, 25-square-block warehouse district that made up the eastern third of downtown. Latimer and his deputy mayor, Richard Broeker, dreamed up the idea of a private development bank, capitalized with foundation money, to catalyze investment in the area. In 1978 they asked the McKnight Foundation for $10 million to back the idea, and got it.

The Lowertown Development Corp. brought in developers, offered loans or loan guarantees, and put together package deals with banks, insurance companies, and anyone else who would listen. Over the previous decade, investors had put only $22 million into Lowertown. In the development corporation's first decade, it triggered $350 million in new investments—leveraging its own money 30 or 40 to 1. Thirty-nine buildings were renovated or constructed; they contained offices, cinemas, retail shops, restaurants and 1,500 units of new housing. By 1988, Lowertown generated nearly *six times* the property taxes it had 10 years before. And the development corporation was turning a profit!

Latimer was a master at using the profit motive. He turned many agencies into "revenue centers," fully or partially dependent on user fees for their income, and let them keep a third of all revenues they generated beyond their budgeted targets, as an incentive to make money. (By 1988, his Department of Planning and Economic Development got 83 percent of its funds from fees and other income.) He constantly set up independent corporations such as the Lowertown Development Corporation. Dick Broeker created a three-day summer festival called "Taste of Minnesota" that turned a profit in its first year, and the Parks and Recreation Department picked up on the idea and sponsored a 12-day "Riverfront Days" festival that became a big moneymaker.

Traditional governments focus entirely on *spending* decisions. City councils detail how much is to be spent for each line item, managers document how closely they have followed these instructions, and accountants check them for accuracy and honesty. Not one person in this process examines anything related to the organization's return on investment. Nor is anyone responsible for developing new (nontax) revenues—otherwise known as profits.

Entrepreneurial managers understand that guaranteed incomes create few incentives to innovate, so they force some agencies to *earn* much or all of their revenue. When profit is out of the question, as it often is with services like welfare, public education, or police protection, entrepreneurial governments still demand a return—whether measured in job placements, improved student performance, higher tax revenues, or greater community health (lower crime rates, lower welfare dependency, lower drug use). Because they define the returns they want and then measure to see if they are achieving them, public entrepreneurs know which initiatives are worth funding and which are not.

LESSON 6: USE GOALS—NOT RULES AND BUDGETS—TO DRIVE YOUR ORGANIZATION

"Never tell people how to do things," Gen. George S. Patton once said. "Tell them what you want them to achieve and they will surprise you with their ingenuity." Most governments do just the opposite. They don't spell out the goals they want programs to achieve. They spell out the exact process by which programs are to be administered and the exact amount managers can spend on every subcategory of every element of every program.

Rule-driven and budget-driven organizations churn out reams of reports on process and spending—but they rarely deliver quality performance. If you want performance, define an organization's mission, spell out the results you want, and then throw out the rule books and line items.

Start with the set of rules known as "civil service." Civil service systems may have made sense 80 years ago, but they make no sense today. They make it virtually impossible to reward people for quality performance, to move people as needs change, or to fire incompetents. This is how you get organizations riddled with employees "who are not capable of doing their jobs," as a former director of your Department of Public and Assisted Housing once described his agency.

If you try to "reform" civil service, the bureaucracy will outlast you. Better to throw it out and start over. You will be accused of grasping for power so you can hire every patronage hack in Washington. (You can point out that your predecessor already did that, despite civil service.)

I realize that abolishing civil service may be politically impossible. But your campaign has given you a precious opening: You promised to get rid of 2,000 bureaucrats; the people supported you; and the civil service system stands in your way.

Strike while the iron is hot. Don't settle for a one-time waiver; if civil service rules don't make sense this year, they're not going to make any more sense next year. You can build in adequate protections against patronage without the absurd rigidities of civil service.

As for the budget system, my advice is similar. Line-item budgets encourage managers to waste money. If a manager does not spend his entire budget by the end of the fiscal year, three things happen: He or she loses the money saved; he or she gets less next year; and the budget director yells because the manager asked for too much last year. Who in their right mind would save any money, under those circumstances? This explains the normal end-of-the-year rush to spend money. Most public managers know where they could save 10 to 15 percent, but they have no incentive to do so. Why go through the pain of transferring or laying people off, if you can't keep the money and use it for something more important?

Under the duress of Proposition 13, Fairfield, California, invented a solution. A handful of other cities have already copied it, and several nations have moved in the same direction. You might call it a "mission-driven budget."

The mission-driven budget makes two simple changes. First, it does away with line items, leaving one basic budget for each program or agency. This gets legislators out of the business of dictating inputs and frees managers to shift resources to where they can be most productive. (If the city council is smart, it shifts into the business of measuring and funding outcomes—which gives it far more genuine control.) Second, it lets managers keep part or all of any money they can save, to use on new priorities. This gets them acting like they're spending their own money, rather than someone else's.

Say the police department is spending $500,000 a year on new squad cars but really needs a new computer system. Normally the chief would not risk asking the city council to shift the money, because he might lose the squad car line item but never get the computer funds. Under a mission-driven budget, he could save $200,000 a year on cars for three years running, then use the $600,000 to buy the computer system.

Fairfield's police department dramatically illustrates the contrast between the two budget systems. Its city budget is set up the new way, but it still hustles a fair number of federal grants, which are set up the old way. "It's amazing," says Chuck Huchel, chief of public safety. "The same people behave differently with the two streams of money. With the federal grants, we prepare a budget in advance, and we put on all the bells and whistles, all the frills—we try to anticipate everything we might need. When we get an authorization, we spend everything that's on the list, whether we need to or not. People don't say, 'Oh, I can save some money here, or I can use it another way now.' Because it's in the plan. You don't have incentives to make the cost savings, because if you don't spend it, you give it back.

"With the city money, they know that any savings they make can be applied to other programs or other equipment. So you say, 'Hey, I don't actually need this to make the program work, so I'm not going to spend it.' Plus they get creative about saving money. We needed a weather covering over a gas pump, to protect people from the rain when they were gassing up their vehicles. The architectural design to make it like a gas station came to around $30,000. We thought that was outrageous. So somebody said, 'What about these bus stop covers—the glass-enclosed ones?' We checked, and they cost $2,500. We put one of those up, and it works fine."

The District's budget deficit gives a new mayor the perfect opening to change the budget system. Normally the DC Council would hesitate to let go of its power to control line items. But if you take responsibility for cutting spending (and thereby inflicting pain) off its hands, it might go along. Bruce Babbitt cut a deal like this when he governed Arizona, and his managers loved it. Once they're rid of their line-item straitjackets, most managers will have no trouble finding ways to cut their spending by 5 or 10 percent.

LESSON 7: DECENTRALIZE AUTHORITY

You campaigned for "decentralized school-based management initiatives," and you were right. Now apply that thinking to the rest of government. Once you have tied spending to outcomes, you can give your mid-level employees a lot more authority to innovate.

The Ford Foundation and the Kennedy School of Government, at Harvard, cosponsor a series of annual "Innovation Awards" for state and local governments. The biggest surprise, to participants at the Kennedy school, has been the discovery that innovation rarely happens because someone at the top has a good blueprint. It happens because good ideas bubble up from employees who actually do the work and deal with the customers.

One of the first Innovation Award winners was a Minnesota program that finds innovators deep within the bureaucracy and gives them the authority they need. It's called STEP ("Strive Toward Excellence in Performance"). Every year employees who have innovative ideas compete to have them designated as STEP projects. The STEP board is co-chaired by the governor and a leading business executive. Its seal of approval does three things: It gives people permission to innovate; it offers them technical assistance; and it forces their bosses to sit up and listen.

One STEP team persuaded the Department of Natural Resources to change its entire attitude toward its customers. During the mid-1980s, use of the state's 64 parks was declining and budget problems were nibbling away at the parks. A group of people within the department decided that they needed a marketing program. They applied for STEP status and won. First they asked park managers to brainstorm about what they could do to make their customers happier; soon the managers were putting in children's play equipment in parks and electric hookups at campsites. Then they created a "Passport Club"—a kind of frequent flier program for park users, to lure them to outlying parks that were not heavily used. Next they began accepting credit cards, running advertising and promoting park permits as Christmas gifts. Sales jumped 300 percent. Then they brought in a private company to improve their gift shops, and gift sales increased by 50 percent. Finally they conducted a customer survey of 1,300 park users.

During the first year after the marketing strategy took effect, the number of park visitors jumped by 10 percent. Numbers like these got the department managers' attention; in 1987 they created a "marketing coordinator" position and hired the STEP team leader to fill it.

Another STEP project, in the department that issues driver's licenses, cut waiting time for the public in half. (Similar innovation, of course, would be a godsend in DC.) Yet another halved the paperwork involved in paying those who provide health care for handicapped children. STEP has since been copied not only by other states, but within the federal government.

The principle is very basic. In today's environment, things work better if those managing public organizations—schools, public housing developments, parks, training programs—have the authority to make many of their own decisions. Centralized, top-down institutions are simply not flexible enough to respond quickly to changing circumstances and customers' needs.

LESSON 8: PUSH CONTROL OF SERVICES OUT OF THE BUREAUCRACY AND INTO THE COMMUNITY

When professionals and bureaucrats have all the control, the people they are serving—their "clients"—have none. They are dependent. This is the situation with most public institutions: our schools, our police departments, our welfare agencies, our public housing authorities. It should come as no surprise when many clients learn dependent behavior—so many that welfare dependency, for example, is among our most intractable problems. Treat people as dependents, and they will eventually become dependent.

The solution is to give communities control over services. Schools controlled at least in part by parents perform far better than schools controlled by "professionals," according to education research. Head Start centers run by parents make the greatest long-term impact on children's lives. The only gleam of hope in an otherwise bleak public housing landscape comes when residents manage or buy their own properties. Why? Because people act differently when they have some control over their own environment.

You have an inspiring example of this lesson right here in Washington. The Kenilworth-Parkside Resident Management Corp., chaired by Kimi Gray, has transformed one of the city's worst public housing developments. The dealers who once used Kenilworth-Parkside as an open-air drug market are gone. Teenage pregnancies have plummeted. More than 600 residents have gone to college. In five years, the crime rate fell from 12 to 15 crimes a month—one of the highest levels in the city—down to 2.

In 1986, the accounting firm Coopers & Lybrand released an audit of Kenilworth-Parkside. During the first four years of tenant management, it reported, rent collections increased 77 percent—seven times the increase at public housing citywide. Vacancy rates fell from 18 percent—then the citywide average—down to 5.4 percent. The Resident Management Corp. helped at least 132 residents get off welfare. If these trends continued, Coopers & Lybrand concluded, the first 10 years of resident management would save the city $4.5 million.

You are undoubtedly familiar with Kenilworth-Parkside's success; in fact, you campaigned in support of "tenant ownership programs." It's time to replicate that success in the city's 59 other public housing developments—and in dozens of other city services.

LESSON 9: CHOOSE PREVENTION OVER CURE

Bureaucratic governments spend little time or money on prevention. Because they are programmed to think of government as service delivery, they typically wait until a problem becomes a crisis, then offer new services to those affected—the homeless on the street, communities victimized by violence, school dropouts, drug users. Hence we spend enormous amounts treating symptoms—with more police, more courts, more jails, more housing programs, more welfare payments, and higher Medicaid outlays—while prevention strategies go begging.

Entrepreneurial governments approach problems very differ-ently. Like Scottsdale, Arizona, they require sprinkler systems in all new buildings rather than paying for ever-larger fire depart-ments. Like New Jersey, they help people before they lose their homes rather than building more shelters. Like Suffolk County, New York, they ban nonrecyclable plastic packaging rather than creating new landfills.

Entrepreneurial governments also do everything they can to an-ticipate the future—to give themselves radar. They practice strategic planning. They use "life-cycle costing," which details not just the initial costs of programs or purchases, but their mainte-nance and other long-term costs. They develop budget and ac-counting systems that force politicians to look at the long-term im-plications of all spending decisions.

Sunnyvale, California, exemplifies anticipatory government. Sunnyvale's budget projects the consequences of every decision out 10 years. If the City Council is deciding whether to repair a highway, the budget makes it clear that the cost will soon quadru-ple if nothing is done. If the council is deciding whether to buy land for a park, the budget shows what it will cost to staff and maintain the park for 10 years.

This process makes the long-term costs of decisions painfully clear to the press and the public. It has changed the behavior of the council. "In the right environment, all of the myths about how elected officials behave have come falling down for me," says City Manager Tom Lewcock. "They don't have to be short-range thinkers, they can be long-range thinkers. They don't have to be people who say, 'I know this is more important than that, but we're going to spend our time on that, because I've got constituents on my back." They don't have to be any of those things."

LESSON 10: WHENEVER POSSIBLE, USE MARKET MECHANISMS RATHER THAN ADMINISTRATIVE MECHANISMS

By changing private investment patterns, government can have a hundred times the impact it has when it uses normal administra-tive programs. Markets are not perfect, and they cannot solve every problem. But they are extremely powerful—and when governments reshape them to serve a public purpose, they can have a tremendous impact.

In 1985, the year before Sandy Freeman became mayor of Tampa, almost a third of the city's housing units needed some degree of rehabilitation. That year the city's Community Redevelopment Agency, a traditional administrative bureaucracy with 41 employees, rehabilitated 37 units.

Freeman and her redevelopment director, Fernando Noriega, decided to use the marketplace to attack the problem. By guaranteeing loans for the first five years, they persuaded several of the city's banks to lend at low interest rates to owners who wanted to renovate their buildings. Last year the program rehabilitated 778 units.

Meanwhile, the Community Redevelopment Agency is down to 22 employees—but according to Noriega, they are "happier, more productive, and better paid employees." Obviously, they have a far greater impact than they did five years ago.

What Tampa did was simple: It used a market mechanism to achieve a public purpose. "We put the market together," Noriega says, "and presented it to the private lenders." You have talked about doing something quite similar with the $100 million "Capital Growth Fund" you want to create. Stick to your guns.

If your opponents question your approach, tell them the story of the 30-year mortgage. In 1930, Americans who wanted to buy homes had to make a 50 percent down payment and repay the mortgage in five years. That's how banks did business. Using the new Federal Housing Administration, the Roosevelt administration pioneered mortgages requiring only 20 percent down and repayment over 30 years. Other government corporations created a secondary market, so banks could resell these loans. And the banking industry converted. Today we take our 30-year, 20 percent down payment loans for granted, because the federal government changed the marketplace. Ask your opponents: Would we be better off if FDR had created half a dozen low- and moderate-income housing programs?

A final point: many of these lessons could be summed up as a shift from administrative mechanisms to market mechanisms. Competition, funding tied to results, customer choice, investment—all are characteristics of functioning markets. In a complex and rapidly changing world, in which our ability to access information is almost unlimited, markets are often more efficient and effective than administrative processes.

But market mechanisms are only half the equation. Markets are impersonal. Markets are unforgiving. Even the most carefully structured markets tend to create inequitable outcomes. That is why we need the other half of the equation: the empowerment of communities. To complement the efficiency and effectiveness of market mechanisms, we need the warmth and caring of families and neighborhoods and other social groupings. As we move away from administrative bureaucracies, we should embrace both markets *and* community.

Washington is an intensely political town, and in Washington people would call this moving right and left at the same time. They would label you a conservative for embracing markets and a liberal for empowering communities. But these ideas are not liberal or conservative. They can be used to implement any agenda. They can help you expand social programs if you choose, or shrink social spending and lower taxes if you choose. They dictate how government should work, not what government should do.

And regardless of what you want it to do, wouldn't it be nice if government *worked* again?

17 Restructuring the Federal Government

William E. Halal, Charles Blake, and
Kathryn Sheldon Hammler

If there is one thing Americans agreed on during the 1992 presidential election, it was the urgent need for fundamental change. The Clinton Administration was brought into office by a demand for restructuring the federal government's role in managing the nation. People everywhere now understand that the old bureaucratic model of government has become cumbersome, costly, and ineffective, and so cities, states, and national governments around the world are inventing an entrepreneurial form of public management.

William E. Halal is professor of management, George Washington University, and served as a consultant responsible for the study reported in this chapter by the International Data Corporation (IDC). **Charles Blake**, was vice president, and **Kathryn Sheldon Hammler** is a research analyst, for the IDC Government Division that supported the original study. This chapter is adapted from the authors' reports "Reinventing Government," and "Fee-for-Service in Federal IRM Departments," (Information Strategies Group, 1992).

This chapter surveys the growth of internal markets in the federal government, drawing mainly on a study of information management departments at major federal agencies. The study shows that market principles are being widely used because they allocate resources more efficiently and encourage creative entrepreneurship, and the practice is expected to spread to most government operations. We also suggest how public managers can restructure their agencies to handle the great changes ahead that amount to a revolution in government.

THE COMING REVOLUTION IN GOVERNMENT

Although the military has been considered the archetype of bureaucratic management since ancient times, a few years ago the U.S. Department of Defense attacked the labyrinth of rules that consume an estimated one-third of the defense budget, delay badly needed work, and destroy morale. An experimental group of base commanders was given the authority to run their installations as they see fit, and a one-page statement, "Principles of Excellence," was developed to replace volumes of regulations. Forty base commanders volunteered to participate. Evaluations showed large gains in performance and suggested that full implementation could save many billions of dollars per year.[1]

This is but one example of a new wave of entrepreneurship that is beginning to flow though the federal government. Business has been struggling to create entrepreneurial structures since the 1980s, and although change has been slower in the public sector, the trend is appearing there also. Studies of David Osborne and Ted Gaebler found a great move underway to "reinvent government":

> As we researched it, we were astounded by the degree of change taking place in our cities, counties, states, and school districts across America.[2]

The various prescriptions for making these changes, such as the previous chapters by James Pinkerton and David Osborne, converge on a few central principles that have been summarized in Box 17–1. These concepts imply a crucial shift in the role of government that is roughly similar to the internal market paradigm being developed in business, as described earlier in this book.

These changes do not involve the liberal view of "more government," nor the conservative view of "less government." They call for

---

──────── *Box 17–1* ────────

PRINCIPLES OF ENTREPRENEURIAL GOVERNMENT

Inject Competition into Service Delivery   Rather than having monolithic agencies dispense public services, governments are allowing
smaller units the freedom to compete for budget funds by serving
their clients in more innovative, effective ways.

Focus on Results Rather Than Inputs   Instead of being concerned
with inputs such as the size of a new program or budget, agencies are
increasingly evaluated and rewarded based on the outputs they have
achieved: the number of clients helped, the benefits they have gained,
and the like.

Empower People to Be Self-Sufficient   These changes are granting
people and communities the choices, knowledge, and control needed
to create a sense of ownership over their lives rather than remain dependent on government.

Provide Facilitating Leadership   There is a general need to find a
middle path between laissez-faire government and industrial policy—leadership that facilitates a dialogue among economic actors to
help them find their own solutions. This is often expressed as "cata-
lytic government" that "steers rather than rows," and "prevents rather
than cures problems."

---

inventing a different type of "entrepreneurial government."[3] Entrepreneurial government is based on the radical idea that the principles of
a free enterprise system can be used within government to produce a
dramatically different logic of public administration. The heart of this
new logic is to reconceptualize public sector functions into their market
equivalents: Large monolithic agencies are broken up into numerous
self-supporting "public enterprises" that compete to sell their services
to clients and other government units; staff offices are redefined as
"internal consultants" offering support on a contractual basis to line
units; cost centers become "service centers" roughly like profit centers,
and so on. All these entrepreneurial units are then free to control their
own operations while being held accountable for performance.

The examples in Box 17–2 illustrate this growing trend toward restructuring governments, which has produced some striking results. If
these preliminary experiments can be widely adopted, today's federal
bureaucracies could be converted into dynamic, creative public enterprise systems able to serve their clients better, adapt to a complex world

---
━━━━━━━━━━━ *Box 17-2* ━━━━━━━━━━━

EXEMPLARS OF ENTREPRENEURIAL GOVERNMENT

New York City Schools   New York City School District 4 had the lowest test scores in the city, with less than 20 percent of the students able to read and write at their current grade level. Teachers were encouraged to form "mini-schools" that stressed different approaches to education, and parents were permitted to choose among these alternatives. In a few years, 64 percent of the students could perform at grade level, test scores rose from lowest in the district to above average, and there is a waiting list for teachers and students wanting to transfer to this school located in one of the nation's most troubled ghettos.

Chicago Public Housing   The Chicago Housing Authority was facing a massive problem as 100,000 public apartment units declined into crime, disrepair, and unsanitary living conditions. Chief Vince Lane decided to form "Tenant Management Councils" that organized, trained, and supervised tenants in managing their own facilities. Soon, graffiti and filth disappeared, repairs were completed quickly, drug dealers were driven from the grounds, and people began helping one another find jobs as they developed a sense of ownership over their community.

Visalia, California City Government   Managers of this city have been allowed wide control over their budgets, including the freedom to move money among line items and to retain unused funds for next year. Employees can receive $1,000 bonuses for good work, as well as 15 percent of any monies they save the city. Now the Visalia city government thinks of itself as a group of entrepreneurs creating innovative solutions to community problems at low cost. "We've got one of the most exciting jobs in the city," said one manager, "We spend whatever time is necessary to get the job done."

---

more easily, and save taxpayers money. Peter Drucker[4] described the need this way:

> Building entrepreneurial management into the existing public-service institution may be the foremost political task of this generation.

The result is that a revolution in government seems imminent in the United States. It is already beginning in education, health care, and the military, and roughly 40 state governments have been making good progress in this direction for years now.[5] Looking ahead, surveys show that

Americans expect better public services without raising taxes significantly, so the federal budget deficit seems destined to exert relentless pressure for major innovation during the 1990s. Senators William Roth and John Glenn have introduced bills to restructure the federal government, and the Clinton Administration has launched its own program. Roth and Glenn described the intent of their bills as follows:

> I think the time has come now. We see all the big private corporations restructuring to get ready for 21st century competition. We have to do that with government, to make it more efficient and compassionate.[6] Rarely in our history have calls for governmental reform come together in such a positive way. We now have what may be just the right mix of political consensus and public pressure to successfully overhaul the government.[7]

Not all government functions lend themselves to this type of entrepreneurial management, so the traditional bureaucracy will still be needed in many situations. But if a client can be identified, almost any public function can, in principle, be converted into a self-supporting enterprise by simply allocating resources in some proportion to the amount and quality of services provided. Even functions that may first appear to serve the broad public welfare can with a little creative imagination be redefined in this way. Basic research and development (R&D), for example, could be viewed as a pooled investment in developing valuable knowledge that is sold to corporate sponsors, much like today's flourishing R&D consortia.

One of the most important changes has been the conversion of support services into the equivalent of profit centers. Throughout many federal agencies, line officers are now paying for information technology, personnel training, use of facilities, and a variety of other services that were once provided free under the old hierarchical system. The study discussed in the following section focuses on the restructuring of Federal Information Resource Management (IRM) departments into self-supporting internal enterprises that sell their services to line units on a "fee-for-service" basis.

FEE-FOR-SERVICE IN FEDERAL INFORMATION MANAGEMENT

The rapid advance of information technology (IT) may offer great new possibilities for improving government, but it has also aggravated a conflict that has long besieged federal IRM departments. On the output end of the IRM function, users have developed insatiable appetites for expensive state-of-the-art information systems; while on the input end, political pressures are forcing managers to reduce budgets. The result is that Chief Information Officers (CIOs) and their staffs are increasingly required to do a lot more with a lot less.

This would be a Herculean challenge under the best conditions, but it was almost impossible under the old concept of IRM in which CIOs had all the responsibility for solving such problems but little control over the parties involved. Users demanded more, top management provided less, and IRM was caught in the middle. One CIO described it as follows: "The problem was that users couldn't get enough IT because they weren't the ones who wrote the checks."

Today, however, a new idea promises to resolve this problem by placing the responsibility for IT decisions where it belongs—on the user. For the past few years, the concept of "Fee-for-Service" (FFS) has been slowly but forcefully restructuring IRM so that users are charged for the services they select, just as any ordinary buyer would pay a vendor in the real world.

Interviews we conducted with managers in some of the largest federal agencies—the Department of Energy, the Department of Transportation, the FAA, and the Department of Defense (DoD)—show that fee-for-service is widely practiced in the U.S. government. Plans are underway to extend it to most remaining federal operations, in some cases through major projects that establish "information utilities." IRM departments are thereby moving from traditional staff roles as cost centers to a new role as "internal IT consultants/vendors." In many cases, these more businesslike IRM departments are selling their services to users outside their agencies, while users are also buying IT services from other IRM departments and from private contractors. One executive called the introduction of FFS, "the most significant change to the organization in the past decade."

The State of the Art

Although FFS has been in use for about two decades, the practice did not gain a serious foothold until the publication in 1985 of Office of Management and Budget (OMB) Circular A130: *Management of Federal Information Resources*. Because of requirements in this document, the concept has been at least partially implemented by all the agencies we studied.

It is now common to find federal IRM managers who have been using FFS for 5 to 7 years, about the time OMB Circular A-130 came out. All the agencies surveyed were either charging for IRM services or had plans to do so, sometimes under another name, such as "Cost Recovery," or "ADP Charge-backs." The type of service covered may include the use of organizationwide mainframe systems, and/or providing hardware, system design, software, and other services to individual offices. There is wide variance in FFS practice, ranging from very little in some organizations to as much as 65 percent in others. A reasonable estimate of the average level of practice in the federal government based on the agencies we studied would be somewhere around 30 percent.

The typical approach has been simply to change existing accounting systems by shifting the cost of IRM equipment and services to user organizations, typically with prices calculated for individual products and services. Another less frequently used approach involves "service-level agreements," sometimes called "interagency agreements," which contract to provide a specified level of support for some period of time at a fixed price. Often, FFS has been initiated indirectly by outsourcing large portions of IRM work to private contractors, who then in turn charge individual federal users for the services provided.

In some cases, agencies have undertaken massive new programs that completely redesign the entire IT system, with FFS being a central part of the new system. The largest such effort is the Computer Resource Nucleus (CORN) Project announced in February 1992 by the FAA, which is considered to be the largest IRM project in the federal government.[8] CORN will integrate all mainframe equipment and services into a single system that handles accounting, payroll, personnel, communications, safety, training, and other organizationwide IT. The scale of the project is enormous. It should cost about $568 million over a 10-year period, serve 14,000 user units, require 11 million lines of software code, provide hundreds of different application systems, and involve major contractors such as EDS and AT&T. The central concept around which CORN is organized is that of an "information utility." Like any public utility, such as telephone service or power generation, services rendered are to be paid by the user organization.

Similar plans underway in Defense are intended to recover all IT costs by charging users for the following services: use of all mainframe systems (the Information Utility for DoD Computing Service, and Project Viable in the Army), standardized reusable hardware and software (the Software Reuse Initiative), maintenance and operations (the

Defense Business Operations Fund), and banking (Defense Finance and Accounting Services Agency). The Air Force Standard Systems Center, for instance, is now moving to sell its inventory of roughly 150 common software systems throughout 500 different Air Force units, and eventually throughout the DoD. It is anticipated that these changes may merge all three military services into one common IT utility. As one officer put it, "The entire DoD system is being restructured."

FFS is inherently a market concept, and since markets can only work effectively if buyers and sellers are free to choose among competing offers, competition is common among federal IRM departments. Contrary to many beliefs, most IRM managers consider it a constructive force. Listen to some typical comments: "Competition is good discipline"; "Competition is OK since we live with it all the time"; "Having a choice of vendors is good for users"; "I like competition—it's more dynamic."

All the agencies in our study use competition, but the type differs. Some have standing arrangements with private firms that bid on projects and service agreements. Others use vendors as an alternative to their internal IRM department. Some federal offices allow their IRM units to work for other agencies.

There are limits to the use of competition. One is the need to ensure that all systems are compatible, but this can be overcome by specifying compatibility requirements, and the problem could be avoided altogether in time by the trend toward open systems. Security precautions also limit bringing outsiders into government, and some special contracts require single-source procurement.

The wide variety of FFS methods used can be understood effectively as lying along a continuum running from the least to the most advanced. One study found eight different levels of charge-back systems being practiced among corporations.[9] Box 17–3 offers brief descriptions

---

Box 17–3

FIVE LEVELS OF CHARGE-BACK SYSTEMS

Level 1. No Charge-Back Charge-backs are not used in some situations for different reasons: The organization's mission or managers are deemed so important that they are accorded free IRM support, tasks are so inherently complex that charge-backs are infeasible, opposition to the concept is too formidable, and the like. Although FFS

(Continued)

Box 17–3 (Continued)

may be used eventually in some of these cases, the concept is probably not appropriate in many situations that should remain subsidized by budget funds.

Level 2. Allocate IT Cost as G&A   The simplest form of charge-back is to allocate all IRM costs among all users according to some formula, in the same way most private firms allocate General and Administrative (G&A) costs. We did not find this approach being used in federal IRM departments, although it may in fact be practiced. The main drawback is that there is little connection between use and cost.

Level 3. Provide Cost Information Only   Many departments report costs of IT usage by each unit for information purposes only—the use of "funny money." The information utilities of the FAA and the DoD initially only report the costs that they would charge to ease users into this difficult adjustment. Receiving this information gradually prepares the users for the reality of paying real bills. CORN is expected to start actually shifting funds from users to IRM in 1995, and the DoD claims it will start charging sometime in 1993 or so. One IRM manager said: "We're only sending out bills now, but we'll start charging at the end of the year when people get comfortable with the idea."

Level 4. Use Break-Even Rates   Most agencies charge users at rates calculated to break even at the end of the year. The intention is to recover only the actual costs of operating the IRM unit since it is considered inappropriate to make a profit or run a loss in government. One IRM manager said he "must have a zero budget balance at the end of the year." This approach produces some difficult problems, such as accumulating a sufficient surplus to permit future capital investments in IT systems, making adjustments to user accounts at the end of the year to balance the IRM budget, and the like.

Level 5. Offer Product Pricing   The most sophisticated approach is to develop prices for all IRM products and services based on the output functions provided: processor time, pages of a printout, number of phone lines, and the like. This requires careful study to determine actual costs in comparison with market rates and other considerations involved in setting prices. When this approach is fully developed, IRM units produce a price list that may run several pages and cover hundreds of individual products and services. Product pricing leads to redefining the IRM unit as a profit center responsible for managing all the normal functions of any business, somewhat like an internal equivalent of the many IT suppliers or consulting firms found in external economies.

of current practices at five most easily distinguished, generic levels along this continuum, ranging from instances where FFS is not feasible to the use of detailed price lists for a hundred or so products and services.

Advantages and Disadvantages

FFS is controversial because it represents a sharp break from traditional government practices. The advantages and disadvantages reported by managers in our study are summarized in Box 17–4. We found that the main advantage most often cited is that the practice encourages a more responsible use of scarce IT resources. The traditional practice produced enormous waste because federal managers were accustomed to using IT lavishly as long as it was free. DoD IRM staff describe the problem as the "Pearl Harbor Syndrome"—the fear of an unknown threat impels military commanders to insist on knowing everything, everywhere, at all times. Stories abound of high-ranking officers demanding multiple copies of huge computer printouts that are never read, and of entire bases equipped with expensive round-the-world phone lines that are used daily by some E-2 to call his or her family in the United States.

Box 17–4

ADVANTAGES AND DISADVANTAGES OF FEE-FOR-SERVICE

Advantages

Places Responsibility on the User   Most IRM managers like the way FFS places the responsibility for IT applications on the user where they feel it belongs. One IRM Manager said, "The main advantage is that clients make the decisions." Users often resist FFS initially, but many soon welcome it as offering a new form of control over their own IT funds and operations, the freedom to choose the systems they prefer, and the like. Some claim they love it.

Allocates Resources More Efficiently   Almost all agree that FFS is essential if expenses are to be held down, especially because there has traditionally been an assumption in government that managers' need to have full access to all available information, regardless of cost. FFS introduces discipline by forcing users to choose which systems will best serve their needs under the reality of resource limitations.

(Continued)

Box 17–4 (Continued)

Improves IT Decisions The preceding changes make IT costs visible and provide an incentive to control them. Without FFS, some users may be paying too much and others too little without knowing it. One user exclaimed when presented his first bill by the IRM department: "We had no idea how expensive our services could be. The costs were hidden in the budget. For the first time, we saw what it was costing us per month." Later this unit changed to a less expensive system with the help of the IRM manager, which not only reduced costs but provided faster, more convenient service for their needs.

Encourages Entrepreneurial IRM IRM departments soon realize after starting FFS that they must become capable providers if they hope to stay in business. This is not a great change, however, because federal IRM managers often describe their roles as entrepreneurs: "I'm always looking for better ways to provide the best possible service." Brandt Allen finds that "companies using [FFS] have more advanced technology and fewer failures. . . . There's less game playing, greater trust, and more harmonious relationships."

Disadvantages

Requires Sophisticated Accounting Systems A sophisticated cost accounting system is necessary to establish prices that are accurate enough to cover all costs, fair enough to be perceived as legitimate, and low enough to be attractive. The system must also efficiently handle many small transactions among numerous accounts.

Increases Transaction Costs New costs are incurred searching for good providers, negotiating and supervising contracts, and conducting other transactions. Some managers claimed that FFS systems produced "high-indirect costs" and was "more expensive." An IRM manager who had to manage FFS for 200 items among 1,000 different users felt the task was an "administrative burden." However, many do not feel these costs are high, and computerized accounting systems encourage market transactions because they can decrease these costs.

Miscellaneous A vague disorientation often results from such fundamental changes in traditional management practices. Some people spoke about a "loss of vertical control and integration," "inhibiting information flow," "contractors overcharging the government," and a general fear of competition.

However, these advantages are gained at the expense of some disadvantages, principally the cost and time required to set up and operate market systems. One IRM manager claimed he "would not use FFS if it were not required. It's a stupid way to do business." Another thought it was "too early to know if it will succeed."

There are justifications for these doubts; however, we found remarkably widespread agreement on the validity of the concept. One interviewee put it best: "Most people agree the logic is sound." Professor Brandt Allen of the University of Virginia noted: "Profit-Center control can dramatically improve the way information services are provided."[10]

CONCLUSION AND RECOMMENDATIONS: STRATEGIES FOR RESTRUCTURING GOVERNMENT

This study shows that internal market concepts are being introduced into the federal government with good success. Based on the trends noted here, most IRM functions are likely to be managed using market mechanisms, possibly as soon as 1995 and no later than 2000. A DoD manager said, "The goal is to recover all IT costs in DoD eventually." There is a general sense that similar systems are destined to move into other staff and line operations as well. Many local and state governments are finding that clients can be allowed the freedom to choose among competing government programs, as in the use of "choice" in education. Most importantly, these changes are introducing a general orientation to market behavior within government, including the virtues of competition among agencies, the setting of prices for government services, and the need to allow discriminating clients to select their providers.

There remain nagging doubts about this unusual idea and serious obstacles that require creative solutions. One of the themes we heard throughout this study is the lack of strategic planning to introduce such changes more effectively. Federal administrators seem to be preoccupied with political pressures to make short-term cost reductions, similar to the tendency toward short-term profits in business. The managers we spoke to were often disappointed with the complacency over such issues shown by agency heads: "The Secretary is too busy. He doesn't understand"; "Top management is not good at acknowledging the need for change"; "The Secretary's office should focus on strategic issues." The main problem seems to be that government administrators often dismiss such needs by claiming that they are "different" because "government doesn't operate on a profit motive."

This may be true, but a public form of entrepreneurship is badly needed, and Americans are beginning to see dramatic innovations cutting through city, state, and federal agencies with good results. After all, when people know that even Communist governments are adopting similar policies, why would they accept anything less of their own nation? Federal managers are unanimous in their opinion that powerful political forces in the nation, particularly the budget deficits, are exerting relentless downward pressures to reduce budgets over the next few years. DoD personnel expect to see a 30 percent reduction. This is experienced as a demand that they recover costs through methods such as FFS, and so the concept is "being shoved down the throats of users," as one person put it.

To help public managers move ahead, we conclude this chapter by extending the results of our study of federal IRM to suggest some strategic programs that other public managers should consider to resolve these difficult issues that hinder restructuring the traditional form of government.

Develop Comprehensive Implementation Programs

The biggest problem in implementing internal markets is the shock that hits managers when they realize that they must start paying for the services they receive and begin earning revenue by serving their clients better. IRM managers in our study told of the fierce resistance they encountered when telling their clients about the impending change that FFS would create in their units: "They were stunned"; "It's very unpopular."

The problem is aggravated because many government personnel are technical people who dislike the messy nature of business and economics. They often do not appreciate the need to conserve resources since they think the value of their projects transcends financial matters. For instance, the dilemma scientists face in making tough choices over how to spend their limited budgets was described as deciding "which child they would choose to give up."

In general, resistance persists because of a tenacious grip on the old bureaucratic form of government. Some managers said: "Traditional big government management is still alive"; "Changes like this are loaded with political landmines"; "Turf battles and cronyism must be put aside." Thus, the transition is difficult because it poses a cultural clash between a comfortable old way of doing things versus a dramatically different, wrenching change to market systems. General Pete Kind, who heads the Army's Information Systems Command, summed up the problem:

> In theory, it's the correct thing to do. In reality, it's going to be a little difficult to implement. . . . The cultural change implied by [internal markets] will not be accomplished easily."[11]

The managers we interviewed had some incisive ideas on handling this problem. The most useful solution is to provide sound training that explains the economic rationale for market systems in a comprehensible, logical way. Government managers are usually dedicated to public service, so they are inclined to understand that internal markets are a better way to manage. Training should not simply focus on how these concepts require financial discipline; it should also point out the benefits that usually result, as noted before, such as the greater freedom and self-control that FFS allows.

It is also important that federal managers actively strive to make the idea work by marketing their services to clients, working with them closely to solve problems, and developing methods to evaluate their satisfaction. All the managers we surveyed spoke keenly of the need to develop a strong marketing capability: "I need marketing people"; "Good marketing is absolutely essential"; "If you find yourself dragging the user along, you're in trouble"; "We have to work with users to understand their needs."

We suggest that agencies should design a comprehensive implementation program to help with all phases of the transition. This program should begin with high-level discussions to decide if market mechanisms are appropriate in individual units, it should include training programs to educate managers on key principles of the concept, and should provide assistance in resolving the issues that often arise. This program would be more effective if it were conducted at least partly by managers who have been through the transition.

Develop Effective Pricing and Accounting Systems

All the managers we spoke to felt that establishing an effective pricing system posed one of the most difficult challenges: "Knowing how much to charge is a tough question"; "It's by far the most difficult obstacle"; "Government hasn't done this before, so there are no mechanisms in place." Most agreed this required more effective cost accounting systems that could attribute costs to various IT products accurately, compare these to market prices, and estimate the revenue produced. One said, "We could bill for all systems with the right analytical tools."

A problem unique to government, which we will examine more fully later, is that departments are artificially constrained in their pricing policies because they cannot make a profit. This limitation on entrepreneurial freedom prevents federal managers from considering methods that the private sector finds useful. One corporate CIO, for instance, used a combination of price subsidies and premiums to encourage desirable trends in IT usage.[12]

Rather than having each federal department work alone in developing the complex accounting systems required to implement market systems, it would be more effective to organize central programs in which managers, accountants, and other specialists could develop common, generic systems. To highlight the importance of the internal market concept, these projects themselves could be managed as self-supporting enterprises that sell their products and services to departments throughout the U.S. government and possibly to other governments.

Create Government Equivalents of Market Concepts

The preceding problems are simply part of a larger and more challenging issue—at present, government lacks the type of market concepts, particularly the "profit center," that enable corporations to implement FFS more readily.

This lack conflicts with the natural inclination of federal IRM managers who tend to think of themselves as operating an internal enterprise. Indeed, many claimed, "It's like we're running a business now"; "We talk about internal customers every day." These attitudes reflect the fact that crucial new functions arise when converting to market systems that require entrepreneurial behavior: a need for flexibility in setting prices to compete with other suppliers, an ability to recover capital investments, the use of long-term planning horizons that permit purchases of major equipment, the importance of providing incentives for good performance, and so on.

However, present concepts of government consider most aspects of business inimicable to public service. We constantly heard phrases such as "The profit-center concept is hard to accept in government"; "You can't use the term 'marketing'"; "Government requires tight control." The predictable result is management systems that cannot evaluate performance, limit entrepreneurial freedom, and offer no incentives.

The problem is especially severe in line functions. Programs such as FFS may shift budget funds from staff departments to line organizations, but how are top administrators to decide how much of this money each line unit should get? What standard is to be used to evaluate the effectiveness of these units in handling their funds? These are tough questions because the lack of an equivalent to the profit center excludes that crucial "output" side of any line unit's performance, thereby reducing government management to simply running cost-centers, and making it very difficult to evaluate overall performance effectively. This has traditionally been approached using various surrogate performance indicators, but there is an unavoidably arbitrary, judgmental limitation to these systems because they lack the final test of serving a paying client. That is, there is no "bottom line."

The problem also affects individuals. We heard poignant complaints over the lack of incentives to reward good performance. Federal executive bonuses have been reduced to 5 percent or so, which is considered too small to be significant, while the demands on federal managers have risen considerably, and there is a perceived indifference to their welfare: "Top management doesn't care"; "Good planning goes unrewarded"; "The attention and funds go to problem units"; "I only get attention when I fail."

Government cannot simply copy business, but there is a great need for creative thinking to develop a sound entrepreneurial form of public management since markets seem likely to move into the public sector far more aggressively. For example, consider the following hypothetical concepts that could represent one approach.

Budget funds could be allocated in some rough proportion to the patronage units receive, producing an income stream that might be thought of as "revenue." The difference between revenue and costs would form the equivalent of profit, but might more appropriately be thought of as "operating surplus." Finally, such concepts could allow a government equivalent of the profit center to emerge, which could possibly be called a "self-supporting unit" or "service center" accorded the same entrepreneurial freedom that makes business work far more efficiently.

Such terms are not simply euphemisms for business practices that are unacceptable in the public sector but are essential market concepts if federal agencies are to operate more effectively in a difficult new economic era. Self-supporting units would then be motivated to serve client needs, their performance could be evaluated and compared in more realistic terms, they might be allowed greater freedom to do their jobs better, and managers and staff could be rewarded by incentives based on the results. Managers we spoke to tend to agree with these concepts: "We need a way to evaluate user satisfaction"; "Performance evaluation should be based on services rendered"; "A good incentive system would be great."

To introduce government equivalents of market mechanisms, we suggest that a task force should be organized to develop a framework of acceptable concepts. This would be an unusually difficult, sensitive task requiring persons who fully understand business, economics, and public administration, and who have the creativity to formulate a new government philosophy that is rational, effective, and politically acceptable. Such a task force should include academics in these fields and practicing federal administrators, and their work should be reviewed by politicians to ensure it would not be misunderstood by Congress or the public.

The challenge is formidable, but as we have noted throughout this chapter, market principles seem destined to move forcefully into the public arena. It would be best to define a useful conceptual framework now to prepare the way for managing this transition in public administration as carefully and thoughtfully as possible.

APPENDIX

A NEW CORPORATE DESIGN

Jay W. Forrester

During the last fifteen years, there have emerged several important new areas of thinking about the corporation, its purpose, and its management. When brought together, these ideas suggest a new kind of organization that promises major improvements in the way the corporation can serve the needs of man. As yet, no such synthesis has been implemented.

In technology we expect bold experiments that test ideas, obtain new knowledge, and lead to major advances. But in matters of social organization we usually propose only timid modifications of conventional practice and balk at daring experiment and innovation. Why? Surely it is not that present organizations have proven so faultless. Nor can it be a matter of risk, for we spend far more and drastically affect the lives of

This appendix originally appeared as the article "A New Corporate Design," *Industrial Management Review* (currently known as the *Sloan Management Review*) Vol. 7, No. 1 (Fall 1965), pp. 5–17. Copyright 1965 Massachusetts Institute of Technology; reprinted with permission. It is now available as Chapter 6, pp. 93–109, in *Collected Papers of Jay W. Forrester* (Cambridge, MA: Productivity Press, 1975).

more people with scientific and product experiments, many of which fail, than would be necessary in experiments with new concepts of corporate design. Perhaps we are victims of a preoccupation with scientific experiment. Perhaps knowledge is so compartmentalized that no one person sees at the same time the evidence of need, the possibility of improvement, and the route of advance. Perhaps we are reluctant to permit changes in the framework of our own existence. But it is time to apply to business organizations the same willingness to innovate that has set the pace of scientific advance.

BASIS FOR A NEW ORGANIZATION

Innovation can only be based on new ideas. These are now available. Four areas of thought, developed in the last two decades, form the foundations for the new type of organization that is here proposed. These four areas cover quite different aspects of the corporation but together they offer a mutually enhancing basis for a new type of enterprise:

1. New thinking in the social sciences indicates that moving away from authoritarian control in an organization can greatly increase motivation, innovation, and individual human growth and satisfaction [5, 6, 7, 8, 9].
2. Critical examination of trends in the structure and government of corporations suggests that the present superior-subordinate basis of control in the corporation should give way to a more constitutional and democratic form [1, 2, 3].
3. Recent research into the nature of social systems has led to the methods of "industrial dynamics" as a way to design the broad policy structure of an organization to enhance growth and stability [4, 10, 11, 12].
4. Modern electronic communication and computers make possible new concepts in corporate organization to increase flexibility, efficiency, and individual freedom of action.*

---

* The literature is notably weak in treating the philosophy of how electronic data processing can, in the long run, lead to restructured organizations and to environments more attractive to the individual. There has been a tendency to stress the negative, short-run trends rather than to develop the positive aspects.

When these four lines of thinking are synthesized into a new, internally consistent structure, we find that they point to a very different kind of organization from that common in business today.

CHARACTERISTICS OF THE NEW ORGANIZATION

The proposed organization can perhaps best be conveyed by discussing eleven of its most conspicuous characteristics.

Elimination of the Superior-Subordinate Relationship

The influence of organizational form on individual behavior is central to the proposed corporate structure. A substantial body of thought, derived from several centuries of politics, national government, economics, and psychology, exposes the stultifying effect of the authoritarian organization on initiative and innovation and suggests that, whatever the merits of authoritarian control in an earlier day, such control is becoming less and less appropriate as our industrial society evolves.

From industrial history, the social sciences, and the observation of contemporary organizations, there emerges a relationship between the methods used for organizational control and the effectiveness and growth of individuals within the organization. The authoritarian and bureaucratic control structure molds individual personality so that the environment is seen as capricious, and lacking in orderly structure and in cause-and-effect relationships. Consequently the individual feels little hope of changing that environment and is not open to information and observations that would lead to improvement [5].

If the authoritarian hierarchy with its superior-subordinate pairing is to be removed, it must be replaced by another form of discipline and control. This substitute can be individual self-discipline arising from the self-interest created by a competitive market mechanism.

To depart from the authoritarian hierarchy as the central organizational structure, one must replace the superior-subordinate pair as the fundamental building block of the organization. In the new organization, an individual would not be assigned to a superior. Instead he would negotiate, as a free individual, a continually changing structure of relationships with those with whom he exchanges goods and services. He would accept specific obligations as agreements of limited duration.

As these are discharged, he would establish a new pattern of relationships as he finds more satisfying and rewarding situations.

The guiding policy structure and accounting procedures of the system must be so adjusted that the self-interest of the individual and the objectives of the total organization can be made to coincide. Education within the organization must then prepare each individual to use his opportunities in that self-interest.

The nonauthoritarian structure implies internal competition for resource allocation. Prices of individual skills, capital, and facilities would rise to the highest level that could be profitably recovered by the various managers who sell to the outside economy. An internal price that is higher than an external price for the same resource would reflect a more efficient and effective internal use of that resource than is possible in the external economy. Such internal competitive allocation resources would contrast to allocation by central authority as is now practiced by industrial corporations.

Individual Profit Centers

If resources are allocated not by the edict of higher authority but according to the value of the resource of the individual members of the organization, there must be a basis on which each member can estimate that value. In our economy outside the corporation, price is established in the long run by competitive conditions at a level that allows a profit to both buyer and seller. To achieve a counterpart within the new organization, each man or small team (partnership) should be a profit center and a decision point responsible for the success of those activities in which the center chooses to engage.

Much has been written about profit centers in the corporation. In the larger corporations, profit responsibility is often decentralized to divisional profit centers. Yet, even in the most extensive present use of the profit center concept, only a tiny percentage of the individuals in the organization are personally involved in a profit center frame of reference to guide their own decisions and actions.

The profit center concept is very different from the budget center concept which is so common in financial planning and control. In a budget center the individual governs himself relative to a negotiated expenditure rate. The objective within the budget center is often to negotiate the highest expenditure rate possible (because salary and status are associated with number of employees and size of budget) and then to spend the full budget. Indeed, there are often pressures to overspend because next year's budget is related to this year's expenditures. The budget measures performance in terms of cost compared to promised cost and not in terms of cost compared to accomplishment.

The budget system of control sets up two conflicting chains. On one side are the functional activities responsible for accomplishing the work of the corporation—research, engineering, production, and sales. In each of these functional areas are pressures to accomplish as much as possible, to hire as many people as possible, and to spend as much money as possible. Since these tendencies toward excess cannot go unchecked, there must be an opposing group, such as the controller's office, to impress financial restraint on the first group. The resulting conflict between pressures toward excesses and restraint of those pressures can only be resolved at higher authoritarian levels in the corporation. Once a control system is established that is not based on self-restraint, the authoritarian structure becomes necessary to resolve conflict. Efficiency, motivation, and morale decline rapidly as the command channels become choked, and as the decision-making point becomes so remote from operations that firsthand knowledge is inadequate for sound decisions.

In contrast to a budget center, a profit center values activity and resources in terms of the difference (profit) between input costs and a sale price that is acceptable to others in a competitive market. The incentive is to maximize the difference between cost and value, to produce the most value for the least cost, and to reduce expenditure of time and resources where this can be done without a more than corresponding reduction in the value of the product. To be effective, rewards at the profit center, both financial and psychological rewards, must depend on profit and not on expenditure rate.

The way in which the profit accounting is done and the manner in which rewards depend on profit become of the utmost importance when these are the measures of success. The possible rules for this accounting cover a broad range. It is here that the self-interest of the individual is determined. It is in the profit center accounting rules that the individual meets the policy structure of the organization. It is here that individual self-interest and the objectives of the organization must coincide if a unity of purpose is to be sustained. It is here that the proper balance must be struck between long- and short-term objectives. It is here that the intended pressures must be created for adequate planning, for quality, for integrity, and for stability and growth of the organization as a whole.

The profit center provides the incentive to start new activity but, perhaps even more important, it must create pressures to discontinue old activities. Stopping an activity at the right time is one of the most important management functions. Too often, termination is delayed because it must be forced on an operational group having personal incentives to continue. In this conflict, termination can be imposed only when the external evidence for stopping the activity becomes overwhelming. Since emphasis should focus on the total life cycle of an undertaking—successful beginning, successful mid-life management, and successful termination or transfer—profit center accounting for determining personal compensation should usually occur at the closing of an account to be measured against a compounded return-on-investment basis that extends over the total life of the activity.

The detailed accounting procedures are beyond the scope of this paper. Initially the accounting rules can only be tentative because they will almost certainly need to be changed after observation of the pressures they create in the organization. Unintended pressures, or the inadequacy of intended pressures, must be corrected at their source by changing the accounting methods, not by building a body of compensating rules that would have to be implemented by a superimposed authoritarian control structure.

In the profit center structure there will be similarities to the various legal entities in the outside economy. Some persons will offer personal services as advisers and consultants, others as contractors taking engineering and manufacturing commitments at a bid price, some as promoters and entrepreneurs to coordinate internal resources to meet the needs of the market, and still others in the role of informed investors to allocate the financial resources of the organization where the promise is greatest. Profit centers would prohibit several procedures to the outside economy, such as the cost-reimbursement contract, which reduce the incentive for efficiency and tend to reimpose the budget method of control.

Objective Determination of Compensation

If each profit center is designed to provide a sufficient measure of performance and if the centers correspond to individual people or small groups of people, then salary and bonus compensation can be determined automatically from the accounts of the center. Each man identified with the center would have a status similar to that of an owner-manager.

Above-average performance, as shown in the profit center accounts, would lead to bonus payments, perhaps distributed into the future to give greater personal income continuity. If high performance persists, repetitive bonus payments would be the signal, according to a formula, for base salary increases to transfer more of the man's compensation to a stable income basis.

An "objective" determination of salary here means one that is not the subjective setting of one man's income by the judgment (often interpreted as whim or caprice) of a superior. Instead, income results from the value set on the man's contribution by peers who negotiate for his service. For this peer evaluation to produce more effective internal alignments, there must be enough internal mobility so that the man can find the more satisfying situations. He must have unhampered freedom to test the value of his contribution in a variety of competing outlets. The objective measure of value rests on the freedom to move away from any situation which he believes to result in an unfair evaluation of his worth.

Policy Making Separated from Decision Making

Policies and decisions are conceptually very distinct from one another although they are intermingled and confused in much of the management literature.

Policies are those rules that guide decisions. The policy treats the general case and at least partially defines how specific decisions under that policy are to be made. Conversely, a decision takes the status and information of the system and processes it in accordance with the guiding policy to determine current action.

In their effect on human initiative and innovation, four measures of policy are important—freedom, accessibility, source, and consistency:

By the first measure, policies can differ in freedom, that is, the extent to which they determine the encompassed decisions. A fully defining policy completely determines the decision as soon as the values of the input variables are available; that is, when the existing conditions that are recognized by the policy have been measured, the rules of the policy are explicit and complete and the decision can be routinely computed. Such a policy leaves no freedom of action and can be automatized in a computer as are the policies for ordinary accounting procedures. On the other hand, a policy can establish a boundary within which the decisions must be made but with freedom remaining to adjust the decisions to personal preference or to information that was not foreseen by the policy.

By the second measure, policies can differ in accessibility, that is, the extent to which they are known to the decision maker. That decision maker who must act without being able to discover the policies which are to govern his actions is in a difficult and frustrating position. This inaccessibility of the guiding policies may arise for any number of reasons—the policies may exist but be undetectable, they may exist and be known but be subject to capricious change, or they may be nonexistent until a decision has been made which then may precipitate a contrary and retroactive policy.

By the third measure, policies can differ in source. Personal satisfaction with policies probably varies along the axis marked at one end by self-determined policies that govern one's own and others' decisions and, at the opposite extreme, by policies imposed by another who establishes those policies unilaterally for his own benefit. In a democracy, the source of policy is intermediate between these extremes, being established by compromise between the citizens in a search for the greatest average satisfaction.

By the fourth measure, policies can differ in consistency, that is, freedom from internal contradiction. Often one finds policy structures in which the parts are so fragmented and unrelated that the separate policies operate at cross-purposes. Examples are seen in emphasis on ever-greater sales even with hesitance and conservatism in expanding productive capacity, in stress on quality and customer satisfaction even while overloading the organization till it can perform only poorly, and in the unresolved conflict between pressures for short-term success and long-term strength. Contradictory policy is apt to arise where policy is an interpretation of decisions rather than vice versa. When decisions are made on the basis of local expediencies and policy is formulated to fit, the policy structure becomes an assembly of unrelated pieces. If policy is to be internally self-supporting and consistent, it must reflect a systems awareness. Each part of the policy structure must be appropriate not only to its local objective but must interact with other policies in a manner consistent with the over-all objectives of the total system. In the complex feedback system structure of an economic enterprise, consistent policy can hardly be created in bits and by happenstance.

As measured along these four dimensions—freedom, accessibility, source and consistency—policy often operates in a manner that is unfavorable to individual effectiveness. Policy is most suppressive of innovation when it completely defines action and states exactly what is to be done. Policy is most frustrating to initiative when it is undeterminable and subject to future definition and retroactive application. Policy is most antagonizing when it is imposed on a subordinate for the benefit of the superior. Policy is most confusing when it is internally inconsistent and provides no guide for resolving conflicting pressures. These undesirable extremes are closely approached in some corporations.

By contrast, the more successful corporations are characterized by policies that give coordination without confinement, clarity of forbidden action, objectives that balance the interests of all, and consistency that reduces unresolved conflict. Yet it would appear that only the rare corporation goes far enough in even one of these four measures of desirable policy and none go far enough in all.

Policy should allow freedom to innovate and should have the fewest restrictions compatible with the coordination needed to insure overall system strength, stability, and growth. Policy should be accessible, clear, and not retroactive. The source of policy should be a process that ensures some consensus by those affected that it is a just compromise for the common good. Policies should be consistent by being designed as parts of a total policy structure that creates the desired dynamic behavior in the resulting system. Recent advances in the theory of dynamic systems and in system simulation using digital computers demonstrate that it will be possible to design internally consistent policy structures directly, rather than inferring corporate policy from the implications of past decisions.

Creating such a policy structure, and maintaining it as conditions change and new insights are acquired, would be a full-time task for a small number of the most capable men in a corporation. The past and present of the corporate system must be studied as a background for designing policy changes which will create pressures and incentives toward an improving future.

Policy making ought to be separated from the distractions of operational decision making; otherwise, short-term pressures will usurp time from policy creation, which can always be postponed to the future. Policy making ought to be separated from decision making to give a more objective and impartial outlook to policy design. Policy making ought to be separated from decision making so that the source of the policy is specific and responsibility for policy is clear.

Restructuring through Electronic Data Processing

Vast amounts of electronic communication and computing equipment have already been installed for business data processing. Yet, the equipment is used almost entirely for tasks of the type that were previously done manually. Emphasis has been on doing more data processing within the earlier patterns, or on reducing the cost of work already being done.

The inadequacy of today's data processing objectives is exposed by industrial dynamics studies of corporate systems that show how behavior depends heavily on classes of information channels and decisions that are not today being supported by the electronic equipment. In these more important channels, information flow is haphazard, information is late, information is biased by human filtering, and error is frequent. Computers provide the incentive to explore the fundamental relationship between information and corporate success.

Part of the policy design task is to identify the relative importance of the various decision points and to determine the quality and fidelity needed in each information input. When this is done, information channels will be emphasized which are very different from those presently receiving attention.

Information networks can take several forms. The networks of most organizations are in the form of a complex mesh with many information repositories and large numbers of interconnecting channels. Another kind of network, made possible by the digital computer, takes the form of an information storage and computing hub with radiating spokes to each source or destination.

In the mesh network type of information system that is now common, the task of information storage and processing is subdivided to many small centers. Information is handled in batches, and files lag behind the status of the real-life system that they represent. Also, much of the information must be processed in series through several centers and there are large "inventories" of in-process information scattered throughout the system. Information retrieved from the system to guide decisions does not reflect past actions that are still being recorded and processed. This is often true even in the simple accounting and sales information that is now being handled by electronic computers. It is universally true and seriously detrimental in those informal information channels and decisions at the higher management levels. The mesh network becomes impossibly complex as the number of centers increases, particularly if each center is allowed to interact with every other center. A partial simplification has been achieved in practice by restricting communication channels to the inverted tree pattern of the formal organization chart. When this is done, lateral communication becomes slow and circuitous.

In the mesh network, substantial time and energy are consumed by internal communication that is made necessary by the dispersed storage of information. As a result, the organization becomes preoccupied with itself. It becomes inward looking with vast numbers of internal channels, the maintenance of which draws attention away from the contacts between the organization and the outside world. The organization consequently makes too little use of new technical knowledge; it loses contact with new market trends; and is insufficiently aware of customer attitudes. These communication difficulties can be alleviated through a complete restructuring of the information system.

Modern electronic equipment permits a rearrangement of the information system into a radial or star shape with all files at the center. "On-line" use of computers for both data processing and internal communication can provide an information picture that is up to date and fully processed at all times. Partially processed inventories of information can be substantially reduced, along with a reduction of the internal communication needed to estimate conditions that are not yet reflected in the formal data.

With such a restructured system, information will be directly accessible to persons that now must operate with too little information either to permit good management or to establish a feeling of security and confidence. If the internal information can be reduced, energy can be turned to the even more challenging quest for external information—information about new technical developments, new management methods, new employees, customer satisfaction, product performance in the field, and changing markets.

Freedom of Access to Information

Much of the character and atmosphere of an organization can be deduced from the way it internally extends and withholds information. Corporations are almost all built on the authoritarian hierarchy structure but corporations differ greatly as to the basis on which authority and status are maintained within the hierarchy. In healthy organizations, authority tends to rest on generally recognized ability, ability which is great enough that it need not be excessively bolstered by information monopolies. In an authoritarian position that is not based on recognized ability, security may simply derive from the structure of the bureaucracy and the prerogatives of the office, or position may be maintained by withholding information from both superiors and subordinates.

To possess information is to possess power. A monopoly of information can give a form of security. There are, in all organizations at all levels, a selective withholding and extending of information. Sole possession of information can make others dependent on oneself. Withholding of information can limit the scope and power of others' actions and reduce the threat to oneself. Control of information channels can isolate certain persons from the remainder of the organization and keep them within one's own sphere of influence.

Most persons in most organizations feel that they do not have access to all the information they need. Sometimes they lack the information specifically needed to accomplish their duties. Very often they lack the information needed to create a sense of security and a belief in the fairness and rationality of the system of which they are a part.

Information is often withheld to forestall questions about an authoritarian decision that has no rational defense. The availability of salary information illustrates the point. Wages of workers in a union situation may be generally known because the contract rules have been made explicit; information about individual compensation is made available to show that the rules are being followed. Conversely there are rules to justify the wage so that a subjective decision need not be defended. At the top of the hierarchy, executive salaries are published to stockholders along with information to implicitly or explicitly justify those salaries. In public service, salaries are set by law and are public knowledge. It is in the middle level of the corporation that one finds the greatest secrecy in salary details; this middle level is where salary determination is most subjective and where a guiding policy is least available. One can generalize to the observation that the more obscure the reasons for a decision, the greater are the inclinations to hide both the decision and the information on which it was based.

An organization can be seriously handicapped by the loss of energy consumed in the struggle for information. Time is occupied by attempts to obtain and to hide information. Psychological energy is drained by the nagging belief that others are withholding information that one needs, and by concern lest others learn information that one hopes to withhold.

Just as the individual hoards information, so does the organization as a whole. Competitive position is often believed to rest on secrecy to a far greater extent than is the fact. Information is withheld from individuals inside the organization on the excuse that this keeps information from outsiders. Secrecy is a poor foundation for success compared with competence, and to maintain secrecy reduces competence.

Although one will never succeed in making all information fully available, the goal can be pursued. Access can be given to the information that is recorded in the formal data system of the corporation. Incentives, both the incentive of convenience and the incentives designed into the accounting system, can encourage the entry of information into the central data files, from which it can be electronically retrieved. Design studies of the corporate data system will show the importance of converting many of today's informal information channels to ones in which regular observations are measured and recorded.

A general principle of the new organization should be to give much wider and more ready access to information than is now the usual practice. This can be accomplished by reducing restrictions on information availability, by designing the social and incentive structure to favor the release of information, and to gather and record information in important channels that often remain on an informal basis.

Elimination of Internal Monopolies

On the national level monopolies are forbidden because of their stultifying influence on economic efficiency. Yet within corporations monopolies are often created in the name of presumed efficiency and are defended as avoiding duplication of effort.

For most activities the economies of scale are not as great as commonly supposed. In many situations, where economy is expected from a larger activity it is easy to see that lower efficiency, in fact, results. Very often the problems of planning and coordination rise so rapidly that they defeat the economies from larger size. This is particularly true of many of the service activities such as shops, drafting rooms, and purchasing offices.

Even where the activity itself may become more efficient in terms of local measures, the efficiency of the total organization may suffer.

For example, in the consolidation of model shops, higher shop efficiency may result from a greater load factor on machines and machinists. However, the consolidated shop, now administratively separated from the technical activities, is less responsive to need, requires negotiation of user priorities, and may well cost substantially in the valuable technical and management time of senior people on whom the success of the organization depends.

It should be a principle of the proposed organization that every type of activity and service must exist in multiple. No person is limited to a single source for his needs. No person is dependent on a single user of his output.

Only by eliminating the monopolies of the normal corporate structure can one have the efficiencies and incentives of a competitive system and provide objective and comparative measures of performance.

Balancing Reward and Risk

The new organization should retain and combine the advantages of earlier organizational forms while minimizing their disadvantages. One wishes to combine the stability and strength of the large, diversified business organization with the challenge and opportunity that the small company offers to its founder-managers. At the same time one must avoid the stifling bureaucracy and compartmentalization that is frequent in large organizations wherein the central power holds the right to allocate resources and make decisions. For the larger companies, competition exists on the outside but has no direct and often little indirect personal influence on those inside, except at the top levels of management. Conversely, the extreme risk and threat of failure in the small organization must be minimized since this repels many who might become effective independent managers.

In today's "small-business" world, the risk to the budding entrepreneur is greater than it need be. In general he gets but one chance. There is no opportunity to practice and to improve ability if the first undertaking is not a success. Penalty for failure should be reduced to a tolerable level but not eliminated. This can be done by risk sharing, not unlike the concept of insurance against catastrophe. The penalties should be just high enough to identify and dissuade the manager who repeatedly fails. Rewards should attract and encourage the competent and be high enough so that a normal quota of successes will more than carry the burden of occasional failures.

Offsetting part of the successes to cover the cost of the failures is now done by risk investors in the financial community but under circumstances unfavorable to the individual who seeks financial help. The investor is interested in a quick return on his investment. He has neither the skill nor the opportunity to substantially increase the ability of the new manager, or even to judge the ability in advance. The investor in new ventures is forced into a sorting process of trying prospective managers, staying with the successes, and dropping the failures as soon as they are so identified. Such a process must be contrasted with a more ideal one in which the individual grows from initially managing his own time, to managing small projects, to becoming an entrepreneur who matches customer needs to the abilities of the organization. This evolution without discontinuity from individual worker to entrepreneur can stop or be redirected at any point. At each stage a history of performance is available to the man and to his potential supporters as a basis for deciding the next stage of his growth.

It follows that specific undertakings must be small enough so that the total organization can survive any individual failure. A favorable over-all ratio of success to failure must rest on the greater efficiency instilled in the organization, the greater competence created by the internal educational system, and the personal growth induced by the freedom, competitive challenge, and greater opportunities for the individual.

Mobility of the Individual

In the new organization, in contrast to the conventional corporation, the individual should have much greater freedom of internal movement, and greater ease of voluntary exit, but more restraint on entry.

The nonauthoritarian structure with its internal competitive characteristics lays the basis for internal mobility so that work relationships can continually change toward those that are more satisfying. This potential mobility must be made real by an educational system that prepares the man for new opportunities and by an accounting system that creates pressures to prevent reversion to the superior-subordinate relationship. The latter is one of the many pressures that must be created by the design of the data processing system. For example, mobility should be enhanced by limiting, in the profit center accounting, the credit allowed for income from any one source that exceeds a specified fraction of the year's activity. This would create pressures on each individual to maintain several activity contacts, making it easier for him to gradually shift toward the ones that are more desirable.

Most corporations have reward structures designed to discourage men from leaving. Pension funds and stock options have rules that penalize the manager who leaves before retirement age. The worker is under similar pressures generated by pension rights and union seniority.

The negative consequences of this immobility are serious to the health of the organization just as immobility can retard a country's economic growth. Dissatisfied persons, who therefore lack dedication to their work, stay in the organization rather than find a position elsewhere to which they are better suited. The suppressed turnover rate in personnel makes it easy for management to ignore undesirable internal conditions which might be quickly corrected if they were emphasized by a higher personnel departure rate. Furthermore, we can assume that people who are unwillingly present are less likely to grow to greater competence and responsibility. Finally, the restrictions on leaving fail in their primary purpose by having little effect on the most competent men whose self-confidence and security lie in outstanding ability.

The new organization should hold people because they want to be a part of its kind of society. Any rights or deferred compensation that have been earned by past performance should be readily transportable if the man decides to leave. In fact, one might go further and visualize a placement office to assist any member of the organization in looking for a more attractive outside opportunity. If he finds one, the organization should reexamine itself to see if it is failing to offer the superior environment that is one of its principal objectives. If the man does not find the outside more attractive, he may become even more dedicated to the organization of which he is a part.

Mobility from the outside into the new organization is a different matter. Life in the organization would be very unlike most people's prior experience. The organization would be suitable for only a small fraction of them. It may well be that, if he has adequate information on which to base his decision, a man can judge his own compatibility with the organization more accurately than those within can judge for him. The mutual decision by the applicant and the organization should be based on a far deeper acquaintanceship than precedes employment in most companies. This might be achieved through a series of study and discussion seminars that would expose the applicant, and perhaps his wife also, to the philosophy, history, psychological basis, objectives, and people of the organization.

The growth and stability of the total organization would depend on the mix of human resources and their rate of entry. The over-all policies must provide guidance and incentives for bringing in the proper skills. For this reason also, the inward mobility cannot be as free as interior or outward mobility.

Enhanced Rights of the Individual

Thoughtful writers on the evolution of the corporation have raised challenging questions about the sources and legitimacy of corporate power and its effect on those involved. By law, power rests with the stockholders; but in practice, stockholders have little control over either the acts or the selection of management. Considering the emerging concepts of social justice, there is serious doubt about the moral right of stockholders, acting through management, to the arbitrary power which can now be exercised over individual employees, particularly those in the middle management and technical groups. The precedents set in the last several hundred years by changes in the form of national government suggest that corporate power will also evolve from the authoritarian toward the constitutional. With this evolution, the primary objectives of the corporation would change from the already diluted idea of existence primarily for profit to the stockholders and toward the concept of a society primarily devoted to the interests of its participants.

The present-day protection of the employee against the exercise of arbitrary power by the corporation is weak and unevenly distributed. Production workers, by joining together in unions, have won a few fundamental individual rights regarding seniority, grievance procedures, and rights of arbitration. But, as one moves up the corporate hierarchy, the subordinate has progressively less security against arbitrary decisions by the superior. It is in the technical and management levels, where initiative and innovation are so important, that we find most unrestrained that suppressor of initiative and innovation—capricious, arbitrary authority.

The new organization should develop around a "constitution" that establishes the rights of the individual and the limitation of the power of the organization over him. Corporate policy would be subject to corporate constitutional provisions just as the national constitution has supremacy over laws made by national legislative bodies. To complete the system, there must be means for "judicial review" by impartial tribunals to arbitrate disagreements and to interpret into illustrative precedent the operational meaning of the constitution and policies of the organization.

Education within the Corporation

A modern national democracy rests on an extensive body of tradition and a high level of public education without which the democratic processes fail. This failure has been manifest in the turmoil during the formation of new nations. Without a foundation of education and tradition, premature democratic governments quickly revert to authoritarian regimes. By contrast, democracy in Western Europe and the United States now rests on a massive base of education and on deep traditions regarding rights and responsibilities of the individual.

A corresponding foundation must support the new type of "industrial democracy" that is here being proposed. Such a base of education and tradition lies as far beyond the background possessed by today's average manager and engineer as the United States public background of democracy lies beyond that in the underdeveloped nations. The cycle of change can begin with education that guides practice which matures into different organizational traditions.

The more effective education of the future must permit man's transition to a new, higher level of abstraction in the economic process. The last such change in level of abstraction was man's entry during the last two centuries into our present industrial society. In the days of the craftsman, the most skilled in the population made the consumer products, but, in the more abstract atmosphere of industrialization, the most skilled have become the inventors and designers who crate machines that, in turn, make the consumer products. The skilled designers now operate once removed from direct production.

At the same time, the structure for decision making changed radically to one in which the decisions are now more abstract because they are removed from the point of actual production. The need for coordinating many efforts caused a subdivision and specialization of decision making, similar to the specialization that is so evident in actual manufacturing steps. Where the craftsman had hardly been aware of the distinction between deciding and doing, the industrial society separates the decision from the action. Decision making is separated from the worker because the governing policy is implicit and subjective. It has

not yet been clearly stated. Coordination has been possible only by cen-
tralizing decision making in one individual so that consistency might
then come from all decisions being tempered by the same subjective
policies. But for this coordination we pay a high price in personal values
and in flexibility to innovate and to respond to changing circumstances.
The separation of work from decision making, with the authoritarian
system that it implies, has been at the root of the growing dissatisfaction
with the present trend in corporate government.

In leaving our present stage of economic evolution and moving to a
future "automation society," we must pass through another transition in
man's relationship to production. In this still more abstract society, the
most skilled, on whom the production processes depend, will be those
who create the machines which in turn make production machines
which, again in turn, produce goods. The most skilled will then be
twice removed from actual production. This new complexity of industrialization has already begun.

The conceptual changes in management which must accompany
our progress into the automation society are as sweeping as the change
to centralized decision making that came with industrialization. In the
new phase there must be another restructuring of the decision-making
process.

Our understanding of the industrial system is now reaching a point
where the policy necessary to guide coordinated decisions can be made
explicit and the policy structure itself can be objectively studied and designed. As this explicit treatment of policy is achieved, policy making and
decision making can be completely separated. Policy making can then be
executed by a central group; and decision making, within the framework
of the common policy, can be returned to the individual person.

In such a new industrial organization education must serve two
purposes that are not essential in an authoritarian corporate government. First, understanding of the growth and stability dynamics that in-
terrelate psychology, economic activity, and markets must be adequate
to permit design of a governing policy structure. Second, the citizens of
the new corporate society must understand the origin, meaning, and
purposes of the policy structure well enough to conduct their affairs
successfully in a manner that combines individual freedom with group
coordination.

In preparing men for our present industrialized society we already
devote a third of each lifetime to education. One might ask how a still
higher level of education is to be achieved. There are several answers.

First, as we climb to the next level of conceptual abstraction, much of the earlier educational process condenses into a new, rational framework. Specifically, as we come to understand the fundamental structure and dynamics of social systems, we can learn explicitly and directly the general concepts which earlier had to be taught indirectly by historical incident or learned slowly from personal experience. Most present-day teaching in the humanities and in management is by the "case method" of retracing specific situations, leaving to the student the task of extracting some general principles from the apparently conflicting descriptions. Now, as it becomes possible to work directly with the pertinent system structures in the context of system theory and laboratory simulation, it becomes clearer how certain fundamental characteristics of social systems can produce the diverse modes of behavior that are observed. An understanding of social systems can be acquired much more rapidly if learning can be based on an explicit system rationale than if this rationale is only dimly and intuitively perceived.

Second, time for education can be obtained in the work environment if the confusions and distractions in present practice can be reduced by a clearer structure and a more efficient coordinating process. Estimates indicate that many of today's organizations consume 25 percent or more of their potential effectiveness trying to coordinate internal activity. Much of this coordination is necessary simply because the organization is overloaded and trying to produce beyond its true capability. As the organization tries to do more in the short run, the costs rise rapidly in terms of confusion, coordinating and planning personnel, resolving priorities, and pacifying dissatisfied customers. The toll is especially high at the creative levels of management and engineering. Policies that ensure slight underloading could leave the same actual productive output and make the time now lost through attempted overloading available for a continuing educational program.

Third, time for education will be economically feasible if it results in greater long-term effectiveness. Greater revenue resulting from a higher degree of initiative and innovation can be allocated partly to the educational program. If the organization maintains its vitality and continues to change in keeping with the times, it should sustain a high enough level of contribution to society to justify a perpetual rebuilding of the educational base.

Fourth, education might be more effective if it could be properly coordinated with a man's development. This would require a true educational opportunity as a continuing part of the work environment. Then it would be possible to shorten a man's formal education at the college level and defer the study of many areas until work experience has indicated their importance and until learning motivation is higher. For example, engineers early see the importance of science but they may be well launched on their professional careers before they see reason to understand psychology, the dynamics of industrial systems, law, or even effective writing.

What, then, should be the place of education in the corporate strategy? The arguments are persuasive that some 25 percent of the total working time of all persons in the corporation should be devoted to preparing for their future roles. This means time devoted to competence some five years in the future and does not include the learning that may be a necessary part of the immediate task. Over a period of years this study would cover a wide range—individual and group psychology, writing, speaking, law, dynamics of industrial behavior, corporate policy design, advances in science and engineering, and historical development of political and corporate organizations—the extent and sequence being tailored to the individual person.

Such an educational program would differ substantially from any now offered. It must be derived from the same foundations and social trends as the new corporation itself. It must be at the same time more practical, but also more fundamental and enduring, than existing advanced training programs in either technology or management.

The educational program must become an integral part of corporate life, not a few weeks or months once in a lifetime at another institution. The over-all policies of the organization must create incentives that protect the time for education from encroachment by short-term pressures. Because self-development is so easy to defer, the responsibility for personal growth should probably be shared by the individual and a "career adviser" whose own compensation depends on the growth and success of his protégés.

ANALOGY TO NATIONAL ECONOMIC STRUCTURE

The central feature of today's corporation is its authoritarian power structure, with the superior-subordinate pair relationship as the fundamental building block. Ultimate authority for all decisions lies at the top and this authority is delegated or withheld by the superior at each level. So entrenched in our thinking is this authoritarian structure that few people can visualize an alternative, yet our largest economic unit stands as a striking and successful contradiction.

The growth and strength of the United States as a whole rests on an economic structure in which the superior-subordinate relationship is absent. Legal entities, be they corporations or individuals, are related to each other as equals. Corporations, doctors, lawyers, shop owners, independent contractors, and private businessmen interact with one another in a structure based on self-interest, not on the right of one to dictate to another. The United States' economic structure is not an exact pattern for the new organization. Yet the constitution and legal structure of the country offer many clues to answering the more difficult questions about the proposed organization.

The profit center concept of the proposed organization brings into the corporation the same free-enterprise profit motive that we believe is essential to the capitalist economy. The objective determination of compensation is the same process that determines the profitability of legal entities in the outside economy.

The stress on separation between policy making and decision making has its counterpart in the separation, on the one hand, between congressional and executive branches of the government and, on the other hand, between the policies set by law and the decision-making freedom left to the independent economic units. Laws, viewed as policy to govern economic activity, tend to be boundary policy stating what cannot be done and leaving all else to the discretion of business decision makers. The counterpart of laws would be corporate policy designed to achieve adequate coordination while permitting individual freedom.

Freedom of access to information within the corporation has its equivalent in the freedom of the press.

Antimonopoly legislation rests on reasons that should prevail far oftener when corporations decide whether or not to combine similar functions.

Education as a major function of government has an equivalent in the emphasis that the corporation should place on preparing its people for the future.

IMPLEMENTATION OF THESE PROPOSALS

It is not implied that these ideas for a new corporate design are yet developed to a point where they would fit all types of businesses. But they do seem particularly suited to those industries which feel the impact of rapid change in science and technology in which conventional management approaches have often been found wanting.

An experiment in organization should presume slow growth at first under conditions permitting revision because it must be realized that an enterprise as different as the one here proposed must test and evolve its most fundamental concepts as well as their implementation.

It does not seem likely that such sweeping changes could be implemented by gradual change within an existing organization. The new proposals represent a consistent structure; but they contain many reversals of existing practice. Introducing the changes piecemeal would place them in conflicting and incompatible environments; the changes would be contrary to existing traditions and would give rise to counterpressures high enough to defeat them.

The only promising approach seems to be to build a new organization from the ground up in the new pattern. It might be either a truly new and independent organization or a detached and isolated subsidiary of an existing corporation. It must feel its way, modify ideas where necessary, and create success at each stage as a foundation for further growth.

REFERENCES

Introduction

1. Quoted from "Personal Computers," *Business Week* (August 12, 1991).

2. For instance, see George Gilder, *Microcosm: The Quantum Revolution in Economics and Technology* (New York: Simon & Schuster, 1989), and Walter B. Wriston, *The Twilight of Authority: How Information Technology Is Transforming Our World* (New York: Scribners, 1992).

3. See Jay W. Forrester, "A New Corporate Design," *Industrial Management Review* 7, no. 1 (Fall 1965): 5–17, which is reprinted in this book. We are indebted to Rick Forschler, Boeing Engineering Corporation, for calling our attention to another early article describing a manufacturing plant in Dayton, Ohio, that invented a similar management system: John C. Sparks, "Production Unlimited," *The Freeman: A Monthly Journal of Ideas on Liberty* 12, no. 3 (March 1962).

4. Warren Bennis, *Beyond Bureaucracy* (New York: McGraw-Hill, 1966).

5. Robert Townsend, *Up the Organization* (New York: Knopf, 1970).

6. Robert Townsend, *Further Up the Organization* (New York: Knopf, 1984).

7. William E. Halal, "Facing Transformation: The Great American House Move," *The Futurist* (September–October 1989).

8. "John Scully," *Forbes* (December 7, 1992).

Chapter 1

1. Russell L. Ackoff, "The Circular Organization: An Update," *The Academy of Management Executive,* 3, no. 1 (1989): 11–16.

Chapter 2

1. G. Bennett Stewart, "Remaking the Public Corporation from Within," *Harvard Business Review* (July–August 1990).

2. Tom Peters, "Get Innovative or Get Dead," *California Management Review* (Fall 1990).

3. Levison, *The Decentralized Company* (New York: AMACOM, 1983), 20–21.

4. Quoted from "IBM: As Markets and Technology Change, Can Big Blue Remake Its Culture?" *Business Week* (June 17, 1991).

5. Ibid.

6. Mark Potts, "A New Vision for Leadership from GE's Visionary," *Washington Post* (March 8, 1992).

7. See Douglas Hall and Judith Richter, "Career Gridlock: Baby Boomers Hit the Wall," *The Executive* (August 1990).

8. Welch is quoted from Mark Potts, "GE's Management Vision," *Washington Post* (May 22, 1988).

9. For instance, see "Measuring Business-Unit Performance," *Research Bulletin No. 206* (The Conference Board, 1987).

10. Rosabeth Moss Kanter, "Championing Change: An Interview with Bell Atlantic's CEO Raymond Smith," *Harvard Business Review* (January–February 1991).

11. As reported by David M. Noer in "Ready, Set, Turn a Profit," *Training and Development Journal* (May 1985).

12. Brandt Allen, "Making Information Services Pay Its Way," *Harvard Business Review* (January–February 1987).

13. Susan Walsh Sanderson, "The Vision of Shared Manufacturing," *Across the Board* (December 1987).

14. C. K. Prahalad and Gary Hamel, "The Core Competence of the Corporation," *Harvard Business Review* (May–June 1990).

15. "A Big Company That Works," *Business Week* (May 4, 1992).

16. Peters, "Get Innovative or Get Dead, op. cit.

17. The view of internal markets corresponds to the emerging science of complexity, described by Roger Lewin, *Complexity: Life at the Edge of Chaos* (New York: Macmillan, 1992); and M. Mitchell Waldrop, *Complexity: The Emerging Science at the Edge of Order and Chaos* (New York: Simon & Schuster, 1992).

18. In order, these examples are from "The Bad Boy of Silicon Valley," *Business Week* (December 9, 1991); "A Big Company That Works," *Business Week* (May 4, 1992); "May the Force Be with You," *Inc.* (July 1987); "Nucor's Big Breakthrough," *Iron Age* (February 1987); "The Miracle Company," *Business Week* (October 19, 1987); "Deconstructing the Computer Industry," *Business Week* (November 23, 1992).

19. William Halal and San Retna, "Corporations in Transition" (work in progress).

20. John Walsh, "Videoconferencing Comes of Age," *Telecommunications* (November 1989); Gail Runnoe, "Videoconferencing Set to Soar," *Network World* (July 3, 1989); and Roberta Furger, "The Growth of the Home Office," *InfoWorld* (October 9, 1989).

21. "The Portable Executive," *Business Week* (October 10, 1988): 104. Also see William Davidow and Michael Malone, *The Virtual Corporation* (New York: Harper, 1992).

22. Eliza Collins, "A Company without Offices," *Harvard Business Review* (January–February 1986).

23. Strassmann is quoted from "Information Strategist Paul Strassmann," *INC.* (March 1988): 27.

24. For instance, see Thomas Malone et al., "The Logic of Electronic Markets," *Harvard Business Review* (May–June 1989); Robert Kuttner, "Computers May Turn the World into One Big Commodities Pit," *Business Week* (September 11, 1989); and Thomas W. Malone and John F. Rockart, "Computers, Networks, and the Corporation," *Scientific American* (September 1991): 131.

25. See Oliver Williamson, *Markets and Hierarchies* (New York: Free Press, 1975).

26. David Clutterback, "The Whittling Away of Middle Management," *International Management* (November 1982): 10–16.

27. Charles Handy, *The Age of Unreason* (Cambridge, MA: Harvard Business School Press, 1990).

28. Rosabeth M. Kanter, "The Attack on Pay," *Harvard Business Review* (March–April 1987).

29. For instance, see Kenneth Labich, "Take Control of Your Career," *Fortune* (May 1992), and "I'm Worried about My Job!" *Business Week* (October 7, 1991).

30. "Part-Timers Are In," *Conference Board's Monthly Briefing* (March 1988); "And Now, 'Temp' Managers," *Newsweek* (September 26, 1988).

31. Harvey Wagner, "The Open Corporation," *California Management Review* (Summer 1991).

32. Anne Fisher, "CEOs Think That Morals Is Dandy," *Fortune* (November 18, 1991).

33. William Halal, "The New Management: Business and Social Institutions for an Information Age," *Business in the Contemporary World* (Winter 1990).

34. See Gregory Tassey, "Structural Change and Competitiveness: The U.S. Semiconductor Industry," *Technological Forecasting & Social Change* (March 1990), and Richard Florida and Martin Kenney, "Silicon Valley and Route 128 Won't Save Us," *California Management Review* (Fall 1990).

35. "Learning from Japan: How a Few U.S. Giants Are Trying to Create Homegrown *Keiretsu*," *Business Week* (January 27, 1992); Rosabeth Moss Kanter, "Becoming PALS: Pooling, Allying, and Linking across Companies," *Academy of Management Executive* (August 1989).

36. Reported by Laura Landro, "Electric Switch," *Wall Street Journal* (July 12, 1982).

37. "Surprise! The New IBM Really Looks New," *Business Week* (May 18, 1992), "IT's PCs vs. Mainframes at IBM," *Business Week* (September 21, 1992).

Chapter 3

1. Thomas S. Kuhn, *The Structure of Scientific Revolutions* (Chicago: University of Chicago Press, 1962), 210 pp.

2. Jay W. Forrester, *Industrial Dynamics* (Cambridge, MA: Productivity Press, 1961), 464 pp.

Jay W. Forrester, *Urban Dynamics* (Cambridge, MA: Productivity Press, 1969), 285 pp.

Jay W. Forrester, *World Dynamics*, 2nd ed. (Cambridge, MA: Productivity Press, 1973), 144 pp.

Jay W. Forrester, *Collected Papers of Jay W. Forrester* (Cambridge, MA: Productivity Press, 1975), 284 pp.

Edward B. Roberts, *Managerial Applications of System Dynamics* (Cambridge, MA: Productivity Press, 1978), 562 pp.

James M. Lyneis, *Corporate Planning and Policy Design: A System Dynamics Approach* (Cambridge, MA: Productivity Press, 1980), 520 pp.

Chapter 4

1. During the early and middle 1980s, articles began to appear (1) forecasting network forms of organization [e.g., Raymond Miles and Charles Snow, "Fit, Failure and the Hall of Fame," *California Management Review* (Spring 1984)]; (2) describing the form's key characteristics [e.g., Hans Thorelli, "Networks: Between Markets and Hierarchies," *Strategic Management Journal* (January/February 1986), and Raymond Miles and Charles Snow, "Network Organizations: New Concepts for New Forms," *California Management Review* (Spring 1986)]; and (3) debating the costs and benefits of network structures [e.g., "The Hollow Corporation," *Business Week* (March 3, 1986)]. A few years ago, a rash of books and articles appeared exploring and generally endorsing various types of network structures, including strategic alliances, value-added partnerships, global market matrices, and so on [e.g., Peter Drucker, *The New Realities* (New York, NY: Harper & Row, 1989); Charles Handy, *The Age of Unreason* (Boston, MA: Harvard Business School Press, 1990); Robert Reich, *The Work of Nations* (New York: Knopf, 1991); Russell Johnson and Paul Lawrence, "Beyond Vertical Integration—The Rise of the Value Added Partnership," *Harvard Business Review* (1988); and William E. Halal, *The New Capitalism* (New York; Wiley, 1986)]. Most recently, a cover story in *Business Week* ["Learning from Japan," (January 27, 1992): 52–60] details numerous examples of U.S. firms creating and benefiting from network structures.

2. For a brief description of both Rubbermaid and Wal-Mart, see the Special Report, *Business Month* (December 1988): 38, 42.

3. For an early discussion of how large firms have disaggregated their operations and spread them across multiple, smaller elements along the value chain, see Michael J. Piore and Charles E. Sabel, *The Second Industrial Divide* (New York: Basic Books, 1984). See also Johnson and Lawrence, op.cit.

4. A more detailed description of these three types of networks, and the forces shaping them, is provided in Charles C. Snow, Raymond E. Miles, and Henry J. Coleman, Jr., "Managing 21st Century Network Organizations," *Organizational Dynamics* (Winter 1992): 5–20.

5. Cooperative, entrepreneurial behavior of this sort is being increasingly encouraged both inside and across firms. See James Brian Quinn and

Penny C. Paquette, "Technology in Services: Creating Organizational Revolutions," 31 *Sloan Management Review,* (Winter 1990): 67–78.

6. There are two main types of *keiretsu.* Many stable networks in the United States resemble "supply" *keiretsu,* which are groups of companies integrated along a value chain dominated by a major manufacturer. To date there are no American counterparts to "bank-centered" *keiretsu,* which are industrial combines of 20 to 45 core companies centered around a bank. For discussions of *keiretsu* -like networks in the United States, see Charles H. Ferguson, "Computers and the Coming of the U.S. *Keiretsu ," Harvard Business Review* (July/August 1990): 55–70; and "Learning from Japan," *Business Week,* op. cit. See also "Japan: All in the Family," *Newsweek* (June 10, 1991): 37–40.

7. IBM announced a major restructuring along these lines late in 1991. See "Out of One Big Blue, Many Little Ones," *Business Week,* (December 9, 1991): 33. For a complete description, see David Kirkpatrick, "Breaking Up IBM," *Fortune,* (July 27, 1992): 44–58.

8. Thomas Gelb, "Overhauling Corporate Engine Drives Winning Strategy," *The Journal of Business Strategy* (November/December 1989): 91–105.

9. See General Mills, *Annual Report,* 1985.

10. See Nike, *Annual Report,* 1991.

11. See William Taylor, "The Logic of Global Business: An Interview with ABB's Percy Barnevik," *Harvard Business Review* (March/April 1991): 91–105.

12. See Jason Magidson and Andrew Polcha, "Creating Market Economies within Organizations: A Conference on Internal 'Markets'," *Planning Review,* 20 (January/February 1992): 37–40.

13. *Business Week* used the term "hollow corporation" pejoratively in its March 3, 1986, cover story, op. cit. However, recognizing that thoughtful outsourcing does not cause an organization to lose its critical expertise, Quinn, Doorley, and Paquette discuss how firms are "learning to love the hollow corporation." See James Brian Quinn, Thomas L. Doorley, and Penny C. Pacquette, "Technology in Services: Rethinking Strategic Focus," 31 *Sloan Management Review,* (Winter 1990): 83.

14. These and other examples are discussed in companion articles in the February 1992 issue of *The Academy of Management Executive* (Richard A. Bettis, Stephen P. Bradley, and Gary Hamel, "Outsourcing and Industrial Decline," pp. 7–22; and James A. Welch and P. Ranganath Nayak, "Strategic Sourcing: A Progressive Approach to the Make-or-Buy Decision," pp. 23–31).

However, while both pieces bemoan the negative impact of faulty outsourcing decisions on U.S. competitiveness, each recognizes that outsourcing, if properly handled, can be an important management tool, and Welch and Nayak propose models to assist with strategic outsourcing decisions.

15. See James Daly and Michael Sullivan-Trainor, "Swing Your Partner, Do-Si-Dough," *Computerworld* (December 23, 1991/January 2, 1992): 21–25.

16. In contrast to the widely publicized and potentially damaging alliances emerging among major computer firms, many small Silicon Valley firms have built profitable dynamic network relationships. In these networks, many firms do nothing but design custom computer chips while others specialize in manufacturing these designs. In some instances, designers have even shared some of their expertise with large concerns in return for access to manufacturing competence. Such networks emerge and are maintained by trust and by the recognition of unique competencies and mutual dependencies. See John Case, "Intimate Relations," *INC.* (August 1990): 64–72.

17. Miles and Snow (1986), op. cit., p. 65.

18. "Learning from Japan," *Business Week*, op. cit., p. 59. Similar relationships based on full cost and profit information sharing among Silicon Valley chip designers and manufacturers are described in John Case, op. cit.

19. Snow, Miles, and Coleman, op. cit.

20. "Learning from Japan," op. cit., p. 59.

Chapter 5

1. J. D. Sterman, "Modeling Managerial Behavior: Misperceptions of Feedback in Dynamic Decision Making Experiment," *Management Science,* 35 no. 3 (1989): 321–339; and "Misperceptions of Feedback in Dynamic Decisionmaking," *Organizational Behavior and Human Decision Processes,* 43 no. 3 (1989): 301–335.

2. See P. M. Senge, *The Fifth Discipline: The Art and Practice of the Learning Organization* (New York: Doubleday/Currency, 1990), Chapter 3.

3. C. Kampmann, and J. D. Sterman, (1992, May), "Do Markets Mitigate Misperceptions of Feedback in Dynamic Tasks?" (Working Paper 3421-92-BPS, Sloan School of Management, Massachusetts Institute of Technology, May 1992) E. Mosekilde, E. R. Larsen, J. D. Sterman, and J. S. Thomsen, "Nonlinear Mode-Interaction in the Macroeconomy," *Annals of Operations Research,* 37 (1992): 185–215; M. Paich, and J. D. Sterman, "Boom, Bust, and

Failures to Learn in Experimental Markets," Working Paper 3441-92 BPS, Sloan School of Management, Massachusetts Institute of Technology, July 1992) Forthcoming, *Management Science*; V. Smith, G. Suchanek, and A. Williams, "Bubbles, Crashes, and Endogenous Expectations in Experimental Spot Asset Markets," *Econometrica,* 56, no. 5 (1988): 1119–1152.

4. See, for example, C. Argyris, *Overcoming Organizational Defenses,* (Boston: Allyn & Bacon, 1990).

5. E. Jacques, *Requisite Organization* (Arlington VA: Cason & Hall, 1989); E. Jacques and S. D. Clement, *Executive Leadership,* (Arlington, VA: Cason & Hall, 1991).

6. For example, "Catch the Team Spirit: The Great Experiment in Team Management," *Across the Board* (May 26, 1989): 5; J. Hoerr, "The Payoff from Teamwork," Business Week (July 10, 1989): 56; R. Johansen, et al., *Leading Business Teams* (Reading, MA: Addison-Wesley, 1991).

7. For example, E. Lawler, *Strategic Pay: Aligning Organizational Strategies and Pay Systems* (San Francisco: Jossey Bass, 1990); R. J. Doyle, and P. I. Doyle, *Gain Management,* (New York: American Management Association, 1992).

8. C. M. Savage, *5th Generation Management: Integrating Enterprises Through Human Networking* (Maynard, MS: Digital Press, 1990); Granier, R. and G. Metes, *Enterprise Networking: Working Together Apart,* (Maynard, MS: Digital Press, 1992).

9. P. Senge, "The Leader's New Work: Building Learning Organizations," 32, no. 1 *Sloan Management Review,* (Fall 1990), 23 pp.

10. I. Nonaka, "The Knowledge-Creating Company," *Harvard Business Review* (November–December 1991): 96–104.

11. Nonaka, ibid., 97.

12. W. E. Deming, *Profound Knowledge* (Cambridge, MA: MIT Center for Advanced Engineering Study, 1993).

13. B. Bakken, *Learning and Transfer of Understanding Dynamic Decision Environments.* (PhD dissertation, Sloan School of Management, Massachusetts Institute of Technology, 1993).

14. For example, Nonaka describes the role of metaphor and "models" in surfacing and disseminating tacit knowledge. Seely Brown has established a "corporate research process" at Xerox to study and improve work practices at all levels: See J. Seely Brown, "Research That Reinvents the Corporation," *Harvard Business Review,* (January–February 1991): 330–339.

15. See P. Wack, "Scenarios: Uncharted Waters Ahead," *Harvard Business Review* (September–October 1985) and "Scenarios: Shooting the Rapids," *Harvard Business Review* (November–December 1985); and A. P. de Geus, "Planning as Learning," *Harvard Business Review,* (March–April 1988).

16. For more detail on tools and capabilities, see P. M. Senge, "Transforming the Practice of Management," forthcoming in *Human Resource Development Quarterly* (1993); P. M. Senge, "The Leaders' New Work," ibid., or P. M. Senge, *The Fifth Discipline: The Art and Practice of the Learning Organization* (Doubleday/Currency, 1990); for regular discussions, see *The Systems Thinker,* a newsletter published by Pegasus Communications, Cambridge, MA.

17. W. Isaacs, "Generative Dialogue: Environments for Collective Inquiry" (Organizational Learning Center Working Paper, Massachusetts Institute of Technology, 1993).

18. For more on system archetypes, see *The Fifth Discipline,* op. cit.; and D. Kim, *Systems Archetypes: Diagnosing Systemic Issues and Designing High-Leverage Interventions,* Pegasus Communications, Cambridge, MA.

19. For more on Corporate Flight Simulators, see *A User's Guide to STELLASTACK* (High Performance Systems, 1988); George P. Richardson, and Alexander L. Pugh, III, (eds.), *Introduction to System Dynamics Modeling with DYNAMO* (Cambridge, MA: Productivity Press, 1990) (previously published by MIT Press, 1981); Nancy Roberts, et al., *Introduction to Computer Simulation: A System Dynamics Modeling Approach* (Reading, MA: Addison-Wesley, 1983; (out of print).

20. For more on left-hand column cases, see C. Argyris, *Strategy, Change, and Defensive Routines* (Boston: Pitman, 1985); and C. Argyris, *Overcoming Organizational Defenses* (Boston: Allyn & Bacon, 1990).

21. See Argyris, *op. cit.;* and C. Argyris, B. Putnam, and D. Smith, *Action Science* (San Francisco: Jossey Bass, 1985).

22. See S. Mizuno (ed.), *Management for Quality Improvement: The 7 New Tools* (Cambridge, MA: Productivity Press, 1988).

Chapter 6

1. The concept of *planning boards* is especially powerful in addressing the problem of integration in social systems in general, and in internal markets in particular. For a discussion of these boards, see R. L. Ackoff "The Circular Organization: An Update," 3, no. 1 *The Academy of Management*

Executive (1989): 11–16, and *Creating the Corporate Future: Plan or Be Planned For* (New York: Wiley, 1981), pp. 163–168.

2. See H. Mintzberg, "Crafting Strategy," *Harvard Business Review* (July–August 1987), and R. H. Hayes, "Strategic Planning—Forward in Reverse?" *Harvard Business Review* (November–December 1985).

3. Centralized planning and monopolies are the two most important factors responsible for the demise of the Soviet Union's economic system according to many observers. Paul Lawrence, for example, revealed this conclusion to the authors in a conversation shortly after finishing a detailed study of Soviet enterprises reported in P. R. Lawrence and C. A. Vlachoutsicos (eds.) *Behind Factory Walls: Decision Making in Soviet and U.S. Enterprises* (Boston: Harvard Business School Press, 1990).

4. D. A. Hounshell and J. K. Smith, *Science and Corporate Strategy: Du Pont R&D 1902–1980*, (Cambridge: Cambridge University Press, 1988).

5. For a discussion of this approach, see Chapter 11, in this volume.

6. For an argument that measurement systems must be designed to dissolve conflicts on three dimensions: horizontal (between suppliers and customers); vertical (at different organizational levels, for example, between a division and the corporation); and diachronic (short-term and long-term), see J. Gharajedaghi and A. Geranmayeh, "Performance Criteria as a Means of Social Integration," in J. M. Choukroun and R. Snow (eds.) *Planning for Human Systems* (Philadelphia: University of Pennsylvania Press, 1992).

7. Malone and Rockart make a very important observation in this regard. Relative production costs, they argue, have always been lower in markets than in hierarchies. Coordination costs, however, have historically been higher in markets than in hierarchies. This phenomenon has resulted in corporations favoring hierarchies over market mechanisms. Recent advances in information technology have changed this equation altogether. The difference in coordination costs is now negligible between the two modes. Therefore, corporations can take advantage of market mechanisms much more frequently. See T. W. Malone and J. F. Rockart, "Computers, Networks and the Corporation," *Scientific American* (September 1991): 128–136.

8. For one view of these reasons, see Chapter 9, in this volume.

9. A most common reason for internal conflicts in large organizations is their transfer-pricing system. For a detailed discussion, see R. G. Eccles, *The Transfer Price Problem* (Lexington, MA: Lexington Books, 1985) and R. N. Anthony, J. Dearden, and N. M. Bedford, *Management Control Systems*, 6th ed., (Homewood, IL: Irwin, 1989) Chapter 8.

10. There are special situations in which management may decide to remain in a business for strategic reasons. It may choose to subsidize an operation or use it as an offensive or a defensive strategic weapon. Nevertheless, it is better to recognize such subsidies and sacrifices explicitly, because they have a tendency to continue for a long time without producing any significant benefits for other parts of the organization.

11. M. E. Porter, "From Competitive Advantage to Corporate Strategy," *Harvard Business Review,* (May–June 1987).

12. K. E. Boulding, *Beyond Economics: Essays on Society, Religion and Ethics,* (Ann Arbor, MI: University of Michigan Press, 1968).

Chapter 9

1. The Buffett model is defined after the example of Warren Buffett, CEO of Berkshire Hathaway. The Volvo model is based on the Volvo Corporation of Sweden, and the Ackoff model is defined in the chapter by Russell Ackoff in this book.

Chapter 10

1. David M. Noer, "Ready, Set, Turn a Profit!" *Training and Development Journal* (May 1985).

Chapter 11

1. A description of our design and strategy can be found in Ali Geranmayeh and Julio R. Bartol, "Systems Thinking in Corporate Development Strategy: The Case of Armco Latin American Division," 3, no. 2 *Systems Practice* (1990): 159–175.

2. Using this logic, we have been able to find innovative ways to expand our business. We have studied our customers' operations to determine what nonessential parts of their business we can provide more efficiently. In our operations in Brazil, for example, we were able to work with our automotive and appliances customers to redesign their operations in a way that transferred some of their equipment and processing to us for a much more effective total system. The redesigned system reduced costs, improved quality, reduced the need for future capital expenditures, and freed up valuable plant space for our customers. A long-term contract and our guaranteed on-time

delivery provide our customers with more efficient control than they can attain by vertical integration.

3. Miles and Snow present and discuss different architectures for such networks in Chapter 4 in this volume.

Chapter 13

1. Albert B. Crenshaw and Thomas Heath, "Six Blues Said to Be in Trouble," *Washington Post* (November 29, 1992).

Chapter 14

1. For a description of the idealized design concept and the interactive planning methodology, see Russell L. Ackoff, *Creating the Corporate Future* (New York: Wiley, 1981).

Chapter 17

1. Cited from David Osborne and Ted Gaebler, *Reinventing Government; How the Entrepreneurial Spirit is Transforming the Public Sector* (Reading, MA: Addison-Wesley, 1992).

2. Osborne and Gaebler, op. cit.

3. A major conference on this theme, "LEFT AND RIGHT," was held in Washington, DC, October 30, 1991, and was sponsored by both the Progressive Foundation and the Heritage Foundation.

4. Peter Drucker, *Innovation and Entrepreneurship* (New York: Harper & Row, 1985).

5. See David Osborne and Douglas Ross, "Catching the Third Wave," *Washington Post* (July 22, 1990).

6. David Broder, "Doing More with Less," *Washington Post* (January 31, 1993).

7. Stephen Barr, "Reinventing Government Moves Forward," *Washington Post* (March 12, 1993).

8. "Project CORN: Cost Recovery Implementation Plan," (FAA, September 8, 1992).

9. Brandt Allen, "Make Information Services Pay Its Way," *Harvard Business Review* (January–February 1987).

10. Allen, "Make Information Services Pay Its Way," op. cit.

11. Reported in *Government Computer News* (June 1992).

12. "For Services Rendered," *Information Week* (April 29, 1991).

Appendix

1. Adolf A. Berle, Jr., *The 20th Century Capitalist Revolution* (New York: Harcourt, Brace, and World, 1954).

2. Richard Eells and Clarence Walton, *Conceptual Foundations of Business* (Homewood, IL: Richard D. Irwin, 1961).

3. Richard Eells, *The Government of Corporations* (Glencoe, IL: Free Press of Glencoe, 1962).

4. Jay W. Forrester, *Industrial Dynamics* (Cambridge, MA: The MIT Press, 1961).

5. Everett E. Hagen, *On the Theory of Social Change* (Homewood, IL: Dorsey Press, 1962).

6. Mason Haire, *Psychology in Management* (New York: McGraw-Hill, 1964).

7. Rensis Likert, *New Patterns of Management* (New York: McGraw-Hill, 1961).

8. David C. McClelland, *The Achieving Society* (Princeton, NJ: D. Van Nostrand, 1961).

9. Douglas McGregor, *The Human Side of Enterprise* (New York: McGraw-Hill, 1960).

10. Ole C. Nord, *Growth of a New Product.* (Cambridge, MA: The MIT Press, 1963).

11. David W. Packer. *Resource Acquisition in Corporate Growth* (Cambridge, MA: The MIT Press, 1964).

12. Edward B. Roberts, *The Dynamics of Research and Development* (New York: Harper & Row, 1964).

About the Authors

RUSSELL L. ACKOFF is founder and chairman of the board of INTERACT: The Institute for Interactive Management. He is also the August A. Busch, Jr. visitor professor of marketing at the Olin School of Business, Washington University, and the Anheuser Busch professor emeritus of management science at the Wharton School of the University of Pennsylvania. Dr. Ackoff holds a BS in Architecture and a PhD in the Philosophy of Science from the University of Pennsylvania. He is former president of the Operations Research Society and the Society for General Systems Research. He has served on numerous editorial boards. Along with West Churchman, he established the first U.S. graduate program in Operations Research at the Case Institute of Technology in 1951. Later he co-founded the Social Systems Sciences Program at the Wharton School. Dr. Ackoff has authored 19 books and more than 150 articles. He has conducted research for more than 300 corporations and government agencies and participated in executive development programs for a wide variety of universities, corporations, and government agencies. Dr. Ackoff's most recent publications include: *Ackoff's Fables* (1991), *Management in Small Doses* (1986), and *Creating the Corporate Future* (1981), all published by John Wiley & Sons.

JULIO R. BARTOL received his BS in Metallurgical Engineering from the University of Cincinnati. He held various management positions in Armco Inc., including corporate vice president and president of the Latin American Division, before retiring in 1993. He is an international business consultant and president of JRB Associates in Montevideo, Uruguay where he is a professor of business management at the Catholic University. Mr. Bartol has published several articles on strategic planning and is a member of the advisory committee of the Union Institute in Cincinnati. He served in the Presidential Commission "Uruguay: A Center for International Services," and is a member of Presidential Commission for the Promotion of Investments in Uruguay. Mr. Bartol is a director of INSEDE (a graduate business school) and CERES (an economic research institute) in Montevideo, Uruguay.

CHARLES BLAKE has served as vice president of information systems at the American Red Cross, Avon Products, and Cities Service Company, where he was responsible for designing, acquiring, and operating worldwide information, data processing, and communications systems. His recent position was vice president of research and operations for the Information Strategies Group, a wholly owned subsidiary of International Data Corporation where he developed and supervised projects that advised federal and state governments on state-of-the-art applications of information systems. He serves on the boards of several private and public companies.

JOHN A. CHARLTON graduated from the University of Windsor, Canada, with a Bachelor of Applied Science (BASc) degree in Electrical Engineering. He joined the Imperial Oil Company in 1974. He has worked in the Esso Petroleum Canada Division in the fields of engineering, refining, sales, supply, and strategic planning. Presently, he is a manager of strategic planning. For the past four years, Mr. Charlton has been responsible for developing plans and programs to restructure the organization and to improve its competitive positioning for the future.

JAY W. FORRESTER received a BS degree in Electrical Engineering from the University of Nebraska, an MS degree from MIT, and honorary doctorates from eight universities. While director of the MIT Computer Laboratory, he was a pioneer in the early development of digital computers, inventing the device that became the standard memory component in computers for two decades. Later he founded and directed the System Dynamics Program at the MIT Sloan School of Management, where he is now Germeshausen professor emeritus and senior lecturer. Professor Forrester has published numerous books and articles on the application of system dynamics to cities, corporations, national economies, and the globe. He has been awarded the Inventor of the Year Award from George Washington University, the Valdermar Poulsen Gold Medal from the Danish Academy of Technical Sciences, the Medal of Honor and the Systems, Man, and Cybernetics Society Award from the Institute of Electrical and Electronic Engineers (EEE), the Harry Goode Memorial Award of the American federation of Information Processing Societies, and the Computer Pioneer Award from the IEEE Computer Society. Professor Forrester was elected to the National Inventors Hall of Fame, Thomas Watson endowed the Jay W. Forrester Chair of Computer Studies at MIT in his honor, and he received the National Medal of Technology from President George Bush.

JOSEPH GAMBLE received a BS degree in accounting from Benjamin Franklin University, Washington, DC. In 1957, he became assistant controller at Group Hospitalization and Medical Services, Inc. (GHMSI), the parent corporation of the Blue Cross and Blue Shield plan for the Washington metropolitan area. Two years later he was promoted to controller; he then held a variety of senior management positions, eventually becoming president and CEO. Mr. Gamble steered the company through many difficult challenges during his tenure, including the restructuring of the organization in the 1980s. He retired in 1992.

ALI GERANMAYEH is a founding member of INTERACT: The Institute for Interactive Management, where he serves as a director and a senior partner. Dr. Geranmayeh holds a PhD from the Wharton School of the University of Pennsylvania in Systems Sciences, an MS from Stanford University in Operations Research, and a BS from Syracuse University in Industrial Engineering. He has 15 years of experience in management consulting with 40 companies in nine countries. Dr. Geranmayeh has worked with top management of major corporations focusing on strategic planning, organizational learning, business planning, new product development, organizational design, and systems thinking. Previously, he was a senior project manager with the Busch Center at the University of Pennsylvania, strategic planning director of MCTel, Inc., operations research analyst with the Agway Corporation and Omnetics Inc., and an industrial engineer with General Tire and Rubber Co.

WILLIAM E. HALAL received a BS in Aerospace Engineering from Purdue University, and MBA and PhD degrees from the University of California at Berkeley. He served as a Major in the Air Force, an aerospace engineer on the Grumman Apollo Program, and in management positions with various companies before joining George Washington University, where he is now professor of management. An authority on emerging technologies, strategic management, and institutional change, he has conducted consulting and research projects for General Motors, AT&T, International Data Corporation, Japanese firms, the DoD, NASA, the National Institutes of Health, and the Federal Courts. He also serves on several advisory boards. Halal's publications have appeared in numerous journals and news media, such as the *New York Times*. His book, *The New Capitalism* (Wiley, 1986), outlined the new system of business and economics emerging for the Information Age. Professor Halal has received the Honor Medal of the Freedoms Foundation at Valley Forge, and the Mitchell Prize, which includes an award of $10,000.

KATHRYN SHELDON HAMMLER holds a BA from Brown University and is pursuing an MBA in Information Systems Management. Ms. Hammler worked at CACI as an associate marketing consultant, and then joined her present employer, International Data Corporation (IDC), Government Division. At IDC Government, she worked as a research analyst with the Future Technology Service and Custom Research departments, conducting studies in strategic planning, information technology procurement, and the use of emerging technologies. Ms. Hammler presently manages IDC Government's marketing and client services department, which tracks the quality of information services and works with clients to customize the programs they receive. She also manages relationships with the information technology industry.

JOHN D. MACLEAN joined the Canadian Imperial Bank of Commerce (CIBC) in 1983 as the executive vice president and manager of the Systems Division. In 1987, Mr. MacLean was assigned to the office of the chairman with the responsibility for coordinating over-all strategic planning for the Bank. For 27 years prior to joining CIBC, Mr. MacLean was a member of the consulting firm of Peat Marwick and Partners. His functional specialties include the information systems and EDP technology area, strategic business planning, marketing and organization development. During his career with Peat Marwick, Mr. MacLean held increasing levels of responsibility, serving as managing partner of the Toronto practice and providing direction for the entire consulting firm.

RAYMOND E. MILES received his PhD from Stanford University, then joined the faculty of the University of California at Berkeley. He served as dean of the Haas School of Business during 1983 to 1990, director of the institute for industrial relations, and editor of the journal *Industrial Relations.* Miles is now the Eugene and Catherine Trefethen professor of organizational behavior, focusing on the interaction of organizational strategy, structure, and management processes. Professor Miles has been a visiting scholar at Dartmouth College, the University of Texas, and the Tavistock Institute in London. He also consults to many private and public organizations, and serves on the board of directors of The Bank of California. He is the author of numerous articles. His books include *Organization by Design* (BPI, 1986), *Organization Strategy, Structure, and Process* (McGraw-Hill, 1978), *Organizational Behavior* (Wadsworth, 1976), *and Theories of Management* (McGraw-Hill, 1975). Professor Miles is a Fellow in the Academy of Management.

DAVID M. NOER was awarded a BA from Gustavus Adolpus College, an MS in Organizational Development from Pepperdine University, and a DBA from George Washington University. He has held numerous executive positions, focusing on organizational diagnosis and development, management training, workforce revitalization, and managing employee layoffs constructively. He was senior vice president for Commercial Credit Company, dean of the Academy of Management, and president of Business Advisors Division at Control Data Corporation. In addition, Noer founded his own consulting company and worked in line and staff positions in Europe, Australia, and Asia. Dr. Noer is currently vice president for training and development at the Center for Creative Leadership, Greensboro, NC. He is the author of four books: *Multinational People Management, How to Beat the Employment Game, Jobkeeping,* and *Healing the Wounds: Surviving Layoff Trauma and Revitalizing Downsized Organizations.*

DAVID OSBORNE graduated with honors from Stanford University and taught at Yale university. Now an independent scholar, consultant, and author, he is best-known for his two books, *Laboratories of Democracy,* (Harvard Business School Press, 1988) and *Reinventing Government* (Addison-Wesley, 1992). Mr. Osborne has published numerous articles in the *New York Times, The Washington Post,* and *Harpers,* among others. He is a columnist for *Governing* magazine. He is now a senior advisor to Vice President Gore's National Performance Review, Chairman of the Alliance for Redesigning Government, a Fellow of the Progressive Policy Institute, and an Associate of the Council of Governors' Policy Advisors.

JAMES P. PINKERTON is a graduate of Stanford University. Mr. Pinkerton joined the White House's Office of Policy Development and Political Affairs Office in the Reagan Administration. He then moved in 1985 to Vice President Bush's political action committee, the Fund For America's Future, as director of research. He served as director of the Office of Policy Development for President George Bush. In 1989, Pinkerton was sworn in as Deputy Assistant to the President for Policy Planning. He left the White House in 1992 to become the John Locke Foundation Fellow in Residence at the Manhattan Institute in Washington, DC. Mr. Pinkerton is also a columnist for *Newsday,* and he is working on a book.

JOHN POURDEHNAD is an independent consultant and an associate member of INTERACT: The Institute for Interactive Management. Dr. Pourdehnad holds a BS in

Mechanical/Production Engineering from Brunel University in England and a PhD in Social Systems Sciences from The Wharton School, University of Pennsylvania. He has over 20 years of experience in strategic management, functional business planning, engineering, management process consulting, and executive development planning. Since 1979, Dr. Pourdehnad has been practicing interactive planning for both the private and public sectors in developing countries and advanced economies. Prior to his association with INTERACT, Pourdehnad co-founded and served as executive vice president of MCTel, Inc. He has also held a variety of management positions in engineering, manufacturing and consulting.

JAMES R. RINEHART is a graduate of Yale University and holds an AMP from Harvard University. He worked in a variety of positions in engineering and manufacturing at General Motors and Mack Trucks, and then served as general manager of Packard Electric at GM, president of GM Canada, and vice president of GMC. Mr. Rinehart was the chairman and chief executive officer of Clark Equipment Company from 1982–1986. He is the executive vice president and chief administrative officer of Hiram College, Ohio, and senior associate of INTERACT. Mr. Rinehart is a director of Ashland Oil and of Automatic Tracking Systems.

BERT C. ROBERTS, JR. is a graduate of Johns Hopkins University. He joined MCI Communications Corporation in 1972, where he has served in several senior management positions. Roberts become president and chief operating officer in 1985, he was named chief executive officer of MCI in 1991, and chairman in 1992. MCI is headquartered in Washington, DC, and is now the second largest long-distance carrier in the United States, with more than 60 offices in 55 countries. Mr. Roberts is a member of the Association of Governing Boards of Universities and Colleges, the Business Roundtable, and The Conference Board, and he serves on the governing bodies of the National Association of Securities Dealers, Georgetown University, the National Alliance of Business, the American Red Cross, and Valence Technology, Inc.

PETER M. SENGE received a BS in Engineering from Stanford University, and an MS in Social Systems and a PhD in Management from MIT. He is now a faculty member and director of the Center for Organizational Learning at the Sloan School of Management, MIT, where he works with a consortium of corporations using systems theory and research to manage organizational and economic change through advanced concepts of leadership, purpose, and systems alignment. Professor Senge has published numerous articles and books and is the author of *The Fifth Discipline: The Art and Practice of the Learning Organization* (Doubleday/Currency), which has more than 300,000 volumes in circulation. He has collaborated with major organizations, such as Ford, Federal Express, Intel, AT&T, and Royal Dutch Shell. Senge is also a founding partner of the management consulting firm, Innovation Associates.

MICHAEL SHEEHAN earned a BS in business from George Mason University and an MBA from the Collgate Darden Graduate School of Business, University of Virginia. He joined the American Automobile Association (AAA) as manager of planning and research, and was promoted to director of corporate planning in 1984. In 1987 he joined Group Hospitalization and Medical Services Inc. (GHMSI), the Blue Cross and

Blue Shield plan for the Washington, DC, metropolitan area, where he is now director of strategic planning.

SETON SHIELDS obtained a Registered Nurse (RN) degree from Monmouth College, New Jersey, and joined Group Hospitalization and Medical Services Inc. (GHMSI), the Blue Cross and Blue Shield plan for the Washington, DC, metropolitan area in 1970. She served in various administrative positions, and was promoted to manager of provider services. In 1985, Ms. Shields was made vice president and executive director, and started the corporation's new venture, Health Management Strategies, Inc. (HMS), which she manages as president and CEO.

CHARLES C. SNOW received his PhD in Business Administration from the University of California at Berkeley. He is now professor of business administration at the Smeal College of Business Administration, The Pennsylvania State University. Previously, Professor Snow served as chairman of the Department of Management and Organization and director of the Executive Management Program at Penn State. He has conducted in-house development programs for many corporations in the United States and overseas. Snow's work on strategic management has produced numerous articles and four books: *Organizational Behavior* (Wadsworth, 1976), *Organizational Strategy, Structure, and Process* (McGraw-Hill, 1978), *Strategies for Competitive Success* (Wiley, 1986), and *Strategy, Organization Design, and Human Resource Management* (JAI Press, 1989). He serves on the editorial boards of five journals.

JOHN STARR spent over 20 years with Alcoa in a wide variety of capacities, including work in 40 countries. As a chemical engineer, he began his career in manufacturing and operations. Later, he used and built on grassroots experiences in sales, marketing and general management assignments. John was instrumental in building two major businesses for Alcoa—a chemical products operation in Europe that quintupled in size in 4 years, and the separation technology business which went from startup to over $100 million in sales in only 3 years. John left Alcoa when the separation business was sold in 1992 and is currently developing a new business in Colorado.

JOHN H. ZIMMERMAN holds a BS in Economics from Colgate University and an MBA from Kent State University. He was vice president of employee relations and chief labor negotiator at Firestone Tire and Rubber Company prior to joining MCI Communications Corporation in 1982, where he is now senior vice president and chief human resources officer. Throughout his career, Mr. Zimmerman has published and lectured on human resource issues, education reform, and the need for a competitive workforce. In 1990, he was appointed to the Commission on Developing Workplace Skills. He currently chairs the AMA Human Resource Advisory Council, and serves on the Advisory Board of the School of Business and Public Management at George Washington University, the Human Resource Committee of the Business Roundtable, the Council for Workplace Excellence, and the National Center on Education and the Economy.

Index